Vidding

Vidding

A History

Francesca Coppa

University of Michigan Press • *Ann Arbor*

For questions or permissions, please contact um.press.perms@umich.edu

Published in the United States of America by the
University of Michigan Press
Manufactured in the United States of America
Printed on acid-free paper
First published February 2022

A CIP catalog record for this book is available from the British Library.

Library of Congress Cataloging-in-Publication data has been applied for.

ISBN 978-0-472-03852-7 (paper : alk. paper)
ISBN 978-0-472-90259-0 (open access ebook)

DOI: https://doi.org/10.3998/mpub.10069132

The Open Access version of this book was made possible with the support of Muhlenberg
College, the Mellon Foundation, The Daniel J. and Carol Shiner Wilson Fund, and the
Harry Potter Education Fanon (HPEF) project.

Cover art by Sally McGrath.

If I can't dance to it, it's not my revolution.

—Emma Goldman, remixed

Contents

This book has also been published in an extended, open access, multimedia edition at https://doi.org/10.3998/mpub.10069132. The extended edition also includes the following appendix material:

1. Spotlight on: MARCHIN' ON, by Hanna

2. Spotlight on: SUPREMACY, by rhoboat

3. Spotlight on: RADIOACTIVE, by Counteragent

List of Hosted Vids

A Note on Formatting

A Note on Names

In his chapter on vidding in 1992's *Textual Poachers*, Henry Jenkins referred to vidders elliptically by their initials: K.F., L.B., M.V.D. Jenkins was writing at a time when vidding was still very much underground as an art, and vidders were afraid that their work was infringing or illegal. The use of these initials shows the fear that vidders felt.

But this is the story of how vidders stopped being afraid; as such, it is making a claim for vidding as a cinematic art. It is also claiming that vidding belongs not just in fan studies but also in film studies, media studies, and women's studies. I am therefore using the names that vidders used to sign their works so they can be credited as the artists that they are.

A Note on Formatting

While some vids have titles different from the songs used to make them, the vast majority have the same names, which can be confusing. I will be therefore following the formatting conventions that Andrew Goodwin established in *Dancing in the Distraction Factory* of putting song titles in quotation marks (Joni Mitchell's "Both Sides Now"), film and television series' titles in italics (*Star Trek*), and vid/music video titles in small caps (Kandy Fong's BOTH SIDES NOW). The first mention of each vid is in boldface type for reference.

A Note on Scope

Vidding: A History is more properly titled *Vidding: A History of Western, Live-Action Media Fandom Music Video*, as it traces a narrow but cohesive cohort of mostly female fan vidders from the 1970s to now. Even so, it is only "a" history—the best I could write based on my research and experience, and the (sometimes fragmentary) oral history of vidders. I hope others will write books that supplement or correct this one.

Beyond live-action science fiction and fantasy vidding are many other fan video traditions that deserve their own histories. Anime music video (AMV) also dates from the VCR era and in many ways follows in parallel to the history I have outlined here. AMVs were also shown at conventions and duplicated onto tapes traded by fans. But anime fandom is also different in many ways from the female-dominated vidding fandom I discuss. AMV-interested readers might start with Mimi Ito's work; there have also been important articles by Dana Milstein and Samantha Close. Ian Roberts's "Genesis of the Digital Anime Music Video Scene, 1990–2001," in the 2012 "Fan/Remix Video" issue of *Transformative Works and Cultures*, also remains a crucial overview. Machinima makers have also made music videos; Paul Marino's work remains central here, and *The Machinima Reader*, edited by Michael Nitsche and Henry Lowood (2011, MIT), is a good first stop. Clive Young's engaging *Homemade Hollywood: Fans Behind the Camera* (2008) remains an excellent history of narrative fan filmmaking, but one that needs updating in the wake of the explosion of fan filmmaking in the post-YouTube era. Finally, YouTube has helped to surface music videos made by soap opera fans, sports fans, news fans, and of course music fans of every possible stripe. As far as I know, there are no scholarly works dedicated to these forms. I hope that this book provides a starting place—or at least an impetus—for historians of these genres.

Acknowledgments

Thanks first and foremost to Naomi Novik and Rebecca Tushnet for inviting me to road trip with them to Harvard for the Signal/Noise 2k5: Creative Revolution conference, which first inspired me to write about vidding. Thanks to Kristina Busse and Karen Hellekson for publishing my first essay on vidding in *Transformative Works and Cultures*, and thanks to Peter Decherney for convincing me that there was a book here. I am grateful to Steve Anderson, founder of Critical Commons and one of the organizers of the 2008 24/7 DIY Video Summit, for inviting me to be part of that historic event. Mary Francis, my first editor at the University of Michigan Press, signed this book and cheered me through the writing of it; my current editor, Sara Jo Cohen, has been my steadfast partner in bringing this nearly decade-long project to a happy conclusion.

This book couldn't have been written without the support of my academic home, Muhlenberg College, which appointed me their first director of film studies in 2006 and which has supported my research at every turn, particularly with the Class of '32 Award and the Daniel J. and Carol Shiner Wilson Faculty Award. I also owe a huge debt of gratitude to the amazing librarians at Trexler Library as well as to our digital learning team. Muhlenberg also helped me apply for a Mellon Community Foundation grant, which has been used to support the creation of the expanded, open access multimedia edition of this book. The Harry Potter Education Fanon (HPEF) project also helped to make the open access version of this book possible. Enormous thanks to my fantastic team of Muhlenberg students who helped to organize, caption, and describe the vids: thank you Kristen Paige, Marlee Schulman, Aubrey Daviau, Juanita Andrade, Dan Burg, and Em Panetta. Karen Hellekson wrestled this incredibly complicated manuscript into shape, copyediting and coding it for print and online.

This book draws heavily on the histories and analyses created and rehearsed by vidders themselves. I am grateful to all the vidders who were interviewed for the Organization for Transformative Works's Vidding Oral History Project or the Media Fandom Oral History Project run by Morgan Dawn and Franzeska Dickson in conjunction with the University of Iowa. I am particularly indebted to the insights of vidders Kandy Fong, Rachael Sabotini, Laura Shapiro, tzikeh, and lim.

This book is dedicated to all the vidders who have passed on, including Abby Albrecht, Diana Barbour, Kathy C., Chris Soto, Zeneyepirate, and, last but not least, self-described Fannish Butterfly and Media Cannibal Sandy Herrold, who had the best, most contagious laugh of any fan I have ever met. I miss you, Sandy.

Introduction

Vidding and the Rise of Remix Culture

In 2005, YouTube went live as a quick and easy (and apparently free to use) way of sharing video on the Internet, with other video hosting and streaming services like Imeem, Vimeo, and Blip soon to follow. The rise of online distribution kicked off an interest in DIY video and "user-generated content," itself a phrase that went mainstream in 2005,[1] though most people didn't, and still don't, realize that many of these so-called YouTube videos were not made for YouTube at all.

In 2005, the Vividcon convention, held annually in Chicago since 2002, celebrated the thirtieth anniversary of vidding, or the making of fan music videos, a grassroots art form in which clips from television shows and movies are set to music as a way of interpreting and reimagining the visual source material. The two cakes wheeled out at the anniversary bash testified to the breadth of vidding's thirty-year history, at least technologically: one cake was frosted to resemble a VHS cassette, and the other was shaped like a compact disc. (See Image A. https://doi.org/10.3998/mpub.10069132.cmp.172) These were the two ways that vids had historically been distributed, though some vidders had begun to offer their vids for download on password-protected sites. (Few were using the nascent streaming services.) All the convention-goers had come to Chicago expressly to see vids (one track of the convention was dedicated to watching vid shows in a theatre-style setting, in a dark room with images projected on a large screen) and to discuss the art and craft of vidding with other vidders (another track featured discussion panels, which were thematic, theoretical, or technical). Some vidders came to show new work; at the time, the Vividcon Premieres show was the Cannes

Film Festival of the vidding world, complete with a full-scale review of premiering vids the morning after the show. But the convention, organized by vidders, didn't advertise itself to anyone outside of vidding fandom. Even its name, Vividcon, gave no clue as to what the convention was about,[2] with the word "vid" only subtly embedded for those in the know. All this to say that in 2005, vidding was a fully developed visual art, albeit one that was highly subcultural and hidden, with its own history and canon, and with a sophisticated artistic and critical language.

In 2005, I attended Signal/Noise 2k5: Creative Revolution, a conference held at the Berkman Center for the Internet and Society at Harvard. It was one of the first conferences on what we now call remix culture, which at the time was framed as "audience creativity . . . enabled by digital technologies."[3] I went because two of my friends had been invited to speak about fanfiction as a form of remix: Rebecca Tushnet, a law professor and intellectual property specialist, and Naomi Novik, a novelist and video game designer who also happens to be the founder of Vividcon. I had met Naomi and Rebecca through my longtime participation in media fandom (broadly speaking, a creative community organized around genre television and movies), and they had been invited to appear on the program by Berkman staffer Erica George, herself also active in media fandom, who had noticed the conference's heavy focus on male scholars and forms of remix dominated by men. George's intervention was crucial; at the time, female-dominated remix arts like fanfiction, fan art, and vidding were still very much underground, though rapidly growing in popularity and visibility due to the Internet. However, there were still (noticeably) only six women out of twenty-five speakers on the program at Harvard that day, and no woman at the conference was given a solo speaking slot.

What I remember most clearly about the conference was director and animator Paul Marino's presentation on machinima, the art of making animated films using video game engines. Marino showcased some work by machinima artists Rooster Teeth, who made *Red vs. Blue* (2003), a comedy series set within the video game *Halo*, and April Hoffmann (aka aprilsghoffmann, aka Atlas Productions), who made videos using *Sims 2* avatars as her actors. Although Hoffmann had made a number of narrative machinima films, notably the three-part series *The Awakening*,[4] that day Marino chose to show LET'S GET IT STARTED (2004) (Video 1 https://doi.org/10.3998/mpub.10069132.cmp.1), a machinima music video made to the Black Eyed Peas song of the same name. In it, various *Sims* avatars appear to sing, dance, and play instruments in time to the music, as if they were performing. Hoffmann used the *Sims* engine to create and direct a series of "actors" through the elaborate choreography she designed, then edited the resulting footage together to create a music video. The result was rhythmic and colorful—more like an anime music video (AMV), with its emphasis on spectacle, than the more interpretive, live-action vids that I was used to, but clearly a related art form. At the end of the presentation, Marino explained that people had been doing creative work like this since the 1990s.

I remember exchanging glances with my friends in the audience. We were all thinking the same thing: these guys don't know that vidding exists. Media fans, mostly female and many queer, had been making vids—remix videos—since the mid-1970s. The scholars I had just seen, and others like them, were going to write the history of remix, and vidding wasn't going to be in it. I remember driving back from the conference ranting that this was the rise of the novel all over again; here were the Samuel Richardsons and Henry Fieldings of remix, come to erase the long history of female scribblers/editors. I was struck by the way remix had become cool, all hip-hop and technogeekism. But fandom, particularly the girl parts, was not cool. Probably some nice women's studies professor, I remember saying bitterly, would come along and find vidding again, but wouldn't it be better if vidding never got lost in the first place?

This book got its start right then.

Vidding and Visibility

Now, in hindsight, I realize that Paul Marino was perfectly correct in his statement: people have indeed been making machinima videos since the mid-to-late 1990s, when the first *Doom* demos and *Quake* movies were made using video gaming's new recording capabilities. But at the time it sounded like Marino was dating remix video from the '90s, when many forms are much older. Jonathan McIntosh has traced the history of political remix video back to 1920s Russia, and he credits Charles A. Ridley with creating "the first viral political mashup."[5] In "Schichlegruber—Doing the Lambeth Walk" (1942), Ridley reedits footage from Leni Riefenstahl's *Triumph of the Will* to make Hitler and the Nazis look like they are singing and dancing in time to the music, turning their marching into the Cockney strut known as the Lambeth Walk and their "Sieg Heil" salutes into jaunty arm swings. Fans of AMVs date their art form to 1982, when Jim Kaposztas made an ironic *Space Battleship Yamato* (aka *Starblazers*) vid, cutting "random violent scenes"[6] to the Beatles' "All You Need Is Love." Vidders date live-action fan vidding, the narrow but rich subject of this book, to the premiere of Kandy Fong's first slideshow in 1975.

By 2005, vidders already had an established canon. Each Vividcon began with a history show that rehearsed that canon, celebrating its innovation, meaning, beauty, and influence on the form. Fans are a self-reflexive bunch, and vidders have constructed much of their own history. In writing this book, I have organized evidence, conducted interviews, and collected primary sources, many of them scattered and ephemeral (VHS liner notes, convention programs, mailing list archives) to verify, flesh out, and occasionally complicate the arc of that history as vidders tell it. I was there myself for some of it, sometimes as a participant, sometimes as a witness or a bystander. (I drove the video projector rented for the first Vividcon from New York to Chicago in the trunk of my car; if that isn't a contribution to vidding culture, I don't know what is.)

In my introduction to *The Fanfiction Reader: Folk Tales for the Digital Age* (2017), I noted that the book had not been written for fanfiction fans, who certainly didn't need me to tell them about themselves or their work. This is true in many ways for this book too, though the technological developments of the last fifty years may mean that some vidders will identify with a particular generation, group, or series of practices I describe, but not with others. There may well be vidders who participated both in the VCR vidding collectives of the 1980s and '90s and in the YouTube multieditor projects of a couple of decades later, but there can't be many, even if the underlying pleasure in collaboration is the same. Online-only vidders may be baffled or even alienated by the rituals and shibboleths of convention-going vid fans, and I'll bet that few vidders ever thought to connect vidding with some of the more avant-garde filmmaking practices I discuss in this book. But the river of vidding, the course of which I attempt to trace, with all of its individual streams, tributaries, and far-flung pools, can usefully be seen as part of the same rich art. Moreover, vidding, a form pioneered and still practiced primarily by "women and those who caucus with women"[7] (to use one fan's notable phrase[8]) is sufficiently different from other remix arts (sampling, hip-hop, mashups, lip synchs, YouTube poop, political remix, autotune, and other forms as described by Owen Gallagher in his excellent overview, *Reclaiming Critical Remix Video: The Role of Sampling in Transformative Works* [2017]), as well as from different forms of fan video (AMV, machinima, fan films, trailer remixes, supercuts, recuts, fan dubs), to make this book worth doing, even as many of these forms have blurred and cross-pollinated in recent years. Vids have been described by vidders themselves as "visual and auditory poetry,"[9] as "condensed and enriched"[10] arguments, and as "emotional creative expression,"[11] and work by scholars and lawyers like Louisa Ellen Stein, Tisha Turk, Alexis Lothian, Katherine Morrissey, John Hondros, Sarah Fiona Winters, Katharina Freund, Sarah Trombley, and Rebecca Tushnet[12] has helped both to raise vidding's profile and to make it something of a poster child for fair use. But in 2005, if you weren't one of a small number of people attached to the vidding community—and most vidders then could trace their genealogy to a few foremothers ("I was taught to vid by Mary Van Deusen," "I learned to vid with Judy Chien")—you probably didn't know that vids existed at all.

Whose fault was it that vidding wasn't better represented that day in 2005? In 1992, Henry Jenkins and Camille Bacon-Smith had both written chapters on live-action fan music videos[13] (both using the older terminology of "song vids" or "song tapes"), but almost nothing had been written since, with the exception of vidder Tashery Shannon's essay in the science fiction magazine *Strange New Worlds*: "Move Over, MTV! Here Come the Song Vids! Fan Music Videos" (October 1993). Shannon was rare for being willing to talk openly about vidding, potentially drawing attention to it at a time when any attention was presumed to be negative. Most vidders, fearing both legal repercussions and ridicule, didn't want anyone to know that vidding as an art form even existed. In fact, they'd taken quite a lot of care to ensure that people didn't know: they worked under pseudonyms, distributing vids only to trusted others via snail mail, or, more recently, offering vids for download on password-protected websites if you swore not to share the password with others. Vidders, working during a time before "remix" was a household word, had deliberately kept their heads down and their work out of the public eye.

However, by the turn of the century, even as vidders remained underground, other forms of fan and remix culture were mainstreaming fast. In 2002, Lucasfilm and Atom Films organized the Official Star Wars Fan Film Awards, an annual contest dedicated to recognizing the best Star Wars fan films. Star Wars fan films have a long and noble history, from 1978's *Hardware Wars*, which won top prize at numerous film festivals in its day, to the Emmy award–winning *Star Wars Uncut* (2010). The first Star Wars awards show was broadcast on the Sci-Fi Channel and hosted by fanboy Kevin Smith. In the same year, 2002, Paul Marino organized the Academy of Machinima Arts and Sciences, which gave out annual awards to the best machinima. Moreover, some machinima had crossed over to becoming a mainstream cultural product: the second season of Rooster Teeth's *Red vs. Blue* premiered at Lincoln Center in 2004, and in 2005, a machinima festival was held at the Museum of the Moving Image in New York.

Fan filmmakers and machinima artists were able to attain this level of public recognition at least partly because they saw themselves as part of the broader filmmaking and gaming communities, and they expected their work to be appreciated by both game creators and their fans.[14] They weren't wrong. Video game creators have by and large embraced machinima, which they see as celebrating and popularizing their games. Consequently, not only have many video game makers explicitly considered the technical and artistic needs of machinima makers in the development of games (much like they allow for hacks and modding), but some have also created blanket legal licenses explicitly allowing noncommercial machinima (for example Blizzard, which makes *World of Warcraft*). Others have gone even further and allowed some machinima makers to bring their creative work to the market—for example Microsoft, which allowed Rooster Teeth to sell *Red vs. Blue* without demanding licensing fees. The series, now in its thirteenth season, has been sold on DVD and Blu-ray and is available via streaming on Netflix. And although some fan filmmakers have received threatening letters from corporate lawyers, this has typically happened after the filmmakers commercially exhibited or distributed their work in a large, mainstream venue, which they apparently felt entitled to do.[15] By the 1990s, most creators had embraced fan films; today, only very large and professional productions (like the $80,000 Star Trek fan film *Prelude to Axanar* and its proposed feature-length sequel) draw legal attention. Lucasfilm not only continues to hold the Official Star Wars Fan Film Awards, but they have made a variety of sound effects and other tools available for fan use. Steven Spielberg sent the kids who made *Raiders: The Adaptation* (1989), a shot-for-shot remake of *Raiders of the Lost Ark* (1981), a letter praising "their loving and detailed tribute" and invited them to meet with him at Dreamworks.[16] Joss Whedon gave "his blessing"[17] to the *Firefly* fan film *Browncoats: Redemption* (2010), but he couldn't stop Fox and Universal from taking issue with it. Studio lawyers cautiously allowed the project to continue after the fan filmmakers agreed not to profit personally from it; consequently, all profit made from film showings, about $113,000, was donated to a variety of charities. Even so, this contrasts with vidding's relationship with the film, television, and music industries.

Vidding as Piracy

Vidders kept under the radar because they feared being perceived as pirates. Like DJs and hip-hop artists who sample, vidders use pieces of existing cultural products—television, music, movies—to make new art. Vidding is an art of the editing room the way that sampling is an art of the turntable and the mashup is an art of the soundboard: it's about combining existing pieces of mass media in a new way. The first vids were made with film slides—castoff, one-of-a-kind pieces of footage—but vidding really took off in the age of the VCR, which allowed vidders to create enormous archives of footage, taping and sharing entire seasons of television on videocassette. This, it should be said, was the only way that footage was available to consumers at that time; new feature films began to be released on VHS, but most television shows and older films were not.

However, as Lucas Hilderbrand notes in *Inherent Vice: Bootleg Histories of Videotape*, videotape enabled access to visual material through alternative mechanisms of preservation and distribution.[18] Fans created their own visual archives, massive libraries of videocassettes, not just for the purposes of viewing but as the raw material for creating fan works. It was not unusual for a fan of a show to send boxes of homemade VHS cassettes to a favorite fan writer or vidder, in the hope that she would write fanfiction or make vids for it. Similarly, fans distributed both raw material and finished vids via post or by creating large duplicating stations at conventions, with VCRs hooked up in strings to facilitate copying. These homey models of distribution are in line with the feminist networks of video sharing that Hilderbrand describes, which "encouraged not only wholly new works but also new interpersonal connections between makers."[19]

But tape, both video and audio, was always an uncomfortable technology for those engaged in creative industries. Both VCRs and audio-tape players had been designed to record from broadcast and were sold for that purpose ("Watch Whatever Whenever" ran the ad for Sony's Betamax), but there were immediately questions about whether it was legal or right to make such copies. This was fought out in court; the case of *Sony v. Universal* (aka the Betamax case) was resolved in 1984, with the Supreme Court ruling that that it was legal to sell VCRs to record television for the purposes of private, noncommercial time-shifting in the home.[20] Although Hollywood tried to get the Supreme Court to set limits on this copying, it refused, and Hollywood eventually dropped the issue because in fact the VCR opened up enormous new commercial markets in the form of VHS rentals and sales. Most people used their VCRs to rent movies from Blockbuster or to tape their favorite shows to watch when they got home from work. But taping continued to have an air of the illicit and the unauthorized—that is to say, the bootleg[21]— and the remix works that were made from these homemade recordings even more so. As Tashery Shannon warned vidders in 1993, "Anyone considering selling song tapes [collections of vids on VHS] should be aware that there is a danger of prosecution under the same laws governing pirating of music or movie tapes."[22] Thus, she explained, vids should only be given away or traded for other vids.

Vidding as Transformative Work

The fear of legal repercussions wasn't the only reason that vidders kept their heads down; they also thought that the vids they were making were likely to be misunderstood or ridiculed by those outside the community. Vids are highly dependent on context; they are an interpretive art form made for an audience that is familiar with the visual source and that wants to think and feel new things about it. In this way, watching a vid is more like reading literary or film criticism than reading a short story or seeing a new movie, and critical analysis is much more interesting and enjoyable if you're familiar with the thing being discussed. If you bring nothing to the vid—no recognition of the characters, no previous engagement with the plot—you may find the vid inaccessible. Tashery Shannon believed that "all but the most slapstick [vids] are incomprehensible to viewers unfamiliar with the source. They become a mere collage of abstract images. The nuances of meaning are lost and nonviewers of the particular shows cannot understand the unique way song vids interact with the source media."[23] While vids purposely created for wider audiences exist, including broad comedy/slapstick vids and so-called recruiter vids (vids designed to seduce people into a particular fandom), even these kinds of vids presuppose that you have some idea of what a fan vid is. Vids are more typically aimed at viewers with an in-depth knowledge of the visual source material, offering an interpretation rather than an entirely new construction. As Paul Marino noted when asked to explain machinima's popularity versus vidding's relative obscurity,

> Machinima has been seen as an extension of intellectual property, offering much more room to grow, whereas vidding is seen as reworking what's already been completed. . . . One could look at vidding as

the practice of "this means something different," whereas machinima leans toward "let's show something different." And to take it a step further into gender-related territory, we could consider that machinima is a more brute force approach, associated with more masculine traits, whereas vidding is a more finessed art, for which women have shown more aptitude.[24]

Vidding's insistence that "this means something different"—something worth arguing for, something not immediately obvious, something worth drawing out from the source text—is what makes vidding transformative, in both the legal and fannish senses of the word. Legally speaking, transformative works are opposed to derivative works and are likelier to be a fair use of existing material. Copyright law gives a creator the right to control the making of derivative works; for instance, the author of a book has the right to author or authorize sequels to the story, or to make a movie telling the same story. But an author does not have the right to stop people from writing reviews or from critiquing, discussing, interpreting, or satirizing the work, and they also do not have the right to stop people from creating transformative works—that is, "altering the first [original] with new expression, meaning, or message."[25]

To turn a television show into a music video is itself a pretty radical transformation. If you're vidding, for example, *Buffy the Vampire Slayer*, you're cutting 144 hours of television into three or four minutes. Or to put it another way, you're selecting hundreds of short clips and building them into rhythmic montages of 180 to 240 seconds. Either way, this is an act of pretty radical sculpture. Every image will have been taken from its original sequence and given a new position within the montage; it will also have new audio, further altering its meaning. This would be interesting just as an act of creative compression, and transformative works have been made through cuts alone. For instance, the Radical Software Group, a group of digital artists, made the video artwork "RSG-Black-1" by cutting all the white people out of the 2001 Ridley Scott film *Black Hawk Down*, about the 1993 US raid on Somalia. The result is "a conceptual investigation of representation and ideology" that highlights the entertainment industry's images of those it sees as "'other.'"[26] On his Tumblr blog, "Every Single Word" (https://everysinglewordspoken. tumblr.com/), actor, writer, and video editor Dylan Marron, whom many people know as the voice of Carlos in the podcast *Welcome to Night Vale*, creates videos that edit down major films to the words spoken by people of color. The entire Harry Potter film series is reduced to five minutes and forty seconds. *E.T. the Extra Terrestrial* (1983) runs for nine seconds. (It is no accident that these race-critical artworks make visible absences and omissions; as I discuss in chapter 5, vidders who have wanted to stage race-based versus gender-based criticisms have had to struggle with representational absences among other problems.) But unlike these works of omission and elision, vids also represent a significant change of genre: vidders remix television and film into music video. As I argue in the next chapter, the aesthetic and formal values of music video are significantly different from those of mainstream commercial television and film; moreover, it is precisely the desire to transform mass media in accordance with those values that makes vidders want to vid in the first place.

Transformativity is not just a legal defense; it also signals a vidder's desire to change the visual text she was given—that is, it is a mark of dissatisfaction. The vidder wants not just more, but different. The difference in the text that the vidder creates might be a relatively small one, like a shift in emphasis. For example, Hanna's Harry Potter vid, MARCHIN' ON (2010) (Video 2 https://doi.org/10.3998/mpub.10069132.cmp.2), focuses its attention entirely on the young people in the film, the Hogwarts class that would go on to form Dumbledore's Army. (See "Spotlight on: MARCHIN' ON" in the online appendix.) Others make more significant transformations. Rhoboat's vid SUPREMACY (2013) (Video 3 https://doi.org/10.3998/mpub.10069132.cmp.3) attempts to reedit the Daniel Craig Bond films to make Judi Dench's M the central character. (See "Spotlight on: SUPREMACY" in the online appendix.) These vids change the story by changing the point of view. Hanna's vid decenters the Harry Potter films by valuing Dumbledore's students as a kind of collective protagonist ("You need us, Harry," chides Hermione at the start of the vid); rhoboat's vid imagines a world in which the mature, female M—the head of MI5—could be at the center of a blockbuster movie. These shifts of emphasis engage the mainstream Hollywood idea of what a protagonist looks like (Harry Potter, James Bond) and change it into something else (the collective, an older woman).

Other vids are even more overtly critical of their source. For example, Counteragent explained in a statement for the 2015 Digital Millennium Copyright Act (DMCA) hearings why she made her *Supernatural* vid, RADIOACTIVE (2014) (Video 4 https://doi.org/10.3998/mpub.10069132.cmp.4):

> My favorite show (*Supernatural*, CW, Season 9) took away the bodily
> agency of a lead character for half of a season and didn't address the

emotional or physiological horror inherent to that kind of invasion. As a woman who worries about bodily agency being taken from me or my fellow women by force or trickery, this hit a nerve. So I made a vid focusing on the horror of that lead character's situation, a horror that was extremely (in my opinion, insultingly) diluted in the source. This vid clearly told its viewer: this is disturbing, pay attention.[27]

Supernatural—a show that, as its title suggests, focuses on supernatural, and often disturbing, events—frequently has plots involving bodily possession by demons, angels, or other creatures. The largely female viewership of the show is well aware of this, but is likely to be sensitive as to how that possession is handled. Counteragent says that the horror of the plot didn't bother her; in fact, arguably that sort of embodied horror speaks slantwise to some aspects of female experience in meaningful ways. But she was bothered by the fact the show, and the characters within the story world, didn't take that horror seriously enough, and their insensitivity was enough to render the show's heroic characters unlikeable to her. Hence RADIOACTIVE, which recuts events of the plot so as to emphasize that "this is disturbing; pay attention." (See "Spotlight on: RADIOACTIVE" in the online appendix.)

Transformational versus Affirmational Fandom

In the eyes of vidders, these kinds of critical alterations—of the perspective, meaning, or value of mass media narratives—differentiate vidders as transformational fans from affirmational[28] or curative[29]/curatorial fans. Broadly speaking, affirmational fans affirm and celebrate the text, while transformational fans transform (interpret, rework, extend, distort) it. Makers of transformative works tend to see affirmative fans as the sanctioned fan base, approved of by creators because they are not threatening. In fact, according to obsession_inc, the fan who coined and defined these terms, affirmational fans further empower the mass media creator, who is considered the ultimate interpretive authority who knows the "truth" of "what really happened" in a particular story. According to this point of view, the author "holds the magic trump card of Because I'm The Only One Who Really Knows, That's Why."[30] Affirmational fandom revolves around figuring out the rules of a particular universe and organizing various kinds of information. This is the culture of wikis, of collecting anime cells or action figures; it is also the culture of arguing on message boards about, for instance, how strong Captain America "really" is,[31] with detailed reference to the text in the form of cited comic panels. Affirmative fandom is related to Bob Rehak's notion of blueprint culture, which he defines as "fan subcultures devoted to drawing, drafting, charting, mapping, and playing the worlds of science-fiction media."[32] It also ties to Matt Hills's idea of mimetic fandom,[33] which produces creative fan artworks that aim to replicate some aspect of the text, by which Hills means things like highly accurate replica props and costumes.

Hills argues that mimetic fan works blur the lines between affirmational and transformational fandoms, if only because some form of transformation is almost inevitable in the creation of the fan work, sometimes because mimetic fan works tend to be handmade and local rather than mass-produced and industrial, with all the artistic variation that implies, and sometimes because the fan-artisan is actually improving on the prop or costume, either by making it more realistic than official, licensed merchandise or by staying closer to some earlier or idealized version of the thing.[34] Fandom shows tremendous creativity in drawing starship blueprints, mapping fantasy lands, forging swords, knitting Gryffindor scarves or Jayne hats,[35] and sculpting lightsabers—though if the artisans' intent is to minimize their personal creativity and work narrowly from an extant blueprint, design, or pattern, then the transformation may be perceived as a bug, not a feature.

However, it is affirmational fandom rather than transformative fandom that tends to be approved by creators, which makes human, if not legal, sense; creators are understandably flattered by the affirmation of their work and irritated by attempts to change or critique it. But in practice, this has been a gendered distinction. Straight white men are more likely to be affirmational or blueprint fans, while women, queer people, and people of color are more likely to be transformational fans. This is frustratingly evident in works like the mainstream 2010 comedy/documentary, *The People vs. George Lucas*, which interviews a host of passionate (and angry) Star Wars fans about their love–hate relationship with Lucas. Almost every shot in the film is of a white man, and out of 110 fans interviewed, there are only five men of color and five women, two of whom are identified as vidders.[36] (There is also a single, silent shot of a cosplaying black Leia—though blink and you'll miss her.) You could easily get the impression that Star Wars fandom is overwhelmingly male and white, when nothing could be further from the truth, as a more recent documentary, *Looking for Leia* (2019), about women and nonbinary Star Wars fans, shows.[37] Moreover, the male fans interviewed in *The People vs. George Lucas* comment explicitly about how supportive of fan works

George Lucas is. These statements run directly counter to the experience of female, queer, and BIPOC fans who make transformative works, who remember that Lucasfilm tried to stop people from writing Star Wars romance as well as slash (homoerotic) fiction. In fact, Lucasfilm executive Jim Ward famously articulated the company's preference for affirmational fans when he declared, "Fandom is about celebrating the story the way that it is."[38]

Transformative fans are obviously shut out by this attitude, but a different kind of shutting out occurs when a long sequence of male fans in *The People vs. George Lucas* register their dissatisfaction with Lucas's later movies and edits by earnestly insisting, one after another in a kind of supercut, that "George Lucas raped my childhood." These fans are not only affirming Lucas's original work to the point of resenting his own edits and sequels, but they are doing so—using "rape" as offhand, casual slang—in an explicitly gendered way. The makers of *The People vs. George Lucas* construct this "rape" sequence without realizing how alienating it is to the female fan or woman spectator. In fact, the sequence is so tone-deaf, and the film's absence of female Star Wars fans so egregious (one has only to look at the outpouring of love and creativity that female fans have expressed for Leia in the wake of Carrie Fisher's death), that one has to wonder if the filmmakers and the male fans they're interviewing are actually trying to set a boundary to keep women out.

Interestingly, the historically gendered and racial positions of affirmational and transformational fandom became confused during the most recent trilogy of Star Wars films. As Kristina Busse points out in *Framing Fan Fiction*, when Disney bought Lucasfilm, they redefined canon, "asking fans to accept a new authoritative framework and to now celebrate the new story 'the way it is.'"[39] Busse argues that this affected "obedient, 'good' fans" who had carefully tracked the canon across the franchise more than it did transformative fans, who were used to disregarding or rewriting large chunks of the story and knew they were doing so without Lucas's approval. But beyond this, the changes that the new films made in terms of gender and racial diversity changed who was—and wasn't—satisfied with canon. Suddenly the story as it was couldn't be affirmed. In the wake of *The Last Jedi*, men's rights activists produced their own transformative work: "The Last Jedi: Defeminized Fanedit," in which "most shots showing female fighters/pilots and female officers commanding people around/having ideas"[40] were cut in a deliberate effort to create a more chauvinist narrative. There was significant racist backlash when Black British actor John Boyega was cast as a stormtrooper.[41]

The character of Rose Tycho, played by Vietnamese American actress Kelly Marie Tran, came in for particular racist and sexist abuse, eventually leading Tran to delete her social media accounts, though she eventually penned a *New York Times* op-ed declaring, "I Won't Be Marginalized by Online Harassment."[42] On the flip side, many white female fans have been increasingly moved to question the racial politics of their own practice, which might be legally transformative but not always socially so. For instance, why wasn't Finn/Poe, an obvious slash pairing suggested by canon (and teased by the BIPOC actors), more popular than the "trash" pairing of Kylo Ren/General Hux, which had been more or less invented out of whole cloth? Is Kylux an outlet for the positive expression of kink, a preference for white bad boys, neither, or both? The female and queer parts of transformative fandom have had to wrestle with their own limitations, including racism and the exclusion of those with other intersectional issues.

Vidding as Supplemental and Affective Art

Just as female fans are likely to be horrified by fanboys' offhand use of the word "rape" in a film like *The People vs. George Lucas*, some male fans may be taken aback or made uncomfortable by the romantic themes and heightened emotions that often characterize transformative fan works such as fanfiction, fan art, and fan vids. You might not notice the male gaze of most mainstream works until you encounter works built with a different gaze in mind—or, to paraphrase Eve Kosofsky Sedgwick's definition of camp, until you encounter works that ask, "What if the right audience for this were exactly *me*?"[43] In "False Equivalence," an issue of the webcomic *Shortpacked*,[44] David Willis stages this difference in gaze by having a male and female fan argue about it. The male fan complains, "I'm tired of you griping that chicks in comic books are sexually objectified! The dudes are, too! They're big, impossibly muscled hulks!" The female fan counters that big muscles are just another male power fantasy, and then draws the version of Batman that she would find attractive. "If I'm gonna get the hots for Batman," she explains, "he has to be built for dexterity, not power. Let's make him more lean. And you know what? Seeing his eyes is important. They should be large and intense. Let's throw in some rosy cheeks and kissable lips." The resulting picture (Figure 1 https://doi.org/10.3998/mpub.10069132.cmp.137) makes the male fan "uncomfortable" but is also a bit of a punch line: this is not the version of Batman that a male spectator is used to seeing. But with

Fig. 1. The concluding panels of "False Equivalence," part of the online comic strip *Short-packed* by David Willis, December 2, 2011.

the casting of Robert Pattinson as *The Batman* (2022), female fans may have the last laugh.

Because transformative works are supplemental to the original text—that is, they assume that you are encountering these fan works in the context of the originals, and that you are therefore seeing them as adding to (and correcting the deficiencies of) a larger transmedia world—they can cut to the chase, artistically speaking. They assume you know the shape of the world, the larger story, who the characters are, and so on. But in the case of transformative fan works, "the chase" is typically not (as the idiom, taken from early silent film, implies) a spectacular action sequence (mass media gives us plenty of spectacular action sequences) but rather a concentrated or highly distilled emotion—a sense of how characters *feel* about what is happening to them. Unlike car chases or elaborately CGIed battle sequences, affective scenes tend to be in short supply in the mass media, particularly in genres like science fiction and fantasy. The few moments we're given are obsessively examined and excavated by fans. Every frame is scrutinized, every look and gesture rendered significant.

For instance, in the wake of the movie *Captain America: The Winter Soldier*, many fans were enthralled by the antagonist, the Winter Soldier/ Bucky Barnes, as played by Sebastian Stan. These fans went back to the first film of the series, *Captain America: The First Avenger*, because the character appears there too, albeit less prominently, as Steve Rogers's best friend. However, his significance in the later films has made his

Fig. 2. GIF set of Bucky Barnes made by Lost-Princess-of-Mirkwood (2014).

earlier appearance more important, and his every facial expression and gesture has been scrutinized for signs of his inner landscape and his (impending) transition into the Winter Soldier. In a GIF set made by Lost-Princess-of-Mirkwood (Figure 2 https://doi.org/10.3998/mpub.10069132.cmp.138), we see a particular moment isolated and scrutinized. This GIF set was captioned, "Wait is this . . . ? I had never noticed this," and the frames seem to show Bucky's smile fading and being replaced by a more complicated and unhappy expression once no one is looking. Note that Figure 2 only approximates the GIF set; in the original, all frames are moving, the characters speaking, their emotions and body language matched to the new story.

Other fans commented on these images, collectively glossing the meaning of the character's microexpressions. For example, they indicate a "realisation of Steve not needing his help anymore" (carryonmy); "it's also Bucky realizing that he can no longer protect his best friend no matter how hard he tries" (edgebug); and "if you watch Bucky through the movies, you'll notice he always makes sure to look like he's 100% fine if other people are looking at him" (phdna). In an essay about *Captain America: The First Avenger* on the pop culture/entertainment website Need to Consume, Hazel Southwell expands on the GIF set in even more detail:

> [It's] the moment when Bucky starts to grieve. It's when Steve's rescued him and they've walked back to camp, when he fully recognises what's happened, when he's close enough back to something approaching normal that he can't avoid analysis, when he has to call him Captain America. Sebastian Stan does a great thing with the dead flatness and grief of coming back from the brink, rescued by a friend and this spelling the end of so many things.[45]

Fans never tire of examining faces on this microlevel—and this image represents only a small section of the larger frame of film. The shot that the GIF set was made from (Figure 3 https://doi.org/10.3998/mpub.10069132.cmp.139) is much more focused on Steve's first triumph as Captain America; Bucky is only one of many background figures, squeezed into the lower righthand corner of the frame. The GIF maker has substantially altered the image, using cropping, editing, and light to move our focus.

In their book *A Billion Wicked Thoughts*, evolutionary psychiatrists Ogi Ogas and Sai Gaddam use fanfiction to argue that women and men's brains process desire differently. Female fans hated the book's methodology and the authors' insistence on explaining gender-based differences as neuroscientifically hardwired through evolution, but the description of female fans' intense scrutiny of fictional characters' bodies, minds, emotional states, and motivations is hard to dispute. Ogas and Gaddam glibly summarize these tendencies as "The Miss Marple Detective Agency"—that is, they argue that women have a neural "system designed to uncover, scrutinize, and evaluate a dazzling range of informative clues."[46] Whether this is neurological or cultural is debatable, but fans do certainly scrutinize the mass media properties they love for clues to characters' interior states, examining still photographs, film clips, and digital images for nuances of feeling.

Vidders use music as a lens through which to view these carefully curated moments, trying to make the spectator see what they see and feel what they feel when they look at them. A vid in that sense is three

Fig. 3. Frame from *Captain America: The First Avenger* (2011) showing Bucky Barnes's position and significance relative to the larger frame (and the larger story).

or four minutes of concentrated emotion, where music is used to create or extend interpretations and feelings associated with that text, or to turn up the volume on subtext. We know, for instance, that Harry Potter cares about Ron and Hermione; that Daniel Craig's James Bond has a deep psychosexual connection to Judi Dench's M (she dies in his arms); that the Winchester brothers are willing literally to go to hell for each other; that Captain Kirk and Mr. Spock are important to each other beyond wives and families, even over the mission itself (Kirk mutinies and blows up the *Enterprise* to save Spock). "But not like that," you might say. "That's too much!" The emotions in a vid might seem overwhelming to a new spectator if the vid is not viewed in the context of a supplement. However, from a vidder's perspective, the three or four minutes of strongly felt emotion that a vid provides barely begins to supplement the three seasons and nine films of the original Star Trek canon, and the emotion is entirely justified by the events of the story.

Vidding as Catharsis, Fandom as Chorus

In a classical tragedy or epic poem, you have the buildup and the battles that we see in much contemporary mass media spectacle, but you would then also be led through to catharsis. After all the reversals and recognitions of the plot, after the climax, there would be narrative time spent on intensifying and purging the emotions built up by the text. The funeral, the rending of garments, the burnt offerings, the chanting and beating of drums; or conversely the victory speech, the dancing and singing, the feasting and celebration—all these are sadly missing from much of mainstream culture, where hours, days, or even years of ever-intensifying drama are likely to end with an ironic smile and a slap on the back: Hey, cool; we saved the world! A cynic might argue that the denial of catharsis is an economic stratagem of mass media: the story ain't over, folks; come back next summer for *The Iliad II: This Time It's Personal.* That's what gets us back into the movie theatre; that's what gets us to tune in next week. Maybe next time there will be emotions and we'll be able to process them—to let these goddamned feelings out.

One might also argue that we are denied catharsis because the expression of strong emotions—or really almost any emotion, like fear, pity, love, or joy—in response to art (as opposed to sport) is now considered effeminate: it's girly, it queers. Today you have to give your superhero buddy a high five rather than hug him, because a hug might be too much; a hug might lead to a kiss, or more. In his influential article "Batman, Deviance, and Camp," Andy Medhurst argues that the fear of queerness has banished Robin the Boy Wonder from the Batman universe. The Bat has been reinvented as a solo act as part of his "reheterosexualization,"[47] but that has also resulted in the Dark Knight's emotional palette going ever darker. Batman is grimmer, more vengeful, less communicative; Robin was also, of course, Batman's friend and confidant. In *Acting Men*, his study of all-male-cast plays, Robert Vorlicky notes that men in plays are only able to able to talk freely to each other—to express themselves, to self-disclose, to emote—under a few highly specific circumstances: in institutional settings or confinement (prison, ships); if they use drugs or alcohol; right after an act of violence. As Vorlicky notes, "Male characters often fight with words or fists before they talk personally."[48] But in mass media storytelling, the fighting-to-talking ratio is out of whack.

Furthermore, what emotions male characters do have often come literally at the expense of women and children, which is particularly hard for the female spectator. Female fans have had to coin words to describe these all too common fictional situations. For instance, there is fridging (a plot device where a female character is raped, killed, or otherwise injured to motivate a male story of adventure or revenge) and manpain (an excessive, characteristically male form of grief that is self-centered and inner directed even though it is ostensibly caused by someone else's suffering). So female fans cry with male characters when their wives are raped and their children murdered, even as the women and children themselves are not seen as important, or even as human beings.

Fridging and manpain are extreme but common versions of Vorlicky's narrow circumstances in which male characters self-disclose and display emotion; now it's not just fistfights in bars but the largescale slaughter of innocents, the blowing up of entire planets. In her vid, THE PRICE (2011),[49] thingswithwings illustrates manpain in a variety of popular fandoms not only as a form of gender and media criticism (why are so many male protagonists burdened by grief for their dead mothers, girlfriends, wives, sisters, and children?) but also as a mode of fannish self-criticism (why are we so desperate for those few, rarely shed male tears?). In her vid notes, thingswithwings explains that she, like many fans, is desperate for cathartic emotion even as she recognizes that when she gets it, it's problematically at her own expense:

> I needed to express the frustration I feel both with the ridiculous/ terrible nature of these tired tropes AND with the entirely predictable (and often problematic) largescale fannish reactions to those tropes. I include my own fannish reactions under that umbrella, of course; I cried when the Doctor cried, I have loved Mulder and Angel and Michael Scofield and Gunn and Harry Potter, I currently watch White Collar and Doctor Who and all. As often as not, when these shows pull shit like this, it still rings a bell inside me and I feel deeply for the characters involved even though I sometimes don't want to, even though it's ham-handed and awful. That's what culture does to you! That's what culture does to me—forces me to identify against myself. So this vid is sort of . . . me trying to loosen those bonds a little bit.[50]

The catharsis offered by these texts forces women to identify against themselves, but by supplementing the text's emotions—by changing the music and the rhythm of television and film—vids can create other forms of catharsis.

Instead of the textual violence and misogyny that result in canonical man tears, vidders create feelings and emotions using the techniques of poetry in the Aristotelian sense, which includes music, drama, rhythm, and movement as well as language. These supplement the canonical film text, intensifying the narrative's emotional arcs or structuring affective responses that it lacks or denies—positive feelings such as joy, victory, affection, desire, awe, as well as grief, sorrow, pathos, longing, doom. And as with theatre making (itself also often dismissed as feminine or queer), fannish vidding is done within and for a community. As with feasts and funerals and other organized emotional occasions, we celebrate and grieve together.

The creation of supplemental emotional content can feel off-putting or inappropriate to those who suspect all feelings of having a queer or feminizing influence. This is a relatively recent phenomenon, maybe even a mass media phenomenon, that stands in contrast to antiquity, where it was understood that all people struggled with strong emotions and that, as Aristotle argued, the purpose of drama was to help us process and regulate those feelings communally. But in today's mass media environment, if it's a "weepie" it's a "woman's picture," if it's a love story it's a "woman's picture," and if it's about children or dancing or the hassles of the workplace it's a "woman's picture," and if it's a comedy drama or a gothic drama it's probably a "woman's picture"—but what if (like me!) you burst out crying in the theatre during *Star Trek III: The Search for Spock?*

An influential vids among vidders is Killa's **DANTE'S PRAYER** (2001) (Video 5 https://doi.org/10.3998/mpub.10069132.cmp.5), a Star Trek vid that uses the haunting Loreena McKennitt song of the same name to create a visual poem illustrating the emotional subtext around Spock's death and resurrection in *Star Trek II: The Wrath of Khan* and *Star Trek III: The Search for Spock* within the context of Kirk and Spock's decades-long relationship. (See "Spotlight on: DANTE'S PRAYER" in the online appendix.) As Joanna Kucharska notes in her analysis of DANTE'S PRAYER in "Also These Voices: Technology and Gender in the Practice of Fanvidding,"[51] the later Star Trek films see the characters aged and moved on from space exploration; however, when fans see them on screen, they cannot help but remember their history together, both chronologically within the narrative (the characters have been nearly inseparable for half a century) and extratextually (we ourselves have lived with these characters in our culture for a very long time). It is this history—the strength and longevity of the Kirk–Spock relationship—that makes Spock's death, and Kirk's actions in the aftermath of that death, a subject suitable for tragedy or epic poetry—or worthy of a vid like DANTE'S PRAYER. In fact, many longtime Star Trek fans were irritated when the reboot movie *Star Trek Into Darkness* (2013) attempted to replay those iconic death scenes with the new, younger characters. The expression of grief didn't have the same significance or resonance when the characters were so young and freshly met; fans felt that the emotion wasn't earned.

But DANTE'S PRAYER tends to leave Star Trek fans breathless, casting its story in lyrical and mythopoetic terms. The title of McKennitt's song alludes to Dante's *Inferno*, and its opening lyrics, "When the dark wood fell before me," confirm that this is a story in which the main character travels into darkness before coming into the light. Dante's journey evokes many others from classical literature. It is the duty of the epic hero (Gilgamesh, Orpheus, Hermes; here, Kirk) to descend into the underworld and to return from that quest with greater knowledge, or with his recently departed beloved. DANTE'S PRAYER celebrates the story of Kirk's successful quest to bring Spock back from the underworld, and the vid ends with a literal moment of anagnorisis, or recognition, as Spock remembers Kirk and all he stands for, and by so doing remembers and recovers himself. Then, as the Greeks would say, "Exit all but the chorus."

Fandom is the chorus, and the chorus continues on even today. Fandom celebrates our contemporary myths in story and song, in every possible media: fiction, sculpture, painting, drawing, plays, films, costumes, jewelry, needlepoint, ceramics, crafts, filk.[52] But in vidding, fans add song to story, and to add music to spectacle or narrative—to make television and film musical—is to create new meanings, to open up new avenues of thinking and new opportunities for collective feeling. Although vidding is certainly a remix art, a form of digital culture, and an exploding creative force on YouTube and many other social media platforms, it's also doing something ancient and human: connecting popular culture to the poetic.

ONE | What Is Vidding?

Vid Watching 101

> Look what you done. You made me whole. Before I met you, I was the song. But now I'm the video.
>
> —*Hedwig and the Angry Inch* (1998)

You have probably already seen one; these days it's easy to stumble across a vid by accident. The Internet is full of streaming video on Facebook and Tumblr and TikTok and Instagram. Your Twitter feed might have recommended a vid to you based on something you like: the Harry Potter movies, say, or the BBC's *Sherlock*. Or you might be Googling around, or searching for something on YouTube, and you find a strange montage of film or television images set to music. You might not be clear on what it is, this musical montage. You might not be able to read its meaning or even understand that it has meaning if you aren't familiar with vidding's visual language. The vid is also likely to feature a lot of rapid-fire cutting, which may take some getting used to. You might wonder who would make such a thing and why anyone would bother, although clearly a lot of people bother; vids online today number in the millions, and they generate more income for record companies than do traditional music videos, even as vidders are gaining recognition as artists and their techniques are being copied by professional filmmakers. You might ask, what the heck *is* this?

A vid (sometimes called a fan vid, song vid, or song tape) is a fan-made music video in which preexisting footage (usually from television or movies) is edited to music (usually, but not always, a pop song). The result is a new multimedia object that tells a story, creates an interpretation, stages an argument, and/or produces a feeling. Fans who make such vids are first and foremost fans of the visual source. As such, a vid is properly labeled a Star Wars vid or a *Game of Thrones* vid (or sometimes a multimedia vid or a metavid), rather than a vid by such-and-such a recording artist. The music serves as the vid's blueprint, its road map, its code and key. The vidder uses all the information in a song—lyrics, melody, beat, tempo, instrumentation—as scaffolding upon which to build a montage that reveals (which is to say, creates) aesthetic and narrative patterns in the footage. In a vid, the ear tells the eye what to see.

This can be a difficult concept for new vid watchers—that the ear is giving the eye a vast second-by-second, moment-by-moment stream of information that the spectator must use as a guide for seeing. The vid spectator's job is one of integration: to see how sound and vision come together meaningfully at each instant, and then how that meaning builds and changes over the course of the vid. This is of course characteristic of all audiovisual works; as Michel Chion points out in *Audio-Vision: Sound on Screen* (1990), the spectator's job has always been to "magnetize" sound and connect it to image;[1] where sound and image don't match, a spectator will try to make sense of the two and join them. But vids require us to do this in a highly concentrated way for several minutes. There's nothing more frustrating than showing a vid and having viewers glance away, or having them turn to look at you in the middle of it; you just can't do that. Vids are intense and information dense. Blink and you'll miss an important moment of audiovisual synchronicity; turn away and you'll lose a piece of the puzzle; miss a beat and you'll lose the whole rhythm.

There's no common word in English for this kind of attention. Gaze? Behold? Or perhaps MARVEL (2014)? (See Video 6 https://doi.org/10.3998/mpub.10069132.cmp.6 and "Spotlight on: MARVEL" in the online appendix.) "Reading" is perhaps the term that comes closest, though it evokes the written word more than the audiovisual text; moreover, reading, unlike vid watching, takes place at the reader's own pace. But watching a vid does require many of the same skills as performing a close reading of, say, poetry. Looking away from a vid is like skipping words in a poem. Like a poem, a vid works diachronically as well as synchronically; each clip has previous associations for the ideal spectator, but it is also being given new meaning by its placement within the montage and against the moment of audio. Like poetry, vids have a rhythm that is not separate or extricable from its narrative meaning but rather is part of it—that is to say, it is constitutive. Vids can also be (frustratingly) intertextual; just as students can be frustrated by poetry's frequent allusions to nightingales, larks, and Grecian urns, vid watchers are expected to recognize densely packed signifiers both within the visual source material and, increasingly, to the history of vidding itself. Discovering these layers may, as with poetry, require significant reviewing. This is easy enough today; the digital world makes it easy not only to rewatch vids but also to examine individual frames if need be. But even analog vidders took pains to distinguish vids that required multiple rewatchings ("living room vids" they called them, meaning you should watch them at home, on a VCR, multiple times to get the layers) from vids that didn't particularly ("con vids," or vids designed to be shown at a public screening and therefore had to make their impact immediately on that first and only viewing).[2]

First Encounters

The first vids I saw were living room vids. I saw them in my own living room, in fact, in the late 1990s, and almost by accident; they had been appended to the end of a homemade VHS cassette. Before Netflix and iTunes, before box sets or professional video releases, the only way to see TV you'd missed (or to get footage for other purposes, like vidding) was if someone had recorded the show off the air and was willing to duplicate tapes for you. Thankfully, there were many fans willing to do this, and one of them had made me this particular box of videocassettes so I could catch up. But when I got to the last episode on the tape, I found it was still rolling. There was more. A song started playing, and there were the characters from the show I'd been watching, with cuts synchronized to the music. That song ended and another started. This one featured not only those same characters but also others from some show I didn't know, intercut.

These were fan vids. The person who had made these cassettes for me had been kind enough—and thrifty enough!—to use up all the space on each tape, adding two or three vids at the end of each, for a total of twelve or so vids. I ended up watching those vids many, many more times than I watched any episode of the show she'd sent me. I discovered that the vids quickly crystalized what I thought and felt about that show; in fact, they seemed to isolate and magnify the very things I was watching for. They were like the crack cocaine of television.

In hindsight, I realize that this was the perfect way to be introduced to vids and the language of vidding. These vids were literally appended to tapes of the show they'd been made from. I knew the characters and the story. The scenes were fresh in my head. The vids, presented to me as "end of tape" filler, were clearly supplemental to that particular show. They'd been curated for me by someone who knew what I was watching. Even so, I had a harder time with vids that intercut characters from shows I didn't know. But the vids taught me how to understand them, and by watching and rewatching them, I began to learn their language. I saw how the vidder of a vid made from many different sources creates visual patterns, drawing comparisons and making distinctions between shows.

I'm going to try to create this experience for you by walking you through a number of vids, moving from easy reads to more complex constructions. I understand that this is complicated by several things, particularly for readers of the print edition—writing about vids is like dancing about architecture—but chiefly because you may not know anything about these source texts. I will try to tell you what you need to know, but let me say this: if you're having trouble grasping vidding as an art or a cultural practice, find a vid for a visual source you're invested in. That's how almost everyone starts and how most people (even vidders themselves) go on. Even those of us who care about vids as an art form prefer to watch vids in fandoms we know, despite the siren call of recruiter vids. Most people don't watch vids of a source they don't know in the same way that they mostly don't read criticism of books they haven't read or films they haven't seen. In a blog post, "Understanding Vidding," Jason Mittell, professor of film and media culture at Middlebury College and author of (among other things) a book on videographic criticism, admitted that despite many sincere attempts, he never really got vidding until encountering Luminosity's ambitious album-length vid, SCOOBY ROAD (2005) (Video 7 https://doi.org/10.3998/mpub.10069132.cmp.7). SCOOBY ROAD remixes the Beatles' *Abbey Road* with *Buffy the Vampire Slayer*,[3] and it worked for Mittell not only because it's "a spectacularly impressive work of editing" but also because he came to it "with strong emotional connections to both works"[4]—that is, to *Buffy* and the Beatles. (See "Spotlight on: SCOOBY ROAD" in the online appendix.) Mittell describes SCOOBY ROAD as offering "emotional resonances within the moment-to-moment stories she spins" as well as "in connection to what a viewer brings . . . via their own media experiences and memories." He also argues that Luminosity's "concept-album" format worked particularly well for him, in that it showcased "how each song offers a narrow slice of the show's scope." I would argue that SCOOBY ROAD created an experience for him that is typical in fandom, but not in academia: Mittell watched sixteen terrific vids in the same fandom, one after the other. That experience of binging—of consuming fan work after fan work, of developing opinions, then taste[5]—no doubt helped; it's how most people come to understand vids. We learn the language of vidding by repetition, by seeing how one vid is not like another. If you only see one or two vids, they've got to be the right vids in the right fandoms. Legal scholar Rebecca Tushnet asks congressional staffers what they're watching when she lobbies for copyright reform, knowing that if she can put the right vid in front of them, they'll get it and want to help.

None of the vids that follow might be that vid for you; in fact, none of the vids in this book might be that vid. But while I can't curate the right vid for you, personally, affectively speaking, I can show you some of the kinds of vids that have been made and some of the ways that they work. In the following pages, I will take you through a series of vids of increasing narrative complexity, and which also happen to demonstrate some of vidding's technological developments. But please do not conclude that recent vids are therefore more complex than earlier ones; there are narratively dense VCR vids and digital vids with simple themes.

Case Studies: Reading Fan Music Video

BEHIND BLUE EYES *(1980), by Kendra Hunter and Diana Barbour* (Starsky and Hutch) *(Video 8 https://doi.org/10.3998/mpub.10069132. cmp.8)*

This is the simplest vid in the world—so simple that you can build it in your own head once I give you the pieces. It's also the first VCR vid anyone knows about, and it was made by Kendra Hunter and Diana Barbour for *Starsky and Hutch* (1975–79), a buddy show/cop drama and at the time a hugely popular media fandom. BEHIND BLUE EYES consists of a single, muddy frame (Figure 4 https://doi.org/10.3998/mpub.10069132. cmp.140) set to "Behind Blue Eyes," by the Who. The song begins: "No one knows what it's like / To be the bad man / To be the sad man / Behind blue eyes." The frame stays on screen for the entire length of the vid, which lasts for three minutes and thirty-six seconds.

But the fact that this vid was made at all is practically a miracle. As fan vidder Kandy Fong tells the story, in the summer of 1980, "Diana lugged her 40 pound RCA VHS machine over to Kendra's house. Kendra had a Magnavox VHS, and a reel-to-reel audiotape player. Diana had been wondering what the 'audio dub' button on her machine was for."[6] It was

Fig. 4. Frame from BEHIND BLUE EYES (1980), by Kendra Hunter and Diana Barbour.

technologically difficult to get a single, stable frame out of a VCR; previous vids, shown as slideshows, had been made from actual film stock. But videocassette footage wasn't as clear, and of course the footage itself wasn't of the highest quality either; it had been taped off the air by a home VCR.

That said, this protovid tells us a lot about how vids work. To listen to the Who's "Behind Blue Eyes" while staring at Detective David Michael Starsky is to make the song about him, and him particularly. It asks us, as fans, to imagine how the lyrics apply to Starsky as we know him. It puts the song into Starsky's voice, giving the character something new, and lyrical, to say beyond the limits of the show's dialogue. It supplements his television story, and it does so in a particular way; it's an aria in which the character articulates his feelings and inner life. The song's metaphor, "behind blue eyes," is about interiority; the vidder is telling us that Starsky has a complex inner life beyond his external appearance. This song in particular also demonstrates what Henry Jenkins has called "emotional intensification":[7] it provides an outlet for a variety of strong feelings—not just badness and sadness, but self-pity, anger, pain and woe, loneliness, vengeance: "Nobody knows what it's like / To feel these feelings / Like I do / And I blame you."

In fact, "Behind Blue Eyes" was always an aria; Pete Townsend wrote the song for his shelved science fiction rock opera *Lifehouse*,[8] where it was intended to express the perspective of Jumbo, the story's villain. The song has a distinct personality; it doesn't feel like it's about just anyone. This bad, sad man is someone specific. M. Blake Wilson argues that the song is an instance of popular tragedy in that competition between the gentle acoustic and the rocking electric sections stages the competing Apollonian and Dionysian forces that Nietzsche saw in the drama of the ancient Greeks and in Richard Wagner's operas.[9] Apollo's songs are defined by "ghostly harp and lyric poetry," Dionysus's by "the satyr's flute and the dissonant nose of the chorus."[10] Certainly fans would recognize Wilson's description of the song as "tearing off and dissolving the 'mask' of Daltry's voice" to give us the song's angry Dionysian bridge, which itself demands that we force open or otherwise get inside the singer with lines like, "When my fist clenches, crack it open," and "Put your finger down my throat"—that is, force me to open up to you. This kind of narrative is catnip to many fans, who are regularly attracted to characters with strong but repressed emotions; fans call them clams.[11] And of course, the thing to do with a clam is to crack it open, which you can do by means of an essay, a fanfiction story, or a vid like this one.

The song does not merely give voice to emotion but also tells a story. We hit climax, achieve catharsis, and at the end, Apollo, and the acoustic guitar, comes back and restores order. "Behind Blue Eyes" is a song in three acts. This, as we'll see, is characteristic of vid songs; because the song is a map, it has to take the listener on a journey. This might be a traditional narrative story, or it might be a melodic, emotional, or somatic one. But, as Tisha Turk argues, a good vid song has got to *go* places.[12]

The song "Behind Blue Eyes" remains a staple in vidding, and it has been used to illustrate the interior life of a variety of blue-eyed characters over the years. But that doesn't mean every vid made from the song is the same; nor does it mean the same thing in every fandom, because the image–music conjunction matters. Starsky isn't Sam Winchester or Neal Caffrey or Rupert Giles or Loki of Asgard. (Thought exercise: if you know any of these characters, think about what it might mean for them to sing, "My love is vengeance.") Starsky has a particular backstory, and Kathleen O'Malley, aka Flamingo, a *Starsky and Hutch* fanfiction writer, archivist, convention organizer, and vidder, didn't hesitate when I asked her how "Behind Blue Eyes" applied to Starsky's character:

> For those of us very invested in the show, Starsky as a character could definitely be seen as the "bad/sad" man in the song. Throughout the series, while he is frequently portrayed in scripts for humor, he had a tragic backstory (father killed in his youth, causing him [we presume]

to be sent to California to live from New York, so separated from his mother and brother). And throughout the series he suffers failed romances with one woman leaving him to hide out with her gangster father, and the other love of his life dying from a vengeful killer's bullet (making Starsky the cause of her death). Starsky also shows a simmering rage that comes through at times, especially regarding anything that threatens Hutch. A favorite fan debate point is whether Starsky deliberately or accidentally shoots out the gas tank of a car with two fleeing felons in it who he thinks may have killed Hutch. (Most of us believe it was very deliberate. The car explodes and cooks the criminals.) He ominously threatens an informant who he thinks might know something about Hutch's kidnapping in "The Fix," and nearly throttles Huggy Bear due to stress when Hutch is dying from the Plague [in the episodes "The Plague: Parts One and Two"]. In "Pariah," he explodes in rage during his and Hutch's search for the man who shot his girlfriend and he considers killing the man in cold blood but a word from Hutch stops him. So, yeah, there's enough in Starsky to fit the song.[13]

These events, tied in Flamingo's mind to specific episodes, are evoked for her by thinking about "Behind Blue Eyes" in conjunction with Starsky. As this answer shows, fans loved *Starsky and Hutch* because they saw it as the precursor to quality television shows like *Hill Street Blues*, where "characters live and change and have darker sides,"[14] rather than as a formulaic 1970s-era cop show of the kind parodied by the Beastie Boys in their commercial music video, SABOTAGE (1994). SABOTAGE presents almost an inverse reading of *Starsky and Hutch*: it's three minutes of car chases and guys with too-wide ties and terrible mustaches and sunglasses running and jumping and sliding over the hoods of cars. As directed by Spike Jonze, SABOTAGE gives us a fast-paced montage of clichéd cop show shots: sirens, explosions, mysterious briefcases and homemade bombs, knife fights, Chevrolets taking air, bags of coke, detectives eating sandwiches. While SABOTAGE was made for nearly half a million dollars, it was successful not in small part because it's a different sort of fan music video, interested (as much of today's vastly mainstreamed fan and geek culture now is) in mimicking and parodying fandom's most beloved pop culture icons. After all, what else is SABOTAGE but an expensive 1970s cop show cosplay? While BEHIND BLUE EYES struggles to give us a glimpse into Starsky's internal state, SABOTAGE is all exteriority, interested in tropes and filmic style. In fact, as I will discuss later in this chapter, many of the most successful commercial music videos share fan vidding's obsession with pop culture; it is arguably part of all music video's DNA.

I've dwelled on BEHIND BLUE EYES not despite the fact that it's a primitive protovid but because of it; it allows me to showcase what music alone can bring to a vid in conjunction with the viewer's web of canonical associations before there's moving pictures or real editing, let alone the fast-paced montage of image–sound associations that characterizes modern vidding. BEHIND BLUE EYES thus represents the most basic form of a character vid as fans have defined the term—that is, a vid that "focuses on a single character; expresses something about thoughts, emotions, actions, or motivations; revels in the character's charm, foibles, or wickedness, etc."[15] (See "Spotlight On: Character Vids" in the online appendix.) It is unusual not only for being one of the last vids made with still images but also because its image was chosen chiefly because it was the best picture that Hunter and Barbour could coax out of a VCR, rather than for its canonical resonance.[16]

That stipulated, let's put authorial intent aside and do the kind of frame analysis one would normally do with a vid. The image is muddy, but we can see that Starsky is well framed by the doorway and well placed within the frame itself; this image obeys the rule of thirds. According to Flamingo, this moment in the show is actually a comic one, but in the frame the vidders have selected, Starsky's expression isn't comic; he seems serious, thoughtful. In fact, at first glance, you might even think he's looking into a mirror, both because of his expression and because you might register, without really seeing it at first, another person in the shot: the back of a head. But it's not a mirror—or it's only metaphorically so. The other person is Hutch, Starsky's partner. So even though this is a character vid about Starsky, and the song seems to speak in a single voice about a single mind, the image has double vision. "No one knows what it's like / To be the bad man / To be the sad man / Behind blue eyes"— but with two people in the frame, mirroring each other, how else might we read that?[17]

WOULDN'T IT BE NICE *(2002), by Laura Shapiro (multifandom)*
(Video 9 https://doi.org/10.3998/mpub.10069132.cmp.9)

WOULDN'T IT BE NICE is a montage of popular twosomes from some of fandom's favorite shows, featuring a number of partners, buddies, and friends presented as yearning lovers. This constructing or foregrounding of queer relationships within mainstream television shows is called slash, named for the punctuation mark that conjoins the names of the characters in a particular pairing or ship (the latter short for "relationship"), like Kirk/Spock.[18] Slash is closely tied up with the history of vidding because making the queer subtexts of certain shows visible—by which I mean literally visible to others on screen—is one of the things that vidders invented vidding to do, and romantic or sexual feelings are some of the easiest to convey by means of contemporary popular music. A slash vid is a (love) story and also an argument. They are so in love; just look.

WOULDN'T IT BE NICE is an early work by vidder and vid activist Laura Shapiro, who describes it as "pure slashy fluff, an argument for gay representation on TV, or an argument for same-sex marriage— depending on how you look at it."[19] The general argument of the vid is relatively simple: Wouldn't it be nice if . . . The characters could be out of the closet? Television featured more same-sex relationships? Gay people were allowed to get married? Any of these may be valid readings, depending on which of Shapiro's proffered descriptions you accept. Is this textual reading, cultural criticism, social activism, or all three at once? Within these broader arguments, Shapiro makes particular lyrics speak to particular televisual stories, telling us how to understand them. "And wouldn't it be nice to live together" is paired with Bodie and Doyle from *The Professionals* standing together by a refrigerator, a clip that, in conjunction with the lyrics, connotes domesticity. "Hold each other close the whole night through" tells us how to understand seeing Jean-Luc Picard of *Star Trek: The Next Generation* in bed with Q (Figure 5   https://doi.org/10.3998/mpub.10069132.cmp.141   and   Figure   6 https://doi.org/10.3998/mpub.10069132.cmp.142). It is perhaps worth saying that in 2002, gay and lesbian representation was nascent on network television.

WOULDN'T IT BE NICE is aesthetically but not technologically complicated. Made more than twenty years after BEHIND BLUE EYES, near the end of the VHS era, WOULDN'T IT BE NICE is, technologically speaking, a transitional vid. It was edited on a computer using iMovie, though made from VHS footage passed through an analog-to-digital converter (the use of which necessitated its own kind of technical competencies). But in 2002, homemade VHS was still the only way to get footage from cult media shows like *The Professionals, I Spy, Wiseguy, The Sentinel, Quantum Leap, Due South,* and *Xena: Warrior Princess.* Although WOULDN'T IT BE NICE was edited on a computer, it still feels like a VCR vid in its aesthetics. There are no effects, no changes in speed or color, although Shapiro did

Fig. 5. "And wouldn't it be nice to live together?"

Fig. 6. "Hold each other close the whole night through."

attempt to brighten some of the darker clips. Early commercial editing software like iMovie didn't have many features, and in any case, converted VHS footage like this couldn't stand up to much alteration without breaking down. Primarily, Shapiro is using a computer to more easily get the precise cuts and musically synchronized internal motion that was characteristic of the best VCR vids of the time. In fact, Shapiro is often categorized as a descendant of the so-called San Francisco School, which

I discuss in more detail in chapter 3, a group of Bay Area vidders known for their particular attention to color and motion in editing.

We see Shapiro's close attention to movement and musicality from the first moments of the vid. The Beach Boys song begins with an instrumental section comprising a series of lilting guitar arpeggios that ends in a crash of drums.[20] In the opening of WOULDN'T IT BE NICE, those arpeggios are paired with a scene from the original *Star Trek* in which Mr. Spock swings, childlike, from a tree, an image that perfectly evokes the playful sound of the instrumentation. The drum crash is synched with an internal motion in the next clip: the falling forward of *The Man from U.N.C.L.E.*'s Napoleon Solo's body (0:06 to 0:13). This continues throughout the vid, so that each clip has a musical and aesthetic meaning as well as a narrative one. For example, Shapiro times it so that *Wiseguy's* undercover cop, Vinnie, kisses his handler Frank's forehead precisely at the climax of the verse's musical phrase, even as the general scene, which depicts the characters cuddling on the sofa, illustrates the narrative lyric at that point in the song: "When we can say goodnight and stay together" (0:36; also note the branded "bug" for CourtTV; this is digitized VCR footage taped off the air).

The choreography is both aesthetically and narratively satisfying. The landing of the kiss at the right moment musically is pleasing even as the story of the song is made to match the story of the visuals. Something similar happens later, in the first bridge section:

> Maybe if we think, and wish, and hope, and pray, it might come true
> Baby, then there wouldn't be a single thing we couldn't do
> Oh we could be married
> And then we'd be happy
> Oh wouldn't it be nice!

This section features the only canonical love stories of the vid; these are the ones that came true. We see Beecher/Keller, the two convicts whose twisted and psychopathic love story was one of the primary soap opera plots on the HBO drama *Oz*, then Willow/Tara, the two (canonically) lesbian witches of *Buffy the Vampire Slayer*. Willow and Tara are close dancing in midair, giving a literal as well as metaphorical meaning to the lyric, "There wouldn't be a single thing we couldn't do": Their love is literally magical. The verse rounds out with Stuart and Vince of the UK's *Queer as Folk*, holding hands in public; fans of the program know that it has taken them the entire run of the show to come to this comfortably coupled place. Stuart and Vince leap joyfully into the air like dancers at the song's climax: "Oh wouldn't it be nice!" (1:30).

WOULDN'T IT BE NICE demonstrates a vid's ability to be a story, an argument, and a carefully choreographed dance all at the same time. "Behind the Sounds," a YouTube documentary on the making of the Beach Boys album *Pet Sounds*, describes the song "Wouldn't It Be Nice" as "a happy song about not having what you want."[21] That sentiment applies equally well to this vid. In WOULDN'T IT BE NICE, Shapiro creates the sort of television she wants and doesn't have.

SNAKES ON A PLANE *(2007), by Dualbunny (Harry Potter)*
(Video 10 https://doi.org/10.3998/mpub.10069132.cmp.10)

Vids create both analytical (interpretive) and emotional (lyrical) meanings; because of this, I argue that vidding ought to be understood as a filmic analog to poetry, an art both like speech and like song. Analytical meanings are created by attending to the sound–image conjunctions, moment by moment; to attend to analytical meaning is to figure out what the vid is saying, and a vid can speak in various ways. It can speak literally through song lyrics, which can function as dialogue, narration, or description: "*Nobody knows what it's like* to be Starsky," or "*Wouldn't it be nice if* Bodie and Doyle could have been partners and lovers at the same time?" But vids also speak musically through such things as instrumentation, rhythm, and syncopation. What visual elements are synchronized with that guitar line or that cymbal crash? What happens in the chorus versus the verse? What visual elements are present at the song's climax, and how does that structure the vid's themes? Here we use music as a guide to seeing, and we use what we see to create a new story or reinterpret the visual source.

But a vid's meaning is not only analytical—or rather, analytical meaning is rarely the crucial part. While vids do tell stories, make arguments, and create interpretations, they are not—to paraphrase Walter Pater—a mere translation of fiction, essays, or criticism. Rather, vidding is its own art, and one that by design affects the body and creates feeling, as music does. Pater famously said that all art aspires to the condition of music,[22] though it was Noël Coward who noted the extraordinary potency of cheap (popular) music in particular. Music sets up its own expectations; it sets patterns and invites you to anticipate and be moved by the resolution of those patterns. Vids as an art form are concerned with somatic, emotional meaning, not secondarily but simultaneously with the pleasures of analytical insight. Pater praised music as the highest art for its perfect blending of matter and form. Similarly, vids make us feel as well as think. They can even can show us how feeling and thinking—the body's way of knowing and the mind's way of knowing—are intertwined, or perhaps actually the same thing. This integration of thinking and feeling, of mind and body, is also, in our dualistic and hierarchical age, one of the grounds for considering vidding a feminist art.

If vidding is pop media aspiring to the condition of music, then we must try to articulate the ways in which vids turn plot-driven or visually spectacular mass media texts into felt experiences. As Pater reminds us, we must not ignore the "peculiar and untranslatable sensuous charm" specific to a particular art.[23] In the case of vidding, this means the pleasures of rhythmic editing, which includes the musical flow of images and the choreographed conjunctions between the audio and the visual—which is to say, precisely the sort of thing that is hard to describe in words. But here goes.

Dualbunny's Harry Potter vid SNAKES ON A PLANE (2007) was made for Vividcon's Club Vivid dance party, so it was designed to affect the body; you are literally supposed to get up and dance to it. (For more about Club Vivid and dance vids, see chapter 4.) SNAKES ON A PLANE might not be the sort of vid you think of as poetry; it doesn't have any of the epic seriousness we might associate with poetry or with a vid like DANTE'S PRAYER. It's not a big "message" vid, and it doesn't have a complicated plot: There are a lot of different kinds of snakes in the Harry Potter movies, and Harry would really like to survive his encounters with them. The vid's Cobra Starship song is big and explosively cheesy, the kind that you want to dance to, or sing along with at the top of your lungs in the car. So far, so bad—because that doesn't explain what's good about this vid. I can say that it's well made; indeed, it's exquisitely edited and structured so as to have fantastic build. I can say that the vid has consistently clever image–music conjunctions, and it doesn't repeat itself; as in the best poetry, we see repetition with a difference, where repeated images and refrains mean something different each time they're encountered. I can also say that Dualbunny, working in 2007, is fully using the features of her computer to edit. But what does any of that mean? No textual explanation will substitute for seeing the vid itself, but let me analyze some moments in a few of these categories.

Repetition with a Difference

While the subject matter of Cobra Starship's "Snakes on a Plane (Bring It)" is unusual—how many songs about snakes can you think of?—the song's structure is fairly conventional: verse, prechorus, chorus, bridge/ middle eight. Curiously, the song interprets the (literal) snakes of the 2006 Samuel Jackson movie metaphorically. The snakes of the song, depicted as "lounging in their suits and ties," seem mostly to be "venomous" music industry hacks. In the middle eight, we're told,

> Ladies and gentlemen,
> These snakes is slitherin'
> With dollar signs in their eyes
> With tongues so reptilian
> This industry's venomous
> With cold-blooded sentiment
> No need for nervousness
> It's just a little turbulence

These words bring to mind Hunter S. Thompson's line about how "the music business is a cruel and shallow money trench, a long plastic hallway where thieves and pimps run free, and good men die like dogs."[24] In Dualbunny's SNAKES ON A PLANE, the snakes that Harry Potter has to fight are both literal (a series of terrifying fanged monsters) and metaphorical (all the Dark Wizards of the story come from the house of Slytherin, whose symbol is a serpent).

So one kind of repetition with a difference in SNAKES ON A PLANE comes from the variety of snakes on offer: literal snakes like boa constrictors and black serpents as well as monsters like the Basilisk and Nagini; snake-faced wraiths like the Dementors; a host of Slytherins, including Snape, Draco and Lucius Malfoy, Barty Crouch Jr., and of course Lord Voldemort; and the Dark Mark, a skull with a snake coming out of its mouth. When Dualbunny begins the vid with a skillful sound edit that makes Harry seem to yell Samuel L. Jackson's famous line from the film—"That's it! I have had it with these motherfucking snakes on this motherfucking plane!"—we grin and feel his pain; the guy's dealing with a lot of fucking snakes.

However, a more striking repetition with a difference happens in the song's prechorus, which is framed as a call-and-response between sing-

ers: "Oh, I'm ready for it!" "Come on, bring it!" The line is repeated
four times each time it occurs, which is three times over the course of the
song. Dualbunny not only makes it mean something different each time
but also uses it to structure an arc that moves Harry's story along and
raises the vid's narrative and emotional stakes. The call-and-response first
occurs at the end of the first verse, which shows Harry getting invited to
Hogwarts. In this context, it is used to show Harry's eagerness for the wizarding experience: He's ready for it! Harry enters the wizarding world;
he shops in Diagon Alley, stares at his inherited pile of gold, clutches
his new magic wand. We also see him riding the Hogwarts Express and
taking the boat across the lake; he's oh so ready for his new magical life.
But by the time the prechorus swings around again, the situation has
changed. Harry is no longer a starry-eyed innocent agape at the wizarding world. The second verse narrates Harry's conflicts with the Slytherin
boys, both in school and on the Quidditch field; correspondingly, the
call-and-response now functions as trash talk between Harry and Draco
Malfoy. For example, in one of the four repetitions in this section, the
lines give voice to the boys' thoughts as they face off in a duel of wands,
with Harry thinking, "Oh, I'm ready for it," and Draco, "Come on, bring
it!" (1:16–1:20).

By the third repetition of the prechorus, the situation has escalated
past this sort of boyish confrontation. Harry is now fighting an all-out war
for his life against Lord Voldemort, which he may really *not* be ready for.
The stakes couldn't be higher: Cedric Diggory is slain. Finally Voldemort
is rushed by the ghosts of all the people's he's murdered, including Harry's parents, Lilly and James. The song's closing lines instruct
Voldemort to "grab your ankles and kiss your ass goodbye," which is as
much of a victory for Harry as Dualbunny can coax out of the first four
movies, which was all the footage available at the time. But the vid has
skillfully led us to this climatic victory, using the repeated prechorus to
frame a story in three acts.

Lyric–Image Conjunctions

I've been describing the overall narrative arc: Harry confronts a new
world, has interpersonal confrontations at school, then goes to war. Now
I want to turn to particular moments of lyric–image conjunction. The
matching of lyrics to image is so well done that one might think that the
song was written about the Harry Potter franchise. I could reel off a list
of lovely moments: "We've got a free upgrade / For snakes on a plane"

paired with a close-up of Harry's Hogwarts invitation, which becomes the upgrade (0:16–0:19); "The sky's alive / With lizards serpentine / Lounging in their suits and ties" paired with a slow pan up the green uniforms of the Slytherin Quidditch team, who do indeed fly in the sky (1:09–1:11). The entire middle eight quoted above (1:58–2:12) is fabulously worked: these snakes are indeed slitherin'—or Slytherin. Lucius Malfoy has dollar signs in his eyes; Barty Crouch is gibbering, flicking his reptilian tongue; Severus Snape is the embodiment of cold-blooded sentiment, at least as far as Harry is concerned. These lyric–image conjunctions are perfect to the point of wit.

But I want to point out one smaller moment that always strikes me as particularly lovely. In the vid's first verse, which Dualbunny uses to stage Harry's first encounters with the wizarding world, we get the lyric "Pop the cheap champagne." This is paired with a rhythmically edited clip from a scene where Harry's house is flooded with invitations to attend Hogwarts. Envelopes come flying in from everywhere—windows, chimney, letter slot—and go whirling around in the air (Figure 7 https://doi.org/10.3998/mpub.10069132.cmp.143, 0:23–0:27). Harry is leaping up ecstatically, arms raised, trying to grab some of the envelopes, but what I want you to see is the way in which this gesture evokes, slantwise and poetically, the popping of champagne. Just like a bottle of champagne explodes up and foams over, so Harry's house has popped (letter box flying open, flue opening) and now overflows with these invitations (the "free upgrade" alluded to earlier), which spurt upward (see Harry leaping) into a fountain and spill over just as champagne would. Even the color of the envelopes is evocative. This is also a moment of celebration in the first film, in that Harry's destiny has reached him. Good vids are full of these moments of perfect audiovisual metaphor, which can be read as I've just done—see, it's like champagne; listen, here's what it means—but it's like explaining jokes or music.

Sound–Image Conjunctions

Not all of a vid's perfect moments are tied to song lyrics; audiovisual poetry is not all narration or description. Many of the best moments in SNAKES ON A PLANE are nonverbal sound–image conjunctions. For example, Dualbunny times a clip so as to make an owl seem like it's doing a taunting hip-hop shoulder shrug in response to the music (0:29–0:32); she orchestrates the "Oh!" in the second iteration of "Oh, I'm ready for it!" with Draco throwing an elbow into Harry on the Quidditch field,

Fig. 7. "Pop the cheap champagne."

so that the "Oh!" is a huff of air, an exclamation marking that violence (1:23); she pairs a moment in which Cobra Starship's song mechanically slows down with a clip of Harry swimming underwater, so that the song's aural distortion is synchronized with the slow motion and distorted sound associated with being submerged (2:50–2:53). These perfect audiovisual moments come one after the other like beads on a string, together creating the vid's choreography and meaning.

Use of Brightness to Structure Climax

Cobra Starship's "Snakes on a Plane" is notable for its dynamics. The song ramps up several times from a vocal line very like normal speech to power-pop heights: a multitracked vocal crescendo of long-held notes. This is particularly characteristic of the song's chorus: "So kiss me good-bye!" with the "bye" held for an entire measure. Dualbunny structures that line explosively each time it appears, literally lighting up the screen. Flames explode on *good-BYYYYYYE*, blinding Harry and us; Tom Riddle explodes into light; wands flash with lightning. These bright clips emphasize the song's structure and create a series of visual narrative climaxes.

By means of these techniques—repetition with a difference, clever lyrical and aural conjunctions, use of brightness to structure climaxes—Dualbunny creates a montage of rhythmic moments that contain poetical meaning and build. Together, they tell a story you can dance to.

FLOW *(2013), by lim (multifandom) (Video 11 https://doi.org/10.3998/mpub.10069132.cmp.11)*

Like poetry, vids run the gamut from lines of simple doggerel to complexly structured works dense with spoken and felt meaning. There are vids in which every moment—every frame, motion, and pixel—may be significant, especially now that vidders have access to sophisticated tools that allow them to work over a piece of video frame by frame. The vidder lim is known not just for her musicality and the quality of her editing but also for her willingness to make each and every frame a canvas. Lim draws and paints over mass media images, manipulating and remaking them, turning them into something hand worked. In her most famous vid, US (2007) (Video 12 https://doi.org/10.3998/mpub.10069132.cmp.12), lim altered each frame to make it look like cross-hatched pencil animation, then choreographed the path a hand would take erasing and coloring and scribbling and further embellishing the televisual images. (For more discussion of US, see chapter 5.)

FLOW, like US, is made of highly worked frames that are both aesthetically pleasing and meaningful; also like US, FLOW is in part about what it means to make television into art. Because of this, FLOW is impossible to explicate in a few paragraphs or even a single essay. It is not only a beautiful and complex work, but it is also about the process of making meaning with all of its complexities, pleasures, obsessions, and compulsions. Lim constructs FLOW both as an information-dense puzzle and as a story about solving a puzzle. It is also a story about *how good it feels* to solve a puzzle, find a pattern, make art. In other words, FLOW is a vid about vidding and how it feels to create patterns out of the formlessness of television. As such, the "flow" of the title signifies in two different directions. Flow is the noise of television from which a vidder must extract a meaningful signal; that is, it is flow in Raymond Williams's sense of an always-on broadcast, a stream of information. "Flow" is also a term of art in psychology, used to describe the feeling of being in the zone—that is, the pleasure of being fully immersed in a task, energized and focused, present in the moment to the point of neglecting the rest of reality.

FLOW is thus not only a work of art and analysis but also a self-portrait of the vidder as detective, obsessively chasing truth by making (finding)

Fig. 8. A collaged murder wall from FLOW by lim (2013, multifandom).

connections (edits) between seemingly disparate things. Moving across a number of Sherlock Holmes and Holmes-inspired TV shows, (including *House, The Mentalist, The X-Files, Person of Interest,* and both the BBC's *Sherlock* and CBS's *Elementary*), lim shows us how detectives follow chains of evidence to find order within chaos. One of her recurring images is the televisual cliché of the so-called murder wall, or the bulletin board, chalkboard, whiteboard, or other surface upon which the TV detective visually organizes his thinking, thereby making it visible to the audience. Murder walls are literally collages of information (Figure 8 https://doi.org/10.3998/mpub.10069132.cmp.144, 2:12–2:22).

Lim turns these murder walls into a metaphor for vidding itself. Like these master detectives, who construct collages of evidence and search for patterns within chaos, vidders also organize information into beautiful visual patterns. They create montages, clip by clip, making meaning—or perhaps only madness. After all, it would be hard to gather a crazier or more obsessive group than Sherlock Holmes, Dr. Gregory House, Fox Mulder, Patrick Jane, et al. But the detective story assures us that there is such a thing as truth, and that it can be found—or as *The X-Files* has it, that the truth is out there.

Lim herself seems more ambivalent on the point, chasing tropes and images from show to show like Alice going down the rabbit hole. In fact, lim literally chases Alice, the Mad Hatter, and the White Rabbit through a series of televisual tea parties in one elaborate sequence, framing vidding as sense and madness both (0:42–1:12). A born-digital vidder who has always made and experienced vids via computer, lim expects—as many VCR-trained or influenced vidders do not—that the spectator will not only watch a vid multiple times, as in the old living room vids, but examine the vid frame by frame. Consequently, in the collage that starts the Alice sequence (Figure 9 https://doi.org/10.3998/mpub.10069132.cmp.145, 0:42), she expects you to notice the highlighted text ("It began with the tea," the Hatter replied) and follow the flow of associations and colors (the Hatter, syringe, and rabbit are all pink; follow the rabbit) along to the teacups and teapots. This is certainly a meaningful chain of associations, but it's also, quite literally, *Alice in Wonderland* logic, beautiful and surreal and dreamlike. FLOW is thus a kind of poetic meditation about ratiocination (the fetish for reasoning beloved of detectives since Poe's Dupin) and pareidolia (seeing patterns where none exist—that is, seeing a face in the moon or pictures in inkblots). The vid argues that the truth may be out there, or the truth may be what we make of it. But making art—finding patterns, creating something beautiful out of chaos—is a profound pleasure that some people must obsessively chase.

This big-picture analysis is built up from countless poetic details, including a sequence where a shot of a book on chaos theory (from *Person of Interest*) cuts to a shot of a butterfly fluttering its wings as *The Mentalist*'s Patrick Jane sips tea ("It began with the tea"), which cuts to a mirroring shot of Cumberbatch's *Sherlock* fluttering his eyelashes in a movement that echoes the fluttering of the butterfly. This montage evokes a conceptual and visual idea—chaos theory's butterfly effect—which is, in part, about the difficulty of finding patterns in or making predictions about large and complex systems. But this is what our detectives (and this vidder) are trying to do.

The attentive reader will have noticed that I've yet to discuss a song lyric or musical line. In fact, FLOW is not named for the song it uses, "Nothing Else Matters," by Orbital's Paul Hartnoll, though, as in any vid, the song is crucial. Its repeated lyric and soaring build gives FLOW much of its emotional intensity: nothing else matters but chasing these patterns, getting into that zone. Moreover, this addictive flow of information is felt viscerally—in fact musically. Sherlock Holmes is canonically a musician as well as a logician; usually he plays the violin, though Dr.

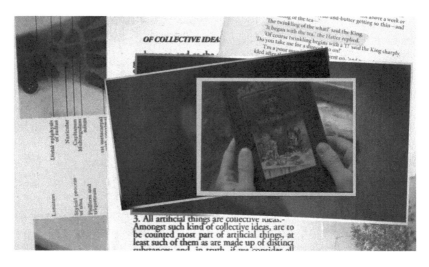

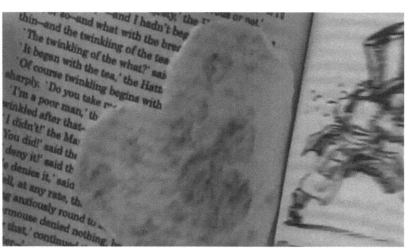

Figs. 9–12. "It began with the tea," the Hatter replied.

House plays the piano. In FLOW, the musical keyboard is related to the computer keyboard. The characters' fingertips tap out the song's piano parts, those beats are translated into binary code, and the binary code is used to interpret and make images, emphasizing that all computer images are code underneath (1:44–1:48). Music is therefore figured as the secret code that underlies everything, just as binary code underpins the digital world. All digital objects are ones and zeros.

As the music builds to a climax, we see the detectives hit full flow. They are sweating, entranced, ecstatic, their arms raised, their eyes

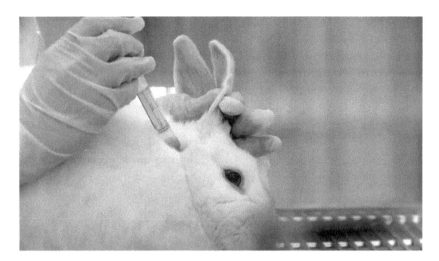

closed or alight; they are transcendent. Lim shows them as soaring through visualized fields of data: millions of screens, streams of ones and zeros. Information flies between frames. Impossible patterns are detected. House throws a ball (past Jonny Lee Miller's Holmes) and Sherlock catches it; in a wonder of motion matching and precision editing, one ball is tossed across three shows (2:29–2:33). Sherlock leaps off a building but Patrick Jane lands; House, working a case at Baltimore Liberty airport, sends the word "Liberty" downstream to Sherlock (3:26–3:34). Clues explode with light. Insight is literalized in the final shot, in which the detective is told those three little words that mean everything: "You were right."

Here I stop, though I haven't even gotten to the relationship between liberty and imprisonment, or the use of static/visual disruption in the vid, or the vid's ideas about fractal geometry and big data, or the importance of the number 42. I haven't talked about any of the television episodes a fan might recognize as central: "Failure to Communicate" (*House M.D.*), "Paper Hearts" (*The X-Files*), "Devil's Cherry" (*The Mentalist*), "The Hounds of Baskerville" (*Sherlock*), and so on. My point is this: not all vids are as complicated (or as rewarding) as FLOW, but vids can be as complicated (and as rewarding) as FLOW.

Some Brief Points of Comparison

I'd like to conclude this chapter with some brief points of comparison between vids and other audiovisual forms. Vids are their own thing, but to understand them, we can draw on what we know of related forms. While many of these forms will be discussed elsewhere in the book, it's worth sketching out some broad intersections and points of contrast. So: Vids are like . . .

Silent Film

As Annabel J. Cohen reminds us, in early film, music served both a practical function (masking the noise of the projector) as well as an aesthetic one (illustrating and explaining the action in emotional terms).[25] Early silent film music was live, and as Martin Miller Marks notes, it was "not all of a piece; it consisted of improvisations, compilations, and original scores, mixed in many ways."[26] In its way, accompanying silent films was a remix art.[27] Early cue sheets and musical anthologies organized music by "mood, dramatic situation, tempo, and meter"—that is, in terms of its emotional effect on the spectator. Before talkies, music was such an intrinsic part of the filmic experience that film was considered more of a musical art than a dramatic or narrative one. Cohen quotes from Hugo Munsterberg's *The Photoplay: A Psychological Study* (1916), arguably the first book of film theory, to make the point. Munsterberg argues:

> We come nearer to the understanding of its [film's] true position in the aesthetic world, if we think at the same time of . . . the art of the musical tones. They have overcome the outer world and the social

world entirely, they unfold our inner life, our mental play, with its feelings and emotions, it's memories and fancies, in a material which seems exempt from the laws of the world of substance and material, tones which are fluttering and fleeting like our own mental states.[28]

In early silent film, when the music was site specific and played live, film was not the standardized mass media object of today; there was still a possibility for local meaning and collaboration. Silent film accompanist Ben Model blogs about the choices he makes when he accompanies film. For instance, he describes how to play for *Nosferatu* so that a modern audience won't laugh but instead has the emotions that Model considers appropriate. "What I wound up doing," Model writes, "seizing on an impulse in the moment, from having been caught up in the emotional arc of the plot from the beginning of the film, was emphasizing the maniacal glee Orlock must have been feeling . . . by playing something much more energetic and demonic."[29]

Nondiegetic Film Music

When the talkies arrived, bringing with them realistic dialogue and sound, many thought that music would be shed as an unrealistic contrivance. But of course it was not. As Cohen explains, "Logically . . . [nondiegetic music] should *detract from* rather than *add to* the sense of reality"[30] of film. But it doesn't. As cultural musicologist Lawrence Kramer reminds us, "Virtually from the outset of the film era, [the immateriality of the film image] prompted a search for sound—a search, that is, for music, not for speech."[31] This search culminated in the development of the soundtrack, where music could merge seamlessly with the spectacle on screen. Siegfried Kracauer has written of the importance of "commentative music"—music that restates the moods, tendencies, or meanings of the pictures it accompanies—and claims it brings the pictures into focus.[32] In *Cutting Rhythms: Shaping the Film Edit*, Karen Pearlman describes how music helps a film attain coherence. Film music "applies a seamless composition to images that are in actuality riddled with seams. Music, which is perceived as a flow rather than a series of individual notes, enhances the flow of images and ameliorates much of the disruptive potential of cutting, thereby making the cuts and the compositions of the cuts' rhythms much harder to see."[33] This was Bernard Herrmann's position too: "Music is a kind of binding veneer that holds a film together, and hence is particularly valuable in the use of montage. It's really the only thing that seals a montage into one coherent effect."[34] While this is particularly true for continuity editing, where we aren't supposed to notice the cuts, it is also true in vidding, which puts editing front and center as an art to be appreciated. Still, the seamlessness of music does add a sense of wholeness to a vid's remixed-and-matched parts.

There are some important distinctions, however. Film music, for both silent and talking films, is often framed as accompaniment,[35] as amplifying or echoing the emotional effects of the pictures on screen rather than producing them, as in vidding. Filmic meaning is thought to be actually in the filmed picture despite what we know of the so-called Kuleshov effect, which Andreas M. Baranowski and Heiko Hecht have shown to be equally true for audio contexts—that is, that music gives meaning to ambiguous situations and can alter our understanding of facial expressions.[36] But film music, also known as the soundtrack, is frequently treated like it's replaceable; indeed, sometimes in practice it is actually replaced. This is typically due to rights issues rather than aesthetic judgment. For example, some TV shows did not have the rights to reuse music when episodes were packaged for DVD, and so sometimes the originally broadcast music was replaced, often to deleterious effect.[37] Similarly, films are frequently scored to "temp tracks" that are later replaced with original (but structurally similar) music.[38] This is impossible in vidding—or rather, you can change a vid's music, but then you're changing the vid's essence. As I hope I have shown with my examples, music is the backbone of fan vids. It is utterly constitutive; it is no mere accompaniment. Vid music is not a soundtrack.

Vid music must be noticed; in fact, it must be actively attended to, mined for information moment by moment. If, as Karen Kalishak says in *Settling the Score*, film music is "a presence we register but don't always notice, a wash of sound to which we respond but whose meaning lies just beyond conscious recognition,"[39] then that is not true of vid music, which we track consciously in order to obtain its meaning. It is not Kalishak's wash of sound; it is not merely the up-tempo, anxiety-producing music that accompanies a shot of galloping horses. It's denser than that. Cohen compares film music to prosody in speech perception—that is, to the patterns of rhythm and sound, stress and intonation—and notes that these patterns "systematically provide emotional meaning to a listener, yet the listener focuses on the meaning and is unconscious of this prosodic source of information."[40] But in vidding, we attend specifically to prosodic information, which is what makes it more like poetry—sound and sense combined—than like narrative film.

The Movie Musical

Like musicals, vids use song to develop characterization and to make visible a character's interior emotional states. Vids create a bridge between genre TV and film and the musical, just as musicals like *The Rocky Horror Show* and *Be More Chill* have from the other direction, and as cult TV shows often now do for themselves, with a musical episode having become almost a standard feature of successful cult TV. *Xena: Warrior Princess* had two musical episodes, one with a song-and-dance sequence that was deemed a "found vid" (see **THE JOXER DANCE** [2003] [Video 13 https://doi.org/10.3998/mpub.10069132.cmp.13], discussed in chapter 4) by vidding fandom, and the musical episodes of *Buffy the Vampire Slayer*, *Community*, and *Scrubs* are now regarded as classics.

But there are other interesting resonances between movie musicals and vids, particularly those vids that use superhero movies and sci-fi television as source. Like those genres, the musical is simultaneously central to and on the margins of American culture. Musicals have been both popular and acclaimed, doing not just enormous box office but also sometimes collecting Oscars. At the same time, they're often seen as middlebrow, and even some best picture award winners (like *The Sound of Music*) are critically disregarded by film scholars. Sci-fi and fantasy has an even worse reputation, as it is considered lowbrow despite its historical association with overeducated geeks and nerds. SFF films are rarely nominated for top awards and almost never win,[41] but like musicals, they are internationally successful tentpole spectacles that bankroll the industry. And they are indeed spectacles. In both musicals and genre blockbusters, there are visually spectacular sequences that don't move the plot forward but are just, well, pleasing to look at, with people and things moving in time to patterns—that is to say, dancing. In one episode of *Every Frame a Painting*, Tony Zhou compares the cinematography, editing, and direction of Michael Bay's chaos-cut action movies to that of Bay's favorite film, *West Side Story*. When shots from both films are put side by side, the influence is clear. Bay's Transformer robots are dancing. Explosions start to have a Busby Berkeley quality. Fighter planes in formation evoke formation in ballroom and cheerleading.

In an interview with the *New York Times*, Bay expresses his admiration for the musical:

> What I like about musicals is that they break the rules of cinema. You know what I'm saying? The old rules of editing where, it's said, you must cut from this to this. You can't cut from here to there. You

can't place the camera there; you have to place it here. When I do my action movies, I break the rules, too. That's one thing musicals and big action movies have in common. With both of them, you can break the rules. One of the things that can make them exciting is that you are breaking the rules.[42]

Bay breaks the rules to create high-concept, but essentially empty, spectacles. His movies borrow some of the techniques of movie musicals, but not their emotion—not the song in the heart. But vidders borrow both aspects, creating what are essentially musical dance sequences out of the visual spectacles of mass media, but in service of character and emotion. Put another way, there's something similarly spectacular about Captain Kirk's energetic fighting style and Riff's, or Captain America flinging his shield and Julie Andrews spinning on a mountaintop. But a vidder will reedit the film to give the captains what they lack: the right song for the moment.

Vids also are extremely condensed—three to four minutes—while the spectacular film, whether sci-fi or musical, is often long and bloated. As Pauline Kael moaned in her review of *Hello, Dolly!*, "I love musicals, but I hate big, expensive musicals, because I have to wade through all the filler of production values to get to what I want to see."[43] Certainly many SFF fans feel this way; fans will sit through any number of long CGI sequences for those few seconds where characters interact or express a feeling. When Kael complains that "so much effort has been expended on the gut-busting things that don't mean anything, that have no feeling attached to them . . . and so little care has been given to the dialogue or to those supine lyrics, or to the characters,"[44] she speaks for every fan who stumbled bleary-eyed out of *Avengers: Age of Ultron*. But a vid can distill that experience, cutting out the filler and drawing meaning out of the spectacle with song.

A last, noteworthy point of comparison: both blockbusters and musicals can be seen to reflect conservative, even retrograde, politics. They're overwhelmingly white, invested in stereotypical gender performance, and almost cheerily heterosexist. At the same time, both forms are at the center of queer subcultures. D. A. Miller has written movingly about the ways in which the musical, as a rare female-dominated art form, has been a site of profound emotional identification for gay men, a place where they can indulge "in the thrills of a femininity become their own."[45] Stacy Wolf, agreeing that the musical is female dominated, argues that "women spectators can find a strong figure in an actor and character of their own gender."[46] In *A Problem Like Maria*, Wolf describes the many creative and "deviant" readings that lesbian spectators make of *The Sound of Music*, declaring that they use the film with "a vengeance."[47] Engagements like these resemble those of media fans, and particularly those of slash and femslash fans. Like Miller's gay male musical fans, slash fans often identify across gender[48] with the overdetermined male heroes of SFF, perhaps thrilling to a masculinity become their own. Like Wolf's lesbian spectators, female fans may find they identify with and/or desire the strong female heroines that SFF sometime provides, and some will work hard to tease out "the contagious pleasure of finding lesbians" when you begin to read generic codes differently.[49] For Wolf, this occurs in reading musical features like duets between women "as" lesbian, or by reading moments of doubling, or women in groups, or gender unconventionality "as" lesbian.[50] Vidders also use these techniques, rereading moments of gender unconventionality and creating visual duets, sometimes across media. Femslash vids (vids that focus on relationships between women) like I'M YOUR MAN (2008, multifandom) (Video 14 https://doi. org/10.3998/mpub.10069132.cmp.14) and BOOM BOOM BA (2004, *Xena: Warrior Princess*) (Video 15 https://doi.org/10.3998/mpub.10069132. cmp.15) by Charmax reinscribe scenes between women to delirious, sensual effect. In HURRICANE (2010, *Battlestar Galactica* and *Farscape*) (Video 16 https://doi.org/10.3998/mpub.10069132.cmp.16), Laura Shapiro constructs a one-night stand between female characters from different shows, imagining an intergalactic bar where military women Starbuck and Aeryn Sun eye fuck, then fall into bed together.

Title Sequences

In their emphasis on cutting and visual musicality as tied to characterization, story genre, and interpretation, title sequences may be vidding's closest professional cousins—closer in function and form than, say, commercial music videos, which I discuss later in this chapter. Vidders themselves have spoken of the importance of title sequences; for example, in her essay "Demystifying Vidding," lim shouts out the opening credits of *Buffy the Vampire Slayer* and *Friends* as sequences to be studied.[51] Lim claims, "The *Friends* titles basically slowly teach you how to edit (very simply) to music—they start off with the characters literally dancing to the music and then gradually over the years replace each dance move with a clip from the show that dances in a similar way." The titles also feature image and motion matching from shot to shot.

Lawrence Kramer calls opening title sequences "the televisual equivalent of lyric poetry" and claims they encapsulate "the fantasies underlying the shows' narrative formulas without the need to rationalize them or bring them to closure."[52] He takes as his case studies the openings of fan favorites *The X-Files* and *NYPD Blue*, two network shows that heralded our current so-called golden age of quality television. Similarly, in "Title Sequences for Contemporary Television Serials," Annette Davison argues that the titles made for premium cable shows like HBO's *The Sopranos* and *Six Feet Under* are "fascinating progenitors of new audiovisual aesthetics."[53] While Davison notes that these influential sequences were themselves influenced by developments in music video and commercials, vidding should also be on that list. All these shows, as well as *True Blood*, *Dexter*, *The Wire*, *House*, and others, feature vid-like aesthetics.

Consider, for instance, the way *The Sopranos* credit sequence repurposes Alabama 3's "Woke Up This Morning," a song inspired by the real-life case of Sara Thornton, an abused woman who killed her husband, to give a voice to Tony Soprano, with whom it is now indelibly associated. Like a vid, the title sequence makes the song absolutely about Tony: It is now the gangster, not the battered wife, who gets a gun, who's born under a bad sign, who has a blue moon in his eyes. Like a good vid, the title sequence forever changes how we hear the song; it's hard to believe it wasn't written for Tony. But of course it wasn't. That's because the title sequence, like a vid, creates a rhythmic montage that puts us up close to Tony, right beside him in the car, as he moves, ascending, out of the Lincoln Tunnel and onto the Jersey Turnpike, going through tollbooths and driving through various neighborhoods and the social classes they represent until he passes through the gate of his own upscale house and comes to a stop.

In *Reading The Sopranos*, David Johansson provides a close reading of this sequence, analyzing all the elements—the tollbooth, the sign that says "Drive Safely," the look on Tony's face when he crests the drive of his house—and reads them through what he admits is knowledge of the character accrued over time, even though we see the credit sequence before we see or know anything else. A title sequence isn't a fan vid, but Johansson is speaking vidding's language when he compares the opening of *The Sopranos* to the overture of an opera, which "introduces conflicts, sets up issue and foreshadows themes, establishing patterns and motifs."[54] He reads each lyric through the lens of Tony's character: "The song encourages the viewer to root for Tony as the heroic underdog, the man who will defeat the curse of his birth, the man whose Papa 'never told him about right and wrong.'"[55] Like a vid, the song has been repurposed, changed to be about what the montage tells us it's about. However, unlike vids, which are typically made by women to express less mainstream perspectives, *The Sopranos* appropriation goes in the wrong direction. As Johansson admits, "Ironically, while 'Woke Up This Morning began as a tale of female rebellion, it's now tied to outsized manliness." The indie blues song about a woman's suffering now gives voice to a big-budget male gangster.[56]

It's worth noting that the above are all television title sequences. TV titles typically work more like fan vids than do film titles, even clever ones by the likes of Saul Bass or Maurice Binder. This is partly because television benefits from repetition and familiarity, as does pop music; while there are film series and serials, even the longest are usually not as long as a single season of TV. Davison notes that a good title sequence must "satisfy the prospective viewer while also remaining interesting to the returning viewer and fan,"[57] and David Lavery gets at this in *Reading "The Sopranos"* when he observes, "It is only after the show has gone on for several seasons that the title sequence increases in richness, as layers of meaning ripple outward over episodes past."[58]

That said, there are always exceptions, and a notably vid-like title sequence occurs in Lawrence Kasdan's 1983 film *The Big Chill*. *The Big Chill* uses music in vid-like ways throughout. The film is at least partly about how the baby boom generation interprets themselves through music. The famous title sequence uses Marvin Gaye's "Heard It through the Grapevine" to introduce the film's large cast of characters as they each get a call telling them that their friend Alex has committed suicide. The montage of their reactions is intercut with shots—not of a man getting dressed, as we first think, but of a corpse with slit wrists being dressed for burial. Like a vid, this audiovisual sequence changes the meaning of the song for those who have seen it. "The grapevine" is now not gossip but the telephone; "it took me by surprise" describes the shock of Alex's suicide; "not much longer would you be mine" is now the death of a friend rather than the loss of a lover. As in a vid, the soulful song gives complexity to the actors' blank expressions and routine actions; it inscribes them with shock and grief. This opening sequence concludes with a second, equally memorable musical appropriation. The Rolling Stones song "You Can't Always Get What You Want," played diegetically on a church organ at the funeral, comes to extend nondiegetically over Alex's entire funeral procession. When Jagger begins to sing, "I saw her today at the reception," we know that what is meant is this funeral, and when the song crests into a choir singing at the end, it seems tailor made for a boom shot of a graveside service.

Sampling, Remix, and African American Vernacular Traditions

Tom Pettitt argues that artworks created in African American vernacular traditions (by which he means sermons, spirituals, blues, the dozens, and jazz, as well as novels and short stories that deploy the idioms of sung and spoken folk narrative) are the immediate predecessors of and have strong commonalities with works produced in our current age of "sampling, remixing, borrowing, reshaping, appropriating and recontextualizing."[59] Similarly, Abigail De Kosnik locates the roots of digital remix in two communities "that had long been (and continue to be) marginalized by mainstream mass media industries," namely "African American men, who, in the mid-1980s, began using digital samplers to cobble together pieces (or 'samples') of existing recordings to form new sonic compositions, and by white American women, who, in the early 1990s, formed online communities on Usenet groups to share fan fiction."[60]

Vidding developed from this same community of fanfiction–writing white women, so despite some commonality of practice with sampling, vidding may be seen as an example of what Mel Stanfill has called "predominantly white fandom,"[61] a term she uses to parallel the "predominantly white institutions" of higher learning that are themselves the (intentionally marked) counterpart to historically black colleges and universities. Vidding's roots are white even to the choice of music, which, as I discuss in chapter 2, initially tended toward lyrical ballads as expressed in folk rock or power pop. While vidders believed that this musical bias represented a bias toward songs with clearly understandable lyrics in the service of literary storytelling, there was little to no unpacking of the bias as to what exactly was comprehensible, and to whose ear.

De Kosnik's work positions African American men and white American women as parallel but separate communities marginalized by media industries. However, there are points of commonality and even intersection, despite the fact that the trajectories of sampling and fan works diverged sharply in the late 1970s and early 1980s, when sampling went mainstream and fandom went underground.[62] For instance, De Kosnik has described how the inventor of remix, DJ Kool Herc, used to spin "two identical records on turntables at the same time, first throwing the needle down at the beginning of the breakbeat on one record and lifting the needle when the breakbeat finished, then immediately throwing the needle down at the start of the breakbeat on the second record,"[63] extending the best, most danceable part of a song potentially ad infinitum. Similarly, as I describe in more detail in chapter 2, vidding foremother Kandy Fong used two slide projectors to cut faster between still images when performing her slideshow vids at conventions, essentially creating the vid live. In both cases, the body and the machine work together to create—or perhaps to perform—a new artwork made out of existing pieces of mass media. And in both sampling and vidding, the artist remakes the work so as to draw out what she likes.

Kevin Glynn specifically shouts out vidding in his analysis of BIN LADEN (2006),[64] a viral YouTube video made from the hip-hop track "Bin Laden" (2004) by Immortal Technique, Mos Def, and DJ Green, with samples from Jadakiss and Eminem. Glynn argues that the history of remix goes from West Africa to the Caribbean and eventually "passes through Jamaica and New York in the birth of hip hop, through the culture of vidders, through that key site of Bush era social commentary, political critique and satire, the *Daily Show*, and through the Internet branches of the Obama movement throughout 2008."[65] The BIN LADEN video is

> a rapid-fire assemblage of miscellaneous images including heavy doses of TV journalists and Fox News commentators, Bush administration politicians, the WTC [World Trade Center] attacks, corporate logos, third world military interventions and death squad victims . . . set to fiercely sardonic lyrics about "fake Christians" and "fake politicians . . . in mansions," the ongoing fight for survival in the ghetto, US war mongering and covert paramilitary actions, and the recurring lines: "Bin Laden didn't blow up the projects. . . . Bush knocked down the towers."[66]

The video is part interpretation and part illustration, sometimes assembling images to match lyrics (for example, showing an image of leeches on "leeches" or a diagram of blood types on "blood"), but sometimes— like a vid—using the song's political narrative to get us to understand the images (and history) differently. As Glynn notes, vidding as an art of appropriation and reinterpretation affected political remixers, and was easily married to the aesthetics of the mixtape. Similarly, artist Kamau Patton credits vidding in his notes to HIP HOP SPA (2011),[67] a music video made for Kuwaiti musician and artist Fatima Al Qadiri's song of the same name. In *Fandom as Methodology: A Sourcebook for Artists and Writers*

(2019), Catherine Grant and Kate Random Love describe how Patton, working like a vidder, stitches together and overlays footage so as to draw comparisons between three cultural experiences in the lives of young black men: watching rap videos alone, enduring solitary confinement, and being in "the isolating experience of the luxury spa,"[68] which gives the work its title.

Also at the intersection of sampling and vidding is THE GRAY VIDEO (2006),[69] made by the Swiss creative team Laurent Fauchère and Antoine Tinguely for the song "Encore," one of the tracks off DJ Danger Mouse's *The Grey Album* (2004), which mashes up *The White Album* by the Beatles with *The Black Album* by Jay-Z. Like a fan work, Danger Mouse's album was made for love and not money, and as Kevin Young explains, Danger Mouse offered it freely to the public, "recognizing the ways in which the Beatles have suffused the culture," so their works "are very much in the air."[70] This claim echoes the fan studies argument that fan works are the result of our need to talk to each other using our shared common culture as a language: that fan works are folk culture in a system where our myths and music are owned.[71] Young claims that *The Grey Album* "returned hip-hop not so much to the streets as to its origins"[72] in informal distribution, "mixtapes and booming systems," and also that it turned pop music "back into the folk forms that begat it."[73]

THE GRAY VIDEO, similarly offered for free, creates a mashed-up visual performance between the Beatles and Jay-Z. Using the televised concert at the end of *A Hard Day's Night* (1964) as the base of the mise-en-scène, the video shows the young Beatles joined by Jay-Z, who performs both on a giant screen the videographers add to the scene and on the original film's monitors in the control booth. Through the power of graphical manipulation, the performances mesh. Ringo moves from his drum kit to a DJ booth, two black female backup singers appear, and John Lennon break-dances. The audience of screaming girls starts to integrate. In "Mashup as Temporal Amalgam: Time, Taste, and Textuality," Paul Booth reads this as staging a clash of temporalities, "a mashup of two distinct sounds, two distinct artists, and two distinct time frames,"[74] the 1960s and 2000s, with particular attention to the "two different time periods' different views of sexuality and fandom."[75] I read the video more as an act of reclamation, broadening representation by interrupting the Beatles performance—or rather returning or recentering black culture within that performance. The Beatles were inspired by early rock records bootlegged into the Liverpool seaport in the 1950s, most of which were what would then have been called race music, and the group cut their teeth performing covers of Little Richard, the Isley Brothers, Arthur Alexander, and others. To me, THE GRAY VIDEO stages a comic desegregation of rock 'n' roll similar to the one John Waters imagines in *Hairspray* (1988), which climaxes with the racial integration of *The Corny Collins Show*. This is supported by the fact that Fauchere and Tinguely repeatedly cut to *A Hard Day's Night*'s shocked TV director (as played by Victor Spinetti), whose aghast reaction shots echo the horrified racism of Waters's similarly over-the-top white characters. In contrast, the Beatles are positively beaming in their close-ups. I would argue that their delight at being brought into a more integrated performance posits them—and not the screaming girls in the audience—as the video's true fans.

While scholars have been considering what fan studies might look like if bell hooks's *Black Looks* (1992) and Tricia Rose's *Black Noise* (1994) had been taken up with the same vigor as *Textual Poachers* (1992) and *The Adoring Audience* (1992), vidders of color and race-critical vidders have created works that sit at the intersection between sampling and vidding (see, for instance, the discussion of ENTER THE WU TANG CLAN: **36 CHAMBERS OF DEATH** [2009] by hapex_legomena in chapter 5) or otherwise enact hooks's "oppositional gaze," which declares, "Not only will I stare. I want my look to change reality."[76] We are also seeing a much more straightforward integration of black heroic protagonists into vids made from predominantly white science fiction and fantasy sources, even as those sources have themselves been challenged to be less insistently white for no real reason other than default whiteness. (See "Spotlight on: Vidding Characters of Color" in the online appendix.)

Avant-Garde/Experimental Film and Art Video

In the next chapter, I will track one strand of experimental filmmakers: that of found-footage artists like Joseph Cornell, Kenneth Anger, and Bruce Conner, whose works affected both commercial music video and fan vidding. But vidding has obvious commonalities with other avant-garde film and video traditions, and particularly with the work of experimental women filmmakers of the 1960s and video artists of the 1970s.

The introduction of cheap Bolex 16mm cameras in the early 1960s made filmmaking more accessible,[77] just as the introduction of VCRs later made vidding and remix art possible. While the majority of so-called underground filmmakers were men, innovators like Barbara Rubin, Carolee Schneemann, and Yoko Ono were also dedicated to exploring what Jonah Mekas calls "the poetic aspect of cinema," creating work that explored feeling even as it countered male ways of looking.[78] Works like Barbara Rubin's *Christmas on Earth* (1963) aimed to create a sensory (in this case erotic and hallucinogenic) experience using some of the same tools vidders later used: cut-up film footage and pop music. Unlike vidders, however, Rubin shot her own disjointed footage (of costumed and painted people having sex), before cutting it up and reassembling it using an editing process that prized randomness—in her words, "chopping the hours and hours of film up into a basket and then toss and toss flip and toss and one by one absently enchanted destined to put it together."[79] The music was either played live—Rubin's film famously played over the Velvet Underground during Andy Warhol's multimedia shows—or serendipitously: Rubin's projection instructions insist that "a radio must be hooked up to a PA system, with a nice cross-section of psychic tumult like an AM rock station, turned on and played loud."[80] Rubin's innovative projection process also anticipates both hip-hop founder DJ Herc's use of two turntables and pathbreaking vidder Kandy Fong's use of two slide projectors. *Christmas on Earth* comprises two reels whose images are layered in the moment of performance by two separate projectors, with a smaller image playing over a larger one. The instructions also note that the film can be enhanced with colored gels "moved and alternated by hand" at the discretion of the projectionist. In all three cases, the mass medium—vinyl records, slides of television, reels of film—is not just a product but material for the production or performance of future art.

The emergence of video offered experimental women artists even more opportunities. In her catalog essay, "The First Generation: Women and Video, 1970–1975," JoAnn Hanley declares that video was "the first time that men and women artists worked in a medium on equal footing."[81] While some video makers continued to turn the camera on "the body and the self," others "used the new medium to create social and political analyses of the myths and facts of patriarchal culture."[82] Straddling both sides was Dara Birnbaum, whose *Technology/Transformation: Wonder Woman* (1978) seems like nothing so much as a deconstructed fan vid. *Technology/Transformation* runs for about five and a half minutes and is in two parts. The first half is a montage of repeating clips from the Lynda Carter *Wonder Woman* series (1975–79), while the second half features the song "Wonder Woman Disco," by the Wonderland Disco Band, playing over a scroll of the song's lyrics.

As T. J. Demos points out, Wonder Woman is often read as figure of female empowerment, but Birnbaum's intention was critique. Using repetition, she shows us a Wonder Woman who does not spin merely as a mode of transformation from secretary to superhero but rather spins and spins and spins in a way that seems helpless, futile, and dizzying. The montage of the first half is characterized by sirens and explosions as Lynda Carter repeatedly spins and explodes into light, sometimes transforming into Wonder Woman but often remaining doggedly ordinary. The repeated explosions and flashes of light make visible "the technological mechanism of special effects" that signals transformation, or perhaps only a desire for it. But is this transformation real? As Dot Tuer points out, by "[isolating] from a global swirl of images those of an office girl and her Amazon double, Birnbaum highlights the simulacrum's fantasy projection of an instant emancipation from the dreary and everyday exploitation of white collar labour."[83] Other clips show Wonder Woman or Diana Prince, her secretarial alter ego, apparently trapped in a hall of mirrors. In one shot, Wonder Woman seems to scratch at her own image; in another, Diana Prince spins and spins, endlessly reflected. In the second part of the vid, Birnbaum deepens her critique like a vidder would, using pop music. The funky groove and sexualized lyrics of "Wonder Woman Disco" show the character's two-sided nature: "Get us out from under / Wonder Woman" posits her as a figure of resistance, if not revolution, but lines like "I just want to shake my wonder maker for you" give the character only the doubtable superpower of sexuality. Like a vidder, Birnbaum appropriated images to talk back to the media,[84] and like a vidder, she had to scheme to get footage. Working in the era before home video recorders, Birnbaum had to ask people in the industry "to steal or pirate these images."[85] Birnbaum notes that there was a question regarding the legality of her practice, but she decided she didn't care: "You're painting my landscape, my landscape constitutes these TV shows like *Wonder Woman*, and I'm allowed to paint them back again. I'm allowed to talk back to you."[86]

Vidders have talked back to Wonder Woman too, and with as much critical sophistication as Birnbaum. Gianduja Kiss's TITANIUM (2012) (Video 17 https://doi.org/10.3998/mpub.10069132.cmp.17) may seem to posit Wonder Woman as a straightforward figure of female empowerment. But as the vid progresses, we see that Diana Prince ("the secretary," in Tuer's terms—that is, the ordinary woman) is heroic too. But the vid doesn't rest there. It moves to critiquing the very idea of an individual superhero, instead showing Wonder Woman not as an isolated figure but as a member of a multigenerational, multiracial coalition of

women. Gianduja Kiss slowly broadens the range of female representation in the vid, constructing a montage of secondary characters who
might well have been forgotten or thought unimportant, showing them
working together.

A more recent Wonder Woman vid, Cyborganize's **TRANSMISSION**
(2018) (Video 73 https://doi.org/10.3998/mpub.10069132.cmp.73)
(further discussed in chapter 5), extends the idea of collectivity even
further, collecting images of Amazons throughout the Wonder Woman
canon, trying to rebuild Diana's home of Themyscira. This use of montage to create an otherwise absent collectivity is typical of vidding and
can be seen in vids like arefadedaway's **ONE GIRL REVOLUTION** (2009).
(Spoiler alert: it was not in fact a one-girl revolution; revolution requires
many women of all kinds, working together.) It is only recently that there
has been enough "heroic" footage of characters of color to be able to
piece together similar vids of racial solidarity and community; one is
bironic's **THE GREATEST** (2018) (see Video 74 https://doi.org/10.3998/
mpub.10069132.cmp.74), which is discussed further in chapter 5.

Commercial Music Video

The most obvious precursor of vidding, or fan music video, is commercial music video—that is, the short promotional films, also known as promos, that were first made in the 1960s and 1970s to send to television
shows when the bands couldn't be there in person, and that later became
the making of MTV. Like vids, commercial music videos are now watched
mostly on YouTube. As I discuss in chapter 2, Kandy Fong points to the
Beatles' videos as her inspiration, and even without that direct testimony,
there are obvious commonalities between the two forms.

Like vidding, commercial music video often works in a poetic mode.
From the first, film has been used to adapt preexisting works like stage
plays and novels, and from this perspective, we can see commercial
music videos as filmic adaptations of poetry: short films made from song.
In *Money for Nothing*, Saul Austerlitz calls the music video director a poet,
though for him poetry is a matter of formal limitation: "A music video
is a challenge for its director, who is like a poet adopting a specific (and
arbitrary) set of rules in which to confine his verse."[87] But poetry adds
as well as limits: crucially, poetry uses music, imagery, musicality and
rhythm to make meaning. E. Anne Kaplan gets at this when she claims
that what makes music video special as a form is

the precise relationship of sound—both musical and vocal—to image. This relationship involves (a) the links between musical rhythms and significations of instrumental sounds, and images provided for them; (b) links between the significations of the song's actual words and images conjured up to convey that "content"; (c) links between any one musical phrase and the accompanying words, and the relay of images as that phrase is being played and sung.[88]

These links could be narrative, conceptual, or simply somatic. Carol Vernalis notes that "all gestures in music video—the flick of a wrist, the flickering of light, or the fluttering of fabric—become like dance."[89] Music videos signify on many levels, asking the spectator to analyze image against music from moment to moment as well as a succession of images over time. This results in what Steven Shaviro calls a "complexly over-determined" form.[90] Gregg B. Walker and Melinda A. Bender describe music videos as "fertile"[91] with meaning, a genre for those who like interpretability and multiplicity. In fact, music video is almost comically polysemic, so that you can have a parody form like "literal music videos" mocking commercial music videos simply by describing what's happening in them. The 2009 literal music video for Bonnie Tyler's 1983 song "Total Eclipse of the Heart"[92] begins: "Pan the room / Random use of candles, empty bottles, and cloth, and can you see me through this fan?" before plaintively asking, "Metaphor?" There must be one somewhere. Music videos like these are like fan music videos in that they're a site of (often embarrassing) semiotic excess: Simon Le Bon strapped to a windmill in ripped leather pants singing "Wild Boys," hair bands doing guitar solos wearing eyeliner and spandex, anything involving shadows or cyborgs or a fog machine, and preferably all three. Why choose? That said, there are significant differences between commercial music videos and fan vids.

First, let's consider the economic environment. While critics are starting to look at music videos made by auteur directors (David Fincher, Spike Jonze, Michel Gondry) as artworks, most of the scholarly work on music video treats it not as a filmic art but as a species of advertising. These scholars can't imagine anyone making music videos within any other context or for any other reason; the history of commercial music video is part of the history of the music industry. This has not been a subtle judgment. In the opening pages of *Music Video and the Politics of Representation*, Diane Railton and Paul Watson assert that "all music videos have an avowedly commercial agenda; they are first and foremost a *commercial* for an associated but distinct consumer product, the music track itself."[93] Austerlitz says that music videos are "first, last, and always about commerce: they are engines meant to drive consumers to stores."[94] Will Straw argues that music video exploded in the early 1980s because it solved problems for the record industry: the aging of the record-buying public and the stagnation of album-oriented radio.[95] Andrew Goodwin makes related claims, arguing that music videos rose to validate and sell music that could not easily be played live.[96] These industrial narratives tell a very different origin story than that of vidding, which emerges out of a mid-1970s combustion of *Star Trek*, technology, and DIY feminism, as I discuss in chapter 2. Vidding remains a subcultural art, and defiantly amateur in the sense of its being made for love rather than money.

Second, as with sampling, there are issues of originality and appropriation. While commercial music videos feature preexisting audio— that is, a song adapted to film—fan vids are made with found footage as well as found audio; it is a *Starsky and Hutch* vid or a Harry Potter vid. In "Music Videos and Reused Footage," Sergio Dias Branco claims that music videos made with reused footage provoke a "double awareness": an awareness that both the music and the images have histories, whereas the more common sort of commercial music video only has one of these layers. Branco cites William C. Wees's work on found footage films, which "invite us to recognize . . . recycled images, and due to that self-referentiality . . . encourage a more analytical reading (which does not necessarily exclude a greater aesthetic appreciation) than the footage originally received."[97] Vids demand that we recognize and analyze reused imagery more than does commercial music video, with its original footage. Vids are an interpretive art.

That said, while one might be tempted to conclude that vidding is also a more derivative art, it is worth noting that commercial music video is intensely appropriative as well. While it doesn't typically remix actual television or film footage,[98] commercial music video frequently recreates, reshoots, or recasts famous footage to make it feature the singer or band—which is part of why commercial music video is so frequently labeled postmodern. I discussed one such video earlier in this chapter, Spike Jonze's SABOTAGE, which stars the Beastie Boys in a 1970s cop show that never was, but a glance at the history of music video produces other examples: Madonna doing the choreography of "Diamonds Are a Girl's Best Friend" in MATERIAL GIRL (1985), The Smashing Pumpkins citing George Méliès in TONIGHT, TONIGHT (1996), Weezer integrating themselves into footage from the TV show *Happy Days* in **BUDDY HOLLY** (1994), Björk dancing in an MGM-style musical number in **IT'S OH SO QUIET** (1995).

E. Anne Kaplan has observed that commercial music videos borrow heavily from horror, suspense, and science fiction[99]—witness, say, Michael Jackson's **THRILLER** (1983) or Duran Duran's **WILD BOYS** (1984)—a claim that Bridget Cherry extends by discussing videos that borrow from cult film and television as a broader category.[100] These are genres that fandom likes too. It seems odd therefore to say that commercial music videos are more original than fan music videos, though it is worth noting that their tone is different. Where commercial videos often reuse familiar shots and genres in a postmodern spirit of ironic detachment, or, Maureen Turim suggests, as a kind of tongue-and-cheek tip of the hat to the ghosts of film past,[101] fan music videos tend to repackage mass footage earnestly (or sometimes critically), rewriting familiar stories to give them emotional arcs that are epic, melodramatic, tragic, or romantic—sincere, in any case.

This brings me to my next point: commercial music videos and fan music videos differ in their relationship to both character and story. Brigid Cherry suggests that postmodern allusions to popular culture in commercial music videos may compensate for their otherwise weak narrative chain,[102] extending Kaplan's analysis that "There is no narrative proper and nothing corresponding to the Hollywood conception of character" in commercial music video.[103] This is different indeed from vidding, whose entire raison d'être is an obsession with explicating character and story; this is often true of title sequences as well. In gesturing toward the styles associated with film and television history, a commercial music video may vaguely invoke its pleasures, but fan music video is an explicitly intertextual and supplemental art form firmly rooted in fondness for and shared analysis of preexisting characters and stories.

Finally, there are gendered differences. Scholarship in music video bluntly admits that commercial music videos are sexist. Saul Austerlitz calls the objectification of women the elephant in the screening room, so commonplace as to be unworthy of mention: "Music videos, for the most part, are intended for men's eyes, providing them with endless opportunities to delectate in the spectacle of beautiful women performing for their pleasure. Videos are male fantasies of controlling and possessing women, and to avoid this subject is to miss one of the most fundamental aspects of music video."[104] One need only consider music video's California Girls or the Robert Palmer girls—or any group of dead-eyed mannequin girls, dancing, dancing; things are worse still for black women, who are objectified, exoticized, commodified. But it's not simply that women are set up to be the object of the gaze; it's also that, to again quote Austerlitz, "with a few exceptions, the male body is wholly absent from the music video."[105] In *Music Video and the Politics of Representation* (2011), Diane Railton and Paul Watson argue that this male absence is tactical: "Very often, the absence of the sexualized male body . . . not only comes to define masculine subjectivity in music video but is also an important process through which hegemonic masculinity maintains its power. Indeed, music videos employ a number of strategies to variously displace, disguise, and disavow the sex of the male body, or even delete it from the field of vision entirely."[106] Downplaying the sexed male body by making women's bodies hypervisible is one stratagem; deleting it through abstraction is another, perhaps through a highly graphical video or the creation of an animated avatar. Railton and Watson give Radiohead's 2+2=5 (2003) and Robbie Williams's cartoon self in LET LOVE BE YOUR ENERGY (2001) as examples, but others immediately spring to mind: Peter Gabriel's SLEDGEHAMMER (1986), the animated characters of Dire Straits' MONEY FOR NOTHING (1985), Daft Punk's entire career, all the way back to the Beatles' *Yellow Submarine* (1968).

But vidding, an art form of female editors, has a very different relationship to male and female bodies. In "Masculinity as Spectacle," Steve Neale claims that traditional film culture creates a culture in which men are tested and women are investigated, but in vidding, we see the opposite: women are tested and men are investigated. When women are the subject of fan vids, they are given agency and narrative centrality; meanwhile, vidding's engagement with mainstream, mass media (and male-centric) storytelling means that it is primarily male characters who are put front and center in fan music videos. Consequently, in fan vids, we see male bodies fetishized, male gestures and expressions scrutinized, male narratives rewritten. It is like a Hollywood mirrorverse where it is the men who are strange and oh so mysterious, in need of intense collaborative scrutiny ("Men—what can they want? If only they could tell us!"). In vids, men are subjectified and objectified, subject and spectacle, while the gaze is female both behind the scenes and in front of the screens. Women are the editors as well as the audience.

So despite some superficial formal similarities, the production context and goals of commercial music video and fan music video are really quite different. In the end, this may come down to something simple: commercial music video creatively explicates a song, while fan vidding creatively explicates a visual source. As Margie, a vidder, explains, "The thing I've never been able to explain to anyone not in [media] fandom (or to fans with absolutely no exposure to vids) is that where pro music videos are visuals that illustrate the music, songvids are music that tells the story of the visuals. They don't get that it's actually a completely different emphasis."[107] Critics debate whether commercial music video is a type of film or a form of music, whether it is advertisement or art, but vidding, for all the complexities and variations that I trace throughout this book, has a central coherence: it is a form developed by women within media fandom to celebrate, extend, critique, and supplement beloved media texts.

TWO | Early Vidding and Its Precursors

In 1975, the book *Star Trek Lives!* by Jacqueline Lichtenberg, Sondra Marshak, and Joan Winston described the explosion of *Star Trek* fan's culture. The book discusses the appeal of the show's themes and characters (Mr. Spock in particular) and explains how fans came together to organize the first *Star Trek* conventions. But the book is most famous for its concluding chapter: "Do-It-Yourself *Star Trek*—The Fan Fiction," which examined the phenomenon of *Star Trek* fanfiction, including the striking fact "that most of it is written by *women*."[1] The authors argue that this is because *Star Trek* "did *not* keep its distance from emotion; did *not* deny close, warm human relationships even among males; did *not* call for a stiff upper lip; did *not* deny the existence and importance of sex; did *not* ban psychological action as a plot-moving force; did *not* deny the possibility of women who might be more than damsels."[2] But in the process of documenting *Star Trek*'s fan culture, Lichtenberg, Marshak, and Winston also vastly enlarged it: as fanzine historian Joan Marie Verba notes in her preface to *Boldly Writing: A Trekker Fan and Zine History, 1967–1987*, "For thousands upon thousands of fans, this was when they became aware that such [fan] activity existed, and that they could join in."[3] The message of *Star Trek Lives!* was that you could indeed do it yourself. You could write *Star Trek*, you could draw it, you could supplement the canonical adventures. *Star Trek Lives!* drew many of its readers into making the kinds of transformative fan works that the book described: zines full of fanfiction and fan art of all kinds, including a nude centerfold of Mr. Spock, published in *Grup* in 1972, the same year as Bert Reynolds's centerfold in *Cosmo* appeared, and a year before *Playgirl* launched.

In 1975, Laura Mulvey published "Visual Pleasure and Narrative Cinema," her essay theorizing the male gaze of traditional Hollywood cinema. Mulvey takes as her starting point the way film "controls erotic ways of looking and spectacle,"[4] and how it projects the phallocentric norms of an active male spectator and a passive female object, where woman is defined by her to-be-looked-at-ness. Mulvey claims that the presence of a woman on screen "tends to work against the development of a storyline, to freeze the flow of action in moments of erotic con-templation."[5] In a fortieth anniversary talk at the British Film Institute, Mulvey contextualized her famous essay as a product of its moment, noting that it couldn't have been written before the women's liberation movement of the early 1970s, nor after her own formal engagement with film studies in the early 1980s. Rather, she describes the essay as a work of feminist advocacy, a manifesto that called for the destruction (via analysis) of the pleasures associated with an erotic gaze that is always male.

But Mulvey's ideas have since evolved. In *Death 24× a Second: Stillness and the Moving Image* (2006), Mulvey explains, "Then, in the 1970s, I was preoccupied by Hollywood's ability to construct the female star as ultimate spectacle," but "now, I am more interested in the way that those moments of spectacle were also moments of narrative halt, hint-ing at the stillness of the single celluloid frame."[6] Hollywood film gave us woman as spectacle and stopped the story to allow us to look at her; it offered a male gaze authorized by the film itself. But today film does not dominate the spectator the way that it used to; we have control, remote and otherwise. Mulvey notes that at the time of "Visual Pleasure and Narrative Cinema," only professionals, directors, and editors had access to the editing equipment that let you slow or stop the flow of cinematic time; today, however, through "electronic or digital viewing,"[7] whether by VCR, DVD, or streaming video, everyone has the ability to fragment a filmic narrative into pieces, into favorite moments, scenes, or single images. Mulvey argues that this stopping—this literal and figurative stilling of cinema—leads to a "feminized" film aesthetic, one that that weakens the propulsive (male) force of cinematic narrative and shifts the power relations "dwelling on pose, stillness, lighting, and the cho-reography of character and camera." It also allows the male figure on screen to become part of the image, so that "he, too, stops rather than drives the narrative."[8] As Mulvey notes, despite the apparent energy of (even, or especially, male) film acting, star performance "depends on pose, on moments of almost invisible stillness, in which the body is dis-played for the spectator's visual pleasure through the mediation of the camera."[9] Men, it turns out, are characterized by to-be-looked-at-ness too, if you can only get them to be still.

In 1975, Kandy Fong, then Kandy Barber, premiered a *Star Trek* slideshow at the Equicon/Filmcon convention called "Amok Time: A Personal Log."[10] Constructed from still images, frames cut from deleted scenes, outtakes, and other cast-off footage,[11] the twelve-minute show was framed as a new episode of *Star Trek*, complete with (still-shot) credit sequence and theme music. Many fans wrote their own episodes of *Star Trek*, but as fanfiction, either in prose or script format. But Fong created something audiovisual using a carousel of slides and an audio track prerecorded on cassette tape. Fong then stood at the projector with her script and made her cuts live, syncing the slides with the audio by forwarding the projector at the appropriate time. Fong uses the device of the spoken "log entry" to structure the narrative. After Kirk's own famous opening monologue ("Space, the final frontier . . .") ends, Fong picks up the tale in her own voice, making herself a character: "Personal narrative, Stardate 7604.15. Since I joined the Starship *Enterprise*, I have noticed many changes . . ." What follows is a series of humorous observations about life on the *Enterprise* from someone purporting to have been there. But around the six-minute mark, story segues into song. Fong's narration gives way first to William Shatner's spoken-word rendition of "It Was a Very Good Year" (1968), then to a home-recorded version of the filk (a fannish bastardization of folk)[12] song "What Do You Do with a Drunken Vulcan?" (an adaptation of the sea shanty "Drunken Sailor"). So, in the show's narrative first half, Fong uses the memoir-like log conceit to organize her disparate images into a coherent narrative. But in the musical second half, she organizes the images rhythmically and uses song to tell two stories: the first, sentimental, about Kirk (**IT WAS A VERY GOOD YEAR** [Video 18 https://doi.org/10.3998/mpub.10069132.cmp.18]), and the second, comic, about Spock (**WHAT DO YOU DO WITH A DRUNKEN VULCAN?** [Video 19 https://doi.org/10.3998/mpub.10069132.cmp.19]). Fong says she got the idea to set images to music this way from the Beatles, whose promos anticipated the first music videos.

While Kandy Fong's original intention may have been simply to entertain fans by making something coherent out of random *Star Trek* frames, what she actually made was neither an episode of narrative television nor a Beatles-style promo but rather something entirely new—a fan vid—that is both an affective artwork and an interpretation of the source text. Similarly, the women who wrote *Star Trek* fanfiction did not write the kind of fiction that substituted for new television episodes or as an equivalent to today's tie-in novels (though many fanfiction writers did and do also write tie-in novels); rather, they invented a genre—fanfiction—that has its own tropes and shared conventions[13] different from those of either commercial or literary fiction.

Star Trek Lives!

Kandy's Fong's first slideshow was an enormous hit. Fong recalls, "This was the only 'new' *Trek* since the show had ended & it had people lined up. We had a small room in the lower level & kept running it over & over."[14] Vidding fandom has used the public debut of this slideshow to date vidding as an art, and remembers WHAT DO YOU DO WITH A DRUNKEN VULCAN? in particular as the first vid, even as "music video" was not yet a mainstream term, or even a mainstream medium, in 1975.

It's unclear why it was DRUNKEN VULCAN and not IT WAS A VERY GOOD YEAR that fans remembered from that first slideshow. Maybe it stayed in the mind because it was the show closer; maybe it was because it addressed the more popular figure of Spock; or maybe female fans enjoyed the idea of a drunken Vulcan (who might be momentarily beyond logic) more than they did a reminder of Kirk's louche profligacy with women. But it's DRUNKEN VULCAN that fans remembered. When I and other members of the Organization for Transformative Works got Fong to recreate her first slideshow at Vividcon 2012,[15] we were surprised to find two vids, not one, in the show. Both use music to organize and interpret a set of (highly disparate) visuals; Fong was working with isolated frames from episodes, outtakes, and promotional events. Still, she could rely on fandom to recognize the characters and episodes, and so add context.

In IT WAS A VERY GOOD YEAR, William Shatner's sung-spoken recording becomes a reflective memoir of Captain Kirk's life and loves. (See Image B. https://doi.org/10.3998/mpub.10069132.cmp.173) "When I was seventeen," Shatner intones nostalgically, chanting more than singing a song made famous by Frank Sinatra, "it was a very good year," and Fong gives us an image of Ruth, a character who (fans know) was a girlfriend of Kirk's from his Starfleet Academy days, when he was presumably seventeen or thereabouts. Moreover, Ruth, who appears in the *Star Trek* episode "Shore Leave," is already a nostalgic fantasy; Kirk literally dreams her into being on a planet that makes illusions real for entertainment purposes. The image of Ruth over this lyric thus ideally suits not just the literal words of the song but also its tone: wistful but satisfied. Later years in the song correlate with Captain Kirk's memories of other girls, and Fong organizes a montage of "small town girls" and "city girls" and "blue-blooded girls" in ways meaningful to fans. So, for example, Edith Keeler, the New York City social worker of the 1930s who is Kirk's great love interest in the famous episode "City on the Edge of Forever," is, satisfyingly and in multiple ways, a "city girl," just as there is no more "blue blooded" a girl than T'Pring of Vulcan, who is not only a woman of independent means, but—if not quite blue blooded then at least literally green blooded, as Vulcans are. These image–word conjunctions land for fans with all the pleasures of multiple meanings or meaningful multiplicity—or like a really satisfying pun.

Similarly, in WHAT DO YOU DO WITH A DRUNKEN VULCAN?, the repeated call ("What do you do with a drunken Vulcan?") and the various responses ("Make him eat an all-day sucker," "Put him in the brig until he's sober," "Make him chug a lug with Scotty") organize and inform the outtakes and stray frames Fong had to work with, like those of Leonard Nimoy sucking on a lollipop. (See Image C. https://doi.org/10.3998/mpub.10069132.cmp.174) Fong gets particularly good mileage out of "Make him go trick-or-treating" because the many alternative universes of *Star Trek* give us images of Kirk and Spock dressed as ancient Greeks, as Nazis, as gangsters, and so on.

The slides technically belonged to her future husband, John Fong, but it was Kandy who saw the bits of film not as something to be owned but as something to be used. She recalls herself asking, "Why don't we do something with this?"[16] Fans were voracious for new *Star Trek* in this empty period between end of *Star Trek: The Animated Series* (1973–74) and *Star Trek: The Motion Picture* (1979). In our transmedia world of sequels, tie-ins, and reboots, it's hard to imagine such scarcity. While there are now hundreds of *Star Trek* novels, between the end of the series and 1975, there had been only one: *Spock Must Die* (1970) by James Blish. But fans of that era were hungry for more *Trek* and so were prepared to make it themselves.

Women had been writing *Star Trek* fanfiction since the late 1960s, a phenomenon documented by Lichtenberg, Marshak, and Winston.[17] A year after Kandy Fong's first slideshow, Marshak and Myrna Culbreath published *Star Trek: The New Voyages* (1976), an all-female anthology of fanfiction with an introduction by Gene Roddenberry and introductions to individual stories by members of the cast. Fans also engaged in making other transformative works—cosplay, sculpture, crafts, music and song, all kinds of visual art—which they shared at conventions. *Star Trek* conventions were themselves a new phenomenon, but one that exploded, as *Star Trek Lives!* documents: the first *Star Trek* convention in 1972, run by

Joan Winston, drew over 3,000 people; the 1973 convention drew 6,000; and in 1974, 15,000 people attended and 6,000 were turned away at the door.[18] Roddenberry supported both conventions and fan works, at least in part because he was trying to reinvent *Star Trek* for the movies. In particular, he saw Kandy Fong's slideshows as proof of the demand for more *Trek*.

The success of "Amok Time: A Personal Log," along with the explicit approval of Gene Roddenberry, encouraged Fong to make more slide-show vids. Roddenberry, who understood the value of an energized fan base, invited Fong to Paramount and gave her additional footage: "They let me pick what I wanted out of the slides they take for publicity shots," she recalls. "Even after the movie had been done, and then the second movie, they let me come in there and take whatever I needed to . . . build up the shows and add things to them." By 1984, she owned more than 6,000 *Star Trek* slides, which she combined into vids in various ways. She took her vids on the convention circuit, not only to small fan-run conventions like Star Con and IDICon, but also to the massive Creation Cons of the late 1970s, which featured the actors and had thousands of attendees.

Fong remembers, "For several years, I would travel from Seattle to San Diego to Boston to Houston showing my shows. I would show the older stuff, then make sure there were 1 or 2 new ones at each con. I ended up with several hours of shows." Eventually Fong moved to using two slide projectors so she could cut between slides more rapidly, still making her edits "live" in the moment, incorporating her body as part of the filmmaking process. These slideshows were therefore as much theatre as they were film, and in fact Fong was also known for writing and staging a number of actual theatrical shows, skits, and playlets for fans to perform at conventions. (These include the hilariously porno-graphic sketch "The Quickie" [aka "Dancing Penises"] (Clip 03 https://doi.org/10.3998/mpub.10069132.cmp.160), featuring Kirk and Spock's person-sized erections dancing and rubbing together.[19]) However, Fong also filmed a few of her slideshows[20] and added clean audio to them, making them more finished filmic objects. These more formal objects were sent to Gene Roddenberry, who wanted copies. They also circu-lated among fans as examples of early vidding, although the vast majority of these slideshows remain unfilmed.[21] However, as a regular on the con-vention circuit for years, Fong influenced a generation of fans with her slideshow vids. It is on this basis that she is regarded as the foremother of vidding, and she was honored as such at the 2005 Vividcon, which celebrated thirty years of vidding by marking the time since the public debut of her first show.

Strawberry Fields Forever

Kandy Fong got the idea to make vids from the Beatles, who in 1966—the year of *Star Trek*'s debut—filmed their first promos, which some identify as the first music videos. The history of commercial music video is a vexed one, with some scholars pointing to early musical film forms like the illustrated songs popular at the turn of the twentieth century, Vitaphone shorts of the 1920s and 1930s, the soundies of the 1940s, and the Scopitones of the late 1950s and after.[22] Others connect music video to the classic Hollywood musical and the rock movies of the 1950s and 1960s. While these differing genealogies of music video produce different claims as to who made the first commercial music video,[23] the Beatles have a strong claim with their 1966 promos of **RAIN** (1966) and **PAPERBACK WRITER** (1966). These promos departed both from the conventions of the performance video (where a band mimes singing and playing their instruments in time to the music) and those of the musical film (where music tends to be used as a soundtrack, as in the famous scene of the ebullient Beatles running around Thornbury Playing Fields in *A Hard Day's Night* [1964]).

In RAIN and PAPERBACK WRITER, the nod to the musical performance video is only gestural. While Paul, George, and John pretend to play guitars during parts of PAPERBACK WRITER, they also stop singing in the middle of lyrics and break up laughing as the song carries on; moreover, their electric instruments don't appear to be plugged into anything. Ringo never plays drums; there's no drum set visible. Rather, he's lounging dreamily against the garden statuary. RAIN makes even less of an attempt at miming realistic performance, instead using various techniques of experimental cinema: blurred focus, cut-off or strangely composed frames, slow motion. (This is no doubt related to the fact that "Rain" was the first Beatles song to use avant-garde techniques in the music, which was at points slowed down or played backward.[24]) Moreover, in RAIN we have a deliberately musical style of cutting, so that the rat-a-tat-a-tat of the drum fills is visualized by the rapid-fire switching between two images: da-da-da-da-da. The film moves to the beat so that the cutting, and not the content, is paramount.

It was the Beatles' third promo, 1967's **STRAWBERRY FIELDS FOREVER**, that so influenced Kandy Fong. In this promo, the Beatles depart entirely from mimicking performance—or rather they turn performance into a surreal experience. An invented instrument that looks like a piano mixed with a harp stands in a field near an enormous and twisted black tree. The Beatles cavort in brightly colored costumes of red and orange and pink. The video is full of absurd and magical moments: the Beatles disappear in one corner of the frame and reappear in another; sometimes they walk backward; sometimes the film runs backward. Events repeat with surprising differences. There are overlays, extreme close-ups, unusual angles, and jump cuts. While the images can be seen as an illustration of the song—certainly in their overall dreaminess, and of course there is a field pictured, evoking if not representing the field described in the lyrics—image has become detached from sound, or rather image is in a new and differently constructed relationship with sound, more metaphorical, slantwise, poetic.

It wasn't that this disjunction between sound and image was new per se; it was characteristic both of early cinema (before the widespread synchronization of sound and image) and of avant-garde film (of the kind that had inspired Paul McCartney in particular). But these Beatles promos were mainstream popular culture, made for the (realist) world of commercial broadcast television. It was the striking disjunction between sound and image that so struck Kandy Fong:

> If you remember back, [before] these dates [*sic*] of so-called professional music videos, you'd have a band up there standing playing their instruments and that's pretty much the video. Well, the Beatles did a video called STRAWBERRY FIELDS FOREVER, and they're doing all kinds of very strange things like jumping out of trees, and they had this deconstructed piano that the wires just go up to the thing up there. . . . And they're just doing all sorts of unusual images. And to my mind I look at this, going, "Okay, we're disconnecting the actual playing of the instruments and singing the song with the images we're seeing. So I can take a song and use images from somewhere else to tell my story—oh, *Star Trek*, oh, of course *Star Trek!*" And that's where I got the idea.[25]

Perhaps not coincidentally, the use of Beatles music to create a sound–image disjunction also later inspired the birth of anime music video. Jim Kaposztas, who is credited with having made the first AMV in 1982, recalls being inspired by the final episode of *The Prisoner* (1967), in which the main character and his compatriots shoot their way out of the totalitarian Village to the tune of "All You Need Is Love." Kaposztas was moved to recreate this ironic contrast in his own video, cutting "random violent scenes"[26] from *Space Battleship Yamato* (aka *Starblazers*) to the same song. Ironically, the finale of *The Prisoner* ("Fall Out," broadcast February 1, 1968) was one of the rare times that Beatles' music was licensed for television, and according to George Harrison's son, Dhani, it was because the Beatles were fans of the show.[27]

The Beatles' Avant-Garde Influences

The Beatles had in turn gotten many of their ideas from anarchist comedy and experimental film. They were also fans of BBC radio's *The Goon Show*, which had launched the careers of Peter Sellers and Spike Milligan, as well as the satire wave that led to *Beyond the Fringe* and *Monty Python's Flying Circus*. Director Richard Lester, hired to create a visual counterpart to the Goons' aural surrealism and silliness, came up with television shows like *The Idiot Weekly, Price 2d* (1956), and *A Show Called Fred* (1956), as well as an experimental film: *The Running Jumping & Standing Still Film* (1959). *The Running Jumping & Standing Still Film* is eleven minutes of lunacy in a field. For example, a charwoman scrubs the grass with a sponge and bucket; later, a man appears on the horizon and approaches the camera in fits and starts until finally, having come close, he is knocked out of frame by a boxing glove. Scenes like these are the direct inspiration not only for the Thornbury Playing Fields scene in *A Hard Day's Night* but also for every Python sketch that begins with a slow pan over the English countryside. Made for £70 on Peter Sellers's own 16mm camera,[28] the film is one step above a home movie: it has no dialogue, though there are a few diegetic sounds—gunshots, flashbulbs—and some faux diegetic birdsong. But as one might expect of a film that reminds you it's a film in its title,[29] *The Running Jumping & Standing Still Film* plays with the conventions of filmmaking. The boxing glove to the face reminds you of the presence of the frame, and in one notable sequence, Spike Milligan makes a tree stump into a phonograph by running around a record very fast while holding a needle attached to a speaker, and the record "plays." (See Clip 4. https://doi.org/10.3998/mpub.10069132.cmp.161) The film makes the conventions of filmmaking visible and makes use of—and has fun with—the makers' own technical limitations.

"I think I have an amateur's approach to filmmaking," Dick Lester told *Vanity Fair* in a 2008 interview, claiming he was never technically trained as a director. Rather, he started as a stagehand in television circa 1950, and was a director by the end of the year back when nobody yet knew what the job of a television director really was. Lester was never "an assistant, or a cameraman, or an editor. I never saw how anybody else made films."[30] This amateur approach suited the Beatles, who had a similar can-do attitude about filmmaking (and everything else) as well as a similarly playful spirit. They recruited Lester on the basis of *The Running Jumping & Standing Still Film*, and *A Hard Day's Night* adopts that film's cheeky attitude toward narrative cinema in scenes like the one where John Lennon seems to spiral down the drain of his bath, or where the Beatles impossibly appear outside a train window, running alongside the train they're supposed to be riding. Lester also directed *Help!*, the Beatles' second film, which has similar moments of filmic surrealism— for instance, the Beatles' four terraced houses are all connected on the inside and furnished with a grass carpet, pipe organ, and vending machines—as well as similarly ebullient performance sequences. Both films have been incredibly influential on the way pop music is filmed, and for his contributions to the development of music video, Richard Lester was among the first recipients of the MTV Video Vanguard award in 1984.

But by the time of their next film, *Magical Mystery Tour* (1967), the Beatles had gotten so defiantly amateurish that they dispensed with a professional director altogether—at least nominally. (They had an uncredited Bernard Knowles on hand.) Made after PAPERBACK WRITER, RAIN, and STRAWBERRY FIELDS FOREVER, *Magical Mystery Tour* features musical sequences that are not straightforward performances, as were those in *A Hard Day's Night* and *Help!* The driving force behind the film, and its de facto director, was Paul McCartney,[31] who by that time had gotten increasingly interested in filmmaking, and particularly in avant-garde film. Like Peter Sellers, McCartney was interested in film and rich enough to be an early adopter of new technology. He had for some time been making avant-garde home movies[32] using techniques like double exposure and running film backward through the projector.[33] In *Revolution in the Head*, Ian McDonald notes with some sarcasm, "McCartney had the cheek to show some of his home movies to Michelangelo Antonioni while he was shooting *Blow Up* in London in 1966."[34]

Both as spectator and maker, McCartney was fueled by his extraordinary access both to films and to technology—access that wouldn't be available to ordinary people until the consumer VCR became available in the late 1970s and early 1980s. The Beatles, too famous to go out to the movies without being mobbed, rented film projectors and screened movies at home, but McCartney's friend, art dealer Robert Fraser, encouraged him to watch movies beyond the mainstream. McCartney recalled: "Robert . . . turned it more into an art thing. So he would hire Bruce Conner's *A Movie.* Kenneth Anger, he'd pull in the harder West Coast stuff. I liked it, it was very liberating."[35]

Kenneth Anger and Bruce Conner are themselves often cited as forerunners to music video, but I would argue that their work shares more with vidding than with commercial music video. Anger's *Scorpio Rising* (1963), which Ara Osterweil describes as "a homoerotic, sadomasochistic homage to a gang of leather-clad bikers,"[36] lets us gaze upon and over male bodies and their sex(y) toys—motorcycles and such that stand in for genitalia—against a '60s soundtrack of popular songs like "My Boyfriend's Back," "He's a Rebel," and "I Will Follow Him." Like *The Running Jumping & Standing Still Film, Scorpio Rising* contains no dialogue. Its soundtrack of thirteen pop songs does all the narrative and emotional work. While Osterweil claims that *Scorpio Rising* "is widely recognized as the prototype for the MTV-style rock music video," I would argue that there aren't nearly enough scantily clad biker boys in conventional music videos, Russell Mulcahy's WILD BOYS notwithstanding; as most commercial music video critics have observed, and as I discussed in the previous chapter, the genre objectifies women.[37]

Fan vidding, on the other hand, typically puts men front and center as objects of desire. Anger's gaze, his interest in men not just as a whole but in (lingeringly appreciated) parts, has more in common with the objectifying gaze of the Clucking Belles vid, A FANNISH TAXONOMY OF HOTNESS (HOT HOT HOT) (2005)[38] (Video 20 https://doi.org/10.3998/ mpub.10069132.cmp.20), than it does with anything in commercial music video. Anger slowly pans up a biker's legs as he zips his fly, encouraging us to enjoy the view; he calls it "the opposite of a striptease: this is the tease of dressing." (See Clip 5. https://doi.org/10.3998/ mpub.10069132.cmp.162) As Diane Railton and Paul Watson have argued, the male body is rarely seen this way in commercial music video, which uses various tactics to "displace, disguise, and disavow the sex of the male body, or even delete it from the field of vision entirely."[39] But this fetishized looking is common in vidding.

In FANNISH TAXONOMY OF HOTNESS, the Clucking Belles (one of the many subgroups of a large fannish collective who call themselves the Media Cannibals) fetishize the bodies, clothes, props, and tropes of mainstream television. The vid is simple enough: it sets images from a wide-ranging number of movies and television shows to Buster Poindexter's dance hit, "Hot Hot Hot." The song isn't complicated, though its refrain is used both to describe others ("See people rocking / Hear people chanting") and express the self ("Feeling hot hot hot!"). This double-ness carries over into the vid: the Clucking Belles not only label various media images as "hot" but also articulate the feelings they induce in the spectator: these images from mainstream TV and film make *us* hot. The Belles tease out the erotics of television by creating montages that stage a fetishistic gaze: men in tight T-shirts, characters nude in the bath, characters writhing in straightjackets. (See "Spotlight on: A FANNISH TAXONOMY OF HOTNESS (HOT HOT HOT)" in the online appendix.)

Similarly, a vid like Danegen's **AROUND THE BEND** (2010) (Video 21 https://doi.org/10.3998/mpub.10069132.cmp.21) is virtually a gender-reversed lesbian version of *Scorpio Rising*, featuring women getting around (and getting off) on various transporting machines: motorcycles, cars, airplanes, tanks, spaceships. Using a combination of media foot-age and found footage of real women pilots, motorcyclists, race car driv-ers, and others (the Motor Maids, aviators Hélène Dutrieu and Bessie Coleman, race car driver Danica Patrick, Dykes on Bikes, and others), the vid creates an inspiring musical montage showing how women, con-trary to stereotype, love technology, machines, speed, driving, sex, and other women, platonically and otherwise. The vidder's summary of the vid was simply "Taking the wheel," which was taken by many as a meta-phor for vidding itself—that is, vidders are women who love the tech-nology of filmmaking, and we're taking the wheel and making our own visual culture. The women of AROUND THE BEND are not only literally in the driver's seat but are also snuggled up in both the front and back seats. Some of the films the vid cites—*Thelma and Louise*, *Boys on the Side*, Gaga and Beyoncé escaping in the Pussy Wagon in the music video for **TELEPHONE** (2010)—are overtly lesbian, while others just give us a male-free version of a love story every girl knows, one involving sex, fast cars, and other girls: women loving women loving cars.

In the commentary to *Scorpio Rising*, Kenneth Anger tells us that he likes boys who like leather unconsciously, not as a deliberate fetish. Similarly, female fan vidders tease out the kinkiness of mainstream media rather than seeking out deliberate pornography (which, in any case, is typically not made with their desires in mind). Anger also claims that he filmed what existed in the world, meaning he didn't stage the sets or tell the bikers how to dress or act. He found kinkiness in the wild.

Like a vidder, Anger uses music to tease out the subtext of found foot-age. For instance, he incorporates a Lutheran Sunday school film called *Last Journey to Jerusalem* into *Scorpio Rising*, wryly setting footage of Jesus leading a procession of apostles against "He's a Rebel" ("See the way he walks down the street / Watch the way he shuffles his feet / My, he holds his head up high / When he goes walking by / He's my guy") (Clip 6 https://doi.org/10.3998/mpub.10069132.cmp.163). The religious film had been delivered to him by mistake ("a gift from the gods," "a magical serendipity"), and Anger decided he could always use extra footage of people getting down on their knees.

Like Anger, Bruce Conner also used music to recontextualize recy-cled images, though unlike Anger, Conner's erotic gaze seems entirely directed at women. Like a vidder, Conner edits rhythmically to create narratively and emotionally coherent montages out of found footage. He also makes a lot out of footage that is disregarded or even typically unseen, like the countdown for the projector and the foot and tail lead-ers. Conner's first film, *A Movie* (1958), moves between soft-core pornog-raphy, B movies, footage of real-life atrocities, and nature footage; the film is one of the first to deal with "the flood of imagery flooding out of Hollywood and Madison Avenue at the dawn of the televisual era."[40] The mushroom cloud (an image of which appears throughout Conner's work in multiple media) appears twice in *A Movie*, in one sequence as the cli-max of erotic looking (a man peering through a submarine's periscope appears to see a starlet sprawled on a bed; missiles launch, explosion!) and in another at the climax of a segment on war that includes news footage of hanging corpses and fields of slaughtered human beings. The music in the film tells us how to feel about what we see: What kind of explosion is it? When is an ocean swell a wave of desire, and when is it a tsunami of impending disaster?

A Movie was incredibly influential, inspiring not just 1960s-era icons like McCartney and Dennis Hopper (who credits it with inspiring the cemetery acid trip in *Easy Rider*), but also the later punk/new wave pio-neers of music video. Conner, who by the late 1970s was hanging around the punk scene, made the collage video MONGOLOID (1978) for Devo and a number of early music videos with Bryan Eno and David Byrne, including the abstract and highly rhythmic MEA CULPA (1981), in which graphic black-and-white shapes—dots, circles, cubes—shudder and dance, frames flickering to the beat. In later years, Conner refused the title of "father of music video," pointedly disavowing the genre with a terse "Not my fault."[41] This may not be surprising considering that he saw himself (as did many of the punk and art house musicians he associated with) as opposed to mainstream commercial filmmaking; as a *New York Times* headline had it, "The Favorite Word in His Vocabulary Is Undermine."[42] Holly Rogers and Jeremy Bartham describe Conner's "interest in found-footage and music, often taken from mass culture," in terms that evoke vidding, claiming that he had "a desire to comment on, and undo, the conventions of pop culture."[43] Martin F. Norden's description of Conner's process similarly evokes the practices of fan vidding much more than of commercial music video: "In the process of reworking footage from such items as cartoons, television commercials, Hollywood movies and newsreels, Conner has gone out of his way to include recognizable emotive or associative concepts, which he then isolates from any former frames of reference. When these concepts are edited together as a montage and exhibited on screen . . . a new structural relationship emerges and offers many interesting effects."[44]

Isolating "emotive or associative concepts" from existing works and putting them into a "new structural relationship" is a pretty good definition of vidding, as experts in found footage cinema have come to realize. In *Joseph Cornell versus Cinema* (2013), Michael Pigott explicitly positions assemblage artist and filmmaker Joseph Cornell as a vidding forerunner and stakes a claim for Cornell's *Rose Hobart* (1936) as the first fan vid.[45] This is not just because the film is a collage of found footage set to music, but also because of its affect and tone. It is "mysterious, lugubrious, atmospheric, oneiric,"[46] a poetic dreamscape made by a pop culture obsessive—what J. Hoberman called "the greatest film fetish of all, made for a cult of one,"[47] which is to say, a fandom of one.

Rose Hobart is radical condensation (today we would call it a remix) of the 1931 film *East of Borneo* starring Rose Hobart, who fascinated Cornell. The film, projected through a piece of blue glass as a form of DIY color tinting, focuses primarily on Hobart's face, her gestures, and her microexpressions, much as a character vid would do today. (See "Spotlight on: Character Vids" in the online appendix.) Cornell also intercuts images from nature: a flickering candle flame, the ripples created by a stone tossed into water, the moon in eclipse. Catherine Corman notes that Cornell "discarded the entire plot" of *East of Borneo*, instead "focusing on the ambiguity of the characters' emotions and the quivering, halting beauty"[48] of Hobart. Cornell wanted to return to the poetry of silent film; he explains what he finds valuable in cinema in his 1941 ode to Hedy Lamarr, which begins: "Among the barren wastes of the talking films there occasionally occur passages to remind one again of the profound and suggestive power of the silent film to evoke an ideal world of beauty, to release unsuspected floods of music from the gaze of a human countenance in its prison of silver light."[49] Corman glosses this passage like so: "Speech creates a 'barren waste.' The 'mute gaze' is profound and overwhelming because, unlike speech, silence can ascend to the sublime."[50] Like a vidder, Cornell attempts to liberate certain sublime passages from the barren wastes of talking films. As Stan Brakhage, his later collaborator, puts it,

> [Cornell] took this movie and . . . cut it down to what he cared about the most. He began making it a film really about the deepest of all possible problems that women can have and how desperate their situation is, and the magics they have and how fragile those are, and made a piece that's, I think, one of the greatest poems of being a woman that's ever been made in film, or maybe anywhere. This is like carving out slowly the deep essence of this movie that he could see because of his love of Rose Hobart.[51]

Brakhage compares Cornell's practice to writing a poem or carving a sculpture, which either way is a profound act of (almost literal) cinephilia. Michael Pigott explicitly compares "Cornell's remixing practice, *photogénie*, cinephilia," with "the practice of 'vidding' as it is known,"[52] arguing that cinephilia and vidding are convergent artistic practices, though they aren't often seen as such. This he (rightfully) attributes to "a gender bias" because "vidding has been primarily associated with women, while the cinephile has been routinely imagined as male."[53] But Pigott sees Cornell's work as bridging these traditions: "Cornell's work in *Rose Hobart* brings together the two practices, and the two figures, of the cinephile and the vidder. He is drawn to the face of Hobart, to the soft marble of her skin, the radiant flesh of her decelerated body. . . . He re-edits as a fan would, cutting out his favorite bits and re-arranging them to alter significance, and tune it to his preferred meaning. Yet he is also drawn to the aberrant detail, the idiosyncratic factor that launches a flight of imagination or even argumentation."[54]

Cornell was attacked by Salvador Dalí at the first screening of *Rose Hobart*; the jealous Dalí leapt up and knocked over the projector, claiming that Cornell was a genius who had plagiarized his unconscious mind. While there were certainly experimental films before *Rose Hobart*, the film is the first of a canon of surreal films set to found music that, having influenced the Beatles and Paul McCartney in particular, came to influence the rest of us, and vidders in particular.[55]

All Together Now

By the late 1960s, the Beatles were committed to making promos, filmed inserts, and movies as a way of escaping the agonies of touring and album support.[56] The music they were making at that point couldn't be played live anyway; an album like *Sergeant Pepper's Lonely Hearts Club Band* is an end product rather than a collection of songs to be performed in concert; it includes within it performance elements like applause. At the same time, McCartney had been exposed to a range of experimental films—Lester's surreal silliness, Anger's fetishizing gaze and rock soundtrack, Conner's found footage techniques and musical animations—that fueled his own desire to experiment, both with image and with soundtrack.

All of McCartney's homemade experimental movies were silent, but, as Barry Miles points out, of course he created soundtracks for them by playing records.[57] Rather than work in the intentional, almost obsessive manner of vidders—carefully matching image to music, shot by shot, frame by frame—McCartney did it in the serendipitous, leave-it-to-chance way characteristic of the late 1960s. Ian McDonald scornfully calls this "the ethos of 1967 itself," in which all meaning is "found" and everything is, to quote the refrain of "All You Need Is Love," *easy*: "All you had to do was toss a coin, consult the *I Ching*, or read a random paragraph from a newspaper—and then start playing or singing. Anyone could do it, everyone could join in. ('All together now . . .')."[58] In the case of his movies, McCartney recalls,

> We discovered that if you put a home movie on, and put a record on at a random point, the record would synchronize with the music. At a number of points it would synchronize magically and at a number of points it would run out of synch. My theory was that in a movie there are probably fifty points that are moving at any time: the cat's tail, the cat's paws, the leaves, the bit of sunlight, the door which was opened and the person that walks through. The arms of the person, the feet of the person, the head turning; there are a lot of points in a movie that were moving; even the camera sometimes. Sometimes it's just the camera that's moving. Camera wobble and the lights will give you movement. And I figured that your eye synchronized these points of movement with the movement in the music.[59]

For McCartney, the internal choreography of film is discovered "magically," whereas in vidding, moments of musicality and movement are drawn out through careful sound–image matching.

This confidence in the found musicality of nearly any footage when set against a record clearly influenced McCartney's direction of *Magical Mystery Tour*, which works very like McCartney's home movies—and indeed were arguably an extension of McCartney's home movies, as his idea was just to load a bunch of interesting-looking actors onto a bus and see what happened. Sometimes the footage seems to be randomly running over the music, while other sections have lovely, if seemingly accidental, sound–image conjunctions. (There's a lovely section of eyes blinking and moving to the beat early in the film, for instance; and small gestures like head tilts and camera motion can have an unexpected and beautiful musicality.) There is also still a lot of running, jumping, and standing still, as well as priests playing blindman's buff, midgets wrestling, and other comic visual absurdities in *Goon Show* mode.

As Miles notes, McCartney wasn't really an innovator—the experimental techniques he used were either borrowed or being developed in parallel by other filmmakers—but he did have a significant role in popularizing them. Miles notes that as early as 1967, Jonas Mekas, founder of *Film Culture* and arguably the godfather of American avant-garde cinema, quoted McCartney in a review of a program of experimental films.[60] So just as the Beatles popularized some techniques of avant-garde music (playing with speed, tape loops, electronic sounds, distortion, nonmusical sounds) and art (pop art, collage, the bed-in, Yoko's bag-ism), they also gave many people, Kandy Fong included, their first taste of experimental film with their promos and *Magical Mystery Tour*. Moreover, they also shared and expanded experimental film's DIY nature.[61] "It was cheeky," McCartney later admitted, "cos people in film school were dying to make a movie, trained to the hilt, and there was us, the beat boys: 'Hey, we'll have a go, I can do that.'"[62] A handmade, homespun ethos was in the air in the late 1960s (George Harrison later called his film production company HandMade films) but obviously, when it came to filmmaking, rich people did DIY cinema first, as they could afford the equipment.

Years later, in a 1991 interview about *Apocalypse Now*, Francis Ford Coppola made a prediction about the emerging culture of cheap (and thus increasingly abundant) video cameras:

> To me, the great hope is that now these little 8mm video recorders and stuff have come around, some—just people who normally wouldn't

make movies are going to be making them. And, you know, suddenly one day some little fat girl in Ohio is going to be the new Mozart, and you know, and make a beautiful film with her little father's camera-corder [*sic*] and for once this whole professionalism about movies will be destroyed forever, you know, and it will really become an art form.[63]

While Coppola seems to believe, at least subconsciously, that the camera rightly belongs to the girl's father, he's obviously saying something true about the importance of technological access to filmmaking, and how that has affected women in particular.

But women have always made what they could with what tools they had.

Both Sides Now

Kandy Fong didn't have a camcorder in 1975, but she had a slide projector and an audio cassette recorder; most unusually for the time, she had access to film footage. Insane as it may seem from the vantage point of today, when we are awash in images, regular people had little access to images until recently. But just as the advent of cheap color printing led to an explosion of grassroots collage art in the 1960s (picture Terry Gilliam's animations or the Sex Pistols' album cover), it wasn't until the home video recorder that people could collect television and film footage to make stuff with. But Fong's future husband, John Fong, had three cigar boxes full of 35mm footage from *Star Trek* (which Fong later jokingly called "his dowry"[64]). The fan culture around *Star Trek* was so strong that the show was, in a sense, prefetishized: Roddenberry cut *Star Trek* footage into frames and sold them to fans and collectors who wanted to literally own a piece of the show. Roddenberry was later accused of more or less stealing this footage from Desilu[65] and selling it and other *Trek*-related artifacts for his own profit. But interestingly, by selling *Star Trek* to fans—by literally giving them the actual cinematic frames—Roddenberry may have engendered a new cinematic gaze.

While Kandy's first slideshow, "Amok Time: A Personal Log," was a mix of narrative storytelling and music, her subsequent works, both those made with slides and those later made with VCR footage, are clearly vids in the modern sense. One of Fong's earliest and most influential vids is BOTH SIDES NOW (c. 1980)[66] (Video 22 https://doi.org/10.3998/mpub.10069132.cmp.22), which was made with slides but, filmed for

Roddenberry, circulated on video beyond Fong's performances on the convention circuit. More recently, it has been featured in museum and gallery exhibitions, including *Spectacle: The Music Video* (2012–15), *Cut Up* (2013) at the Museum of the Moving Image, *Psychic Driving* (2013) in Belfast, and *MashUp: The Birth of Modern Culture* (2016) at the Vancouver Art Gallery. BOTH SIDES NOW is a character vid: it both gives voice to and interprets Mr. Spock. Although the song was written by Joni Mitchell and popularized by Judy Collins, Fong uses Leonard Nimoy's 1968 version and makes it clear that the voice of the song is not Nimoy's but Spock's. Here Spock reflects on his own experiences, which we have shared through the narrative of *Star Trek*. Although the song is of its moment and the cutting is almost unbearably slow by contemporary standards, this early vid does two notable things: first, it creates an intertext between two of Leonard Nimoy's artworks, his acting and his singing; and second, it gives Spock a voice, and it's not the voice a casual viewer of *Star Trek* would expect, despite its being Nimoy's own voice.

The vid's title card/opening frame, that of a bearded Spock contemplating Captain Kirk's profile, signals one kind of bothness: the image is from the doubly titled 1967 episode "Mirror, Mirror," in which Kirk and some of his crew are swapped into a brutal parallel universe. The bearded Spock is the doppelgänger version, and the image has become a pop culture cliché: if we see a normally clean-shaven character wearing a goatee, we know he's the evil version. But actual doppelgängers are only the most obvious form of double vision on display in this vid.

In fact, Fong uses the song "Both Sides Now" to comment on the intrinsic dividedness of Spock's character: his dual nature as a half-human, half-alien caught between two different cultural and expressive traditions. As the only alien crew member aboard the original series' *Enterprise*, Spock is frequently teased for his physical and philosophical differences in a way that would today qualify as workplace harassment. We also learn from Spock's human mother, Amanda, that Spock was regarded as an alien "half-breed" on Vulcan as well.

This otherness has made Spock a stand-in for many minority groups (Jewish people, because of Nimoy's own heritage and incorporation of Jewish gestures and symbols into Vulcan culture; Asian people, for the "slanty eyes" and clichéd inscrutability; people on the spectrum, for seriousness and lack of affect), but Spock has also been an important figure of identification for women. In "Women, *Star Trek*, and the Early Development of Fannish Vidding," I argue that this was partly because Spock was moved into a role in the *Trek* narrative that had originally been designed for a woman: Number One, the female first officer of *Star Trek*'s first pilot, played by Majel Barrett. It was Number One, so identified with the role of first officer that she had no other name, who first occupied the role of aloof, unemotional, mathematically inclined other. Like Spock, she was marked by that otherness; she too falls between worlds. Number One is not one of the men on the bridge, but she's not one of the girls either.[67] Like Spock, she's dismissed as a walking computer, as not fully human, as lacking feelings, though these insults are worse in Number One's case because of course women are supposed to be warm and nurturing, sexual or maternal. For Number One, this is a particularly gendered failure. But *Star Trek*'s insistence on the *Enterprise*'s first officer as an unemotional alien makes particular sense if the character is female. It is a 1960s picture of an unnatural—for which read strong, highly rational, technologically minded—woman,[68] the sort of woman who became a scientist, a computer programmer, a science fiction fan—or a vidder.

It is worth noting the fate of Number One after the pilot, as it is almost a parable of the possibilities for women at the time. Majel Barrett was recast in two nearly opposite roles. She was put into a blonde bouffant wig and a miniskirt to play the more stereotypically female character of Christine Chapel, a nurse who pines for Spock. But Barrett was also cast as the inflectionless voice of the *Enterprise*. While Number One was compared to a computer, the *Enterprise* actually *is* a computer. The voice of female authority was thus detached from embodied, messy female physicality; the metaphor of the scientific woman as machine was literalized and the rational female body removed from the screen. Last, we must note that—Reader, she married him! Majel Barrett married *Star Trek* creator Gene Roddenberry and was subsequently referred to as "the first lady of *Star Trek*." This is also an acceptable female role.

When Number One was eliminated from the narrative, Spock was moved into her position. He is therefore the shadow of a missing woman; a scar. He inherits her (gendered) problems as a strong, highly ranked woman in a male hierarchy. It can therefore be argued that Spock sees "from both sides" of the gender divide, and certainly Kandy Fong positions him as such. As Melissa Dickinson has argued, "There are some clear reasons why women science fiction fans of the '60s and early '70s—many of whom held advanced science and engineering degrees—might have connected powerfully with *Star Trek* (and specifically with Spock) as an expression of their own alienation among peers."[69] Consequently, BOTH SIDES NOW is fraught with gender slippage. The vid constructs an emo-

Fig. 13. "I've looked at love from both sides now," from BOTH SIDES NOW by Kandy Fong (c. 1980)

tional inner voice for *Star Trek*'s most notorious unemotional character, letting him express things he would not otherwise say. But the fact that Fong uses Leonard Nimoy's voice (from his album, knowingly titled *The Way I Feel*) adds legitimacy to the idea that this interior monologue could actually be Spock's, however laughable that might seem to someone reading the text superficially.

The song lyrics tell us that the narrator has looked at both sides of "clouds" (which Fong interprets more or less literally; as someone whose job involves interplanetary flight, Spock has certainly seen both sides of clouds) as well as "love." Fong uses this lyric to unpack a series of significant images, including one where Spock is framed as looking both at Christine Chapel (a textual, if thwarted, love interest of Spock's) and at James Kirk (a subtextual one) (Figure 13).

The sung assertion "I've looked at love from both sides now" in Spock's own voice turns *Star Trek*'s subtextual homoerotics—the reading that gave rise to slash fiction and the Kirk/Spock love affair—into text. It also makes us look at the footage differently. In the slide Fong selects for this lyric, Spock, at the far left, is part of the frame. He stands in for us, and like us, he is doing the looking. We are asked to see the famously logical Spock as a desiring subject. Looking back at him are Kirk and Chapel, and although Kirk is sitting and Chapel is standing, they're paralleled in the frame as blonds of analogous height. Fong's editing choice further asks us to question whether Spock's dual nature as half human, half alien (or perhaps I should say both human and alien) might also imply his bisexuality. We are explicitly asked to consider whether Spock is attracted to both men and women, to read Spock's inner landscape as well as his outer appearance. Spock is, after all, a character whose primary *gestus* is rigid self-control, but who would imagine that the tall, deep-voiced, dignified actor Leonard Nimoy had that much Joni Mitchell in him? If Nimoy has this voice inside him, why not Spock?

Each image in BOTH SIDES NOW can and should be subjected to this sort of analysis. To the extent we recognize these slides and can contextualize them within *Star Trek*, we may find the conjunction of music and image particularly provocative. Fong asks us to reread the images she presents through the lens of the song, sometimes just for amusement— for example, the lyric "But now old friends are acting strange" appears in conjunction with a funny picture of Kirk and McCoy. But Fong also asks questions and makes various sorts of textual/analytical arguments.

For instance, Fong uses the lyric "It's love's illusions I recall" to unpack an image from "The Enterprise Incident" (1968), an episode in which Kirk and Spock conspire to steal a cloaking device from under the nose of a female Romulan commander. (See Image D. https://doi. org/10.3998/mpub.10069132.cmp.175) As part of the plan, Kirk feigns mental illness, fakes his own death, and has plastic surgery so he can go undercover as a Romulan. Meanwhile, Spock subtly romances the Romulan commander, who seems genuinely attracted to him and who offers him a post as her second in command, promising him that she, unlike the humans he currently works with, understands and appreciates him. So when Spock recalls "love's illusions," does he mean Kirk's trickery? His own? The Romulan commander's offer of love and respect, which he must turn down?

This interpretive quality is what makes BOTH SIDES NOW a vid[70] and marks Fong as the founder of the form. There were others who made *Star Trek* slideshows for conventions, mainly random shots of the actors and characters played over a soundtrack, with no image–lyric conjunctions, no musical editing/timing, no interpretative framework, no emotional build. Kandy Fong complained about one (male) fan who didn't understand that the images in her shows were synched, that she was actually telling a story, that "there was a pace for each slide to be shown as far as the words of the song."[71] But BOTH SIDES NOW is a work in which music is clearly used as a narrative and analytical tool. By using image and sound to stage the contrast between Spock's external appearance and inner voice, Fong teases out various kinds of bothness surrounding the text: human and alien, male and female, heterosexual and homosexual, reason and emotion, control and desire.

Women Who Look

Another form of bothness in BOTH SIDES NOW is that of looking and being looked at. The song repeatedly returns to looking (at clouds, at love, at life), a refrain that is all the more striking in a song written by a woman and first sung in a female voice; it articulates a strong and subjective gaze. Fong's visuals, however, present Spock equally as the narrating subject and as the object of the gaze (and also the object of analysis). We spend the vid looking at him as well as at what he sees.

BOTH SIDES NOW thus exemplifies Mulvey's to-be-looked-at-ness as applied to men; it gives us the male image, stilled. This positioning of men as the object of the gaze was present both in the Beatles promos that influenced Kandy Fong as well as in *Star Trek* itself. In STRAWBERRY FIELDS FOREVER, for example, we see the Beatles both as spectacle and as spectators. Each of the Beatles stares directly into the lens, at us, but we also see them stilled, in parts and in fragments. In this way, STRAWBERRY FIELDS FOREVER highlights both the Beatles' to-be-looked-at-ness (their antics, the costumes, the fetishizing close-ups of their eyes, ears, lips, mustaches) as well as their ability to startle us by seeming to look at us directly.[72] (See Image E https://doi.org/10.3998/mpub.10069132. cmp.176 and Image F. https://doi.org/10.3998/mpub.10069132. cmp.177)

The Beatles had the power of the gaze but also presented themselves for interpretation. By the time of STRAWBERRY FIELDS FOREVER, they had the status not only of fictional characters but also of serialized transmedia characters on the level of Sherlock Holmes or James Bond. They'd had themselves scripted into consistency (John was the smart one! Paul was the cute one!) by playwright Alun Owen and other writers in ways that resemble the highly racialized characterizations of *Star Trek*, where all Vulcans are logical and all Klingons are warriors. (This kind of stereo-typing and generalizing is obviously familiar to woman as well as to other minorities; what *do* women want?) The Beatles were thus uniquely open to the gaze not just as fetishized and endlessly photographed rock stars but also as the protagonists of an ongoing transmedia narrative made up of movies, interviews, profiles, and journalistic puff pieces.

Similarly, *Star Trek*, whose 1966–69 run on NBC maps perfectly onto the era of Beatles promos (that is, their late psychedelic period), was also defined to an unusual degree by to-be-looked-at-ness. Like the Beatles promos, *Star Trek* was visually spectacular: boldly colorful, surreal, interesting to look at.[73] In "Minimalist Magic: The Star Trek Look,"[74] Mervyn Nicholson argues for the importance of precisely the aspects of *Star Trek*'s visual style that some might dismiss as low-budget or quaint, like its spare sets and huge blocks of colored light: the blood-orange or neon green skies, the brightly colorful interiors. Moreover, *Star Trek* had more than one episode where the characters wander through land-scapes disguised as alien worlds. Both McCartney in STRAWBERRY FIELDS FOREVER and Spock in "This Side of Paradise" (1967) climb alien trees and confront strange flowers.[75] (See Image G https://doi.org/10.3998/mpub.10069132.cmp.178 and Image H. https://doi.org/10.3998/mpub.10069132.cmp.179)

Nicholson argues that *Trek*'s minimalist visual style deemphasizes objects (props and sets) in favor of actors and their performances. In fact, like Andy Warhol, who also worked in a minimalist style, *Star Trek* focuses particularly on faces bathed in colored light. According to Nicholson, this emphasis on faces was crucial to *Star Trek*'s success; in particular, he gives credit to William Shatner's face and how he used it: "Television is a medium obsessed with faces. The close-up is virtually built into the medium, because of its small size. Shatner's face is remark-ably congenial for television, because he is so skilled in communicating emotion, thought, reactions, in his face by means of his face. He *acts* with his face. The facial mobility is extraordinary, without being in any way freakish. . . . The camera loves his face and dwells on it, allowing constant opportunity to metamorphose through the variety of emotions and reac-tions that constitute the drama." The range and mobility of Shatner's expressions allow Nimoy the advantage of performative contrast. While Kirk and Spock are in many ways a study in opposites, Nicholson claims that this "is especially noticeable in facial expression. Spock's studied immobility doubles the effect of Kirk's expressiveness." I would add that the reverse is also true: Shatner's overt theatricality and constantly changing microexpressions make Nimoy's tiny facial movements seem all the more significant, since the show has trained us to read faces as a primary source of dramatic information. Their faces solicit our scrutiny and demand our interpretation. Kirk's emotions constantly shift, requiring you to watch him at all times; meanwhile, the tiniest lift of Spock's eyebrow or pull of his mouth speaks volumes; he is the rare man with a Mona Lisa smile.

It is worth saying overtly that this to-be-looked-at-ness runs counter to how men normally act on film and TV; in fact, for a contrast, Nicholson directs us to look no further than Jeffrey Hunter's Captain Pike in *Star Trek*'s original (failed) pilot. Hunter is square jawed and (perhaps deliberately) inexpressive ("the typical macho male, feelings always under control," says Nicholson), whereas Shatner "is openly and consistently emotional, expressing a remarkable range of emotion, from rage and panic to love, curiosity, passion, shock, and, yes, even fear—not an emotion always allowed a lead male in an action show." (See Image I https://doi.org/10.3998/mpub.10069132.cmp.180 and Image J. https://doi.org/10.3998/mpub.10069132.cmp.181) Meanwhile Spock's popularity stems at least in part from the intensity of the gaze we direct at him, watching for hints of worry or amusement in his eyes. Like the female character he replaced, Spock is "mysterious"; he is, to borrow Steve Neale's phrase from *Masculinity as Spectacle*, investigated, rather than tested, through being vidded.[76] (See Image K. https://doi.org/10.3998/mpub.10069132.cmp.182)

Nicholson concludes that *Star Trek*'s minimalist aesthetic is politically inflected. For instance, he sees minimalism's emphasis on male faces and male emotions as an assault on conventional patriarchy and male authoritarianism. He also claims that minimalism also disrupts the relationship between spectator and object, what Maurice Berger calls "the traditional relationship between a fixed, static object and a fixated and static viewer."[77] Minimalism appeals to our visualizing power, encouraging us "to fill in the Minimalist spaces assigned to imagination," rather like McLuhan's idea of a "cool media," which was said to characterize television in the 1960s.[78] Lack encourages interpretation as well as participation. This may be one reason why it was *Star Trek* fandom that invented vidding. *Star Trek* gave the female spectator interesting men to look at and provided them with raw footage to interrogate. In the 1970s, women took up tools, built an audience through conventions and fan works, and began to remake film to their liking.

At the end of "Visual Pleasure and Narrative Cinema," Mulvey calls for an experimental cinema (a radical cinema, even an artisanal cinema) that will break down the voyeuristic, scopophilic male gaze by breaking up the traditional narrative editing that constructs and conceals it. She calls for a cinema that makes us aware of framing and editing, and thus aware of ourselves as spectators. Vidding is one answer to this call. It is a new cinematic form with a female gaze, a short-form cinema made in the editing room of stills and fragments by self-conscious participant-observers. Kandy Fong found frames of *Star Trek* that were already cut apart, with the narrative editing already broken down, but it was she who—drawing on the DIY ethos of both 1970s fandom and feminism—looked at them, put them together, and made something new.

THREE | VCR Vidding and the Vidding Collectives (1980–1991)

> The more I see of men, the more I love my VCR.
>
> —Embroidered sampler seen at the Escapade art auction,
> cited by Constance Penley in *NASA/Trek* (1997)

In 1984, Kandy Fong published an open letter in the first issue of the *Starsky and Hutch* letterzine, *Between Friends*: "One of my hobbies is setting some of my 6,000 ST [*Star Trek*] slides to music. . . . Why am I bringing this up in a S&H [*Starsky and Hutch*] letterzine? Because the only knowledge that I have of anyone else doing anything like this is a comment dropped at a con that S&H fans do slide shows all the time. Hello out there—does anyone do slide shows?"[1] In trying to find someone doing "anything like" what she was doing, Kandy Fong had gone to the right place. While *Starsky and Hutch* fans didn't work with actual film slides, as Kandy did in those early days, they are broadly acknowledged as the fandom that invented VCR vidding, a practice that by 1984 had spread to other fandoms. Fans made vids using consumer VCRs from about 1980 to the early 2000s, when digital source files became common and computer vidding became the norm. But to tell the story of analog vidding is to tell a story of female collaboration as well as technological and artistic innovation. Vidding is not just about the development of an art form but also about the development of an art world: a (nearly all-female) community of auteurs, critics, spectators, and fans working together to create what Tisha Turk and Joshua Johnson have called an ecology of vidding[2]—that is, a vibrant system of interactions around a visual art.

Inventing the Archive

Starsky and Hutch became the first fandom to make vids using VCRs partly as a matter of historical timing: the fandom's popularity coincided with the release of the consumer VCR, then called a VTR, or video tape recorder. *Starsky and Hutch* was broadcast on ABC from 1975 to 1979 and was an active fandom for years afterward thanks to the show's rotation in reruns. Sony released the Betamax recorder in 1975, and JVC's competing VHS format followed a year later. VTRs were expensive both to buy and to use, and consequently few people owned them, at least at first. In fact, at a cost of $1,000 and up, they were more typically rented for parties or special occasions than purchased. But media fans—that is, the fans of genre television and film who organized and came together to share their interest in particular story worlds—were early adopters of video recording technology, which they used to build enormous archives of televisual footage at a time when practically nobody had access to such footage. The consumer market for buying individual, professionally made copies of movies or TV shows simply did not yet exist.

Fans didn't build their home video archives in isolation; rather, fandom's community infrastructure helped both to spread out the work of archiving footage and to defray the then-enormous costs of video machines and blank tapes. As *Dark Shadows* vidder Kathleen Reynolds recalls, in 1978 almost nobody had a VCR because they were so expensive. But her friend had one, so they "worked out a deal with each other where she would record the publicly broadcast episodes through the week on her VCR if I provided the blank video tape—which at that time . . . were very expensive: they were like 25 dollars for one blank video tape."[3]

Cooperative cost-sharing agreements like these allowed fans not only to build media libraries but also to grow them by sharing, trading, and duplicating tapes. A group of fans that had clustered around one VCR would partner with another group that had its own VCR. After all, recording a show off the air required only one machine, but duplicating tapes and vidding required two. Some of these fan clusters developed into vidding collectives, groups of fans who made vids together and released them under the umbrella of a single "studio" name. Because of the dependence on shared tools and analog archives of source footage, vidding collectives tended to form in particular regions and were often named for them, like the Chicago Loop, Apocalypse West, or the California Crew. Geographical proximity was important, if only because in those early days a fan needed to physically haul her VCR—and early VCRs were heavy and bulky—to another fan's house and hook the two machines together if she wanted to duplicate tapes or make a vid. Fans also organized enormous chains of VCRs at media conventions, setting up duping rooms where fellow fans could obtain copies of the visual source (that is, the television episodes or movies central to a particular fandom) or of vids themselves. Kandy Fong was at the center of this organizational effort and is thus recognized within fandom as an innovator in vid distribution as well as in vid creation.

Fandom therefore built on previous collaborative models to organize the creative activities that formed around the technology of the VCR. Fans who had come together to stage letter-writing campaigns and conventions, fans who had edited APAs (amateur press associations) and published zines of fanfiction, fans who had put on plays and sewed costumes and painted fan art—they all now turned to the task of figuring out ways to share video tools and vidding techniques. They worked together not only to obtain footage but also to protect it, developing protocols both for archiving and for duplicating videocassettes in order to minimize tape wear over generations, thus conserving image quality. Fans became obsessive experts on the subject of videotape, writing and mimeographing for distribution essays with titles like "The Use and Abuse of Video Tape" and "Tape Care." They also shared information on how magnetic tape is made as well as how best to travel with it, store it, and wind it:

> FWIW, the best way to store magnetic tape of any kind is not re-wound or fast forwarded. The best way to store tape is loosely. . . . Tight winding encourages stretching and "magnetic imprinting" where the tape is pressed against another bit and their magnetic charges, minutely, attract and repel each other. It largely results in just a tiny, tiny amount more of static, but if you use thin (as it found in less expensive or very long tapes) tape you can occasionally actually get a print of one bit on another. In audio once in a while this produces an audible ghosting of the sound that is a neat special effect, but hardly good news for preserving the original material. The longer the tape is left wound tightly, the more chance for problems.[4]

No detail was too small. Here a fan advises others to "pack" or "cycle" their tapes:

Once you buy some quality tapes, take them out of their wrapper and "pack" or "cycle" them. Do this by fast-forwarding the tape to the end and rewinding the tape back to the beginning. Packing tapes helps care for them and your equipment in two ways. First, it removes excess oxides that might be on your new tapes. These oxides can temporarily get lodged in the video heads of your equipment and cause drop-out, a tiny interruption in the recording and playback of a tape which shows up on your screen as little dots or lines of light. By packing your tapes, you allow this excess oxide to fall off the tape, thus making the tape clean and ready for use. Second, by packing your tapes you are smoothing out any variations in how tightly the tape was wound by the manufacturer. These variations could lead to recording problems by causing the tape to flutter through the tape transport mechanism if wound too loosely, or pull on the mechanism if too tight.[5]

Protocols like these were important for archiving and crucial for vidding because vidding put additional strain on magnetic tape, thus affecting the images and sounds it recorded. Even in these early days, quality mattered. Fans noticed distortions, blurriness, and other imperfections.

Media fandom was therefore one of the first places in the pre-Blockbuster, pre-YouTube, pre-Netflix world where people had access to large archives of footage; moreover, likely because of the collaborative and social nature of the archiving enterprise, these collectors were women. Working together, female fans put together enormous televisual libraries for themselves and their friends, making, sharing, and swapping thousands of videocassettes recording not-yet-purchasable runs of fan-favorite television shows like *Star Trek*, *Starsky and Hutch*, *Blake's 7*, *The Man from U.N.C.L.E.*, *The Professionals*, *I Spy*, *Wiseguy*, and others.

It was only a matter of time before these fans began to use their archives of footage and their highly developed talent for collaborative creativity to make something new: to make vids.

Inventing the VCR Vid

What fans made was limited by the technology they were using. This is true in all art making, but early vidding presented particular problems. VCR vidders were using home equipment made for recording, not filmmaking or film editing. The machines weren't designed to do what these first vidders made them do. But these women managed to make precise artworks using these blunt instruments—technological bricolage at its finest.

As I discussed in chapter 1, the first VCR vids we know of were made by Kendra Hunter and Diana Barbour, though according to Hunter, vidding was Barbour's idea. In fact, Barbour and a friend, Terry Adams, turned up at Hunter's house late one night to enthuse about this great idea she'd just had. "It was just an idea!" Hunter insists. "I had talked to them earlier in the day and it had not been a topic of conversation. It was something that came up when they were talking that evening. I had gone to bed because I had a horrible headache . . . and then they dragged me out of bed and said, 'We have to do this.' And that's how it started." Hunter and Barbour spent the next few months struggling to make something. "We were literally working with stone knives and bear skins," Kendra Hunter remembers. "We did the one tape where we made all of our mistakes. This didn't work, or that didn't work. . . ."[6] In the end, they made twenty vids, which they brought to the *Starsky and Hutch* fan convention, ZebraCon[7] aka ZCon, in the fall of 1980.

Those vids started a revolution. According to Kandy Fong and Sandy Herrold's 2008 lecture "Vidding History: 1980–1984," which compiled conversations with vidders of the time, those first vids "blew everyone away—no one had seen anything like that."[8] Some of the vids were shown on a television set in one of the public convention spaces, but Hunter and Barbour were also compelled to do multiple (and packed) showings in their hotel room. They'd brought a VCR from home in order to show their work to other fans at the con, but people wanted to see these vids over and over; they were simply amazed. Hunter and Barbour replayed their tapes all weekend. "What I do remember was watching the women in that room watching what we had created," Hunter recalls. "It was probably one of the best moments I had in fandom."

Hunter and Barbour also spent the weekend explaining how these vids were made. According to Flamingo, this was their most important contribution to fandom, even above and beyond the many notable vids they made: they taught others. The next year, 1981, a remarkable sixteen people brought vids to ZCon. This group included Elaine Hauptman, Carol Huffman, and Terry Martin (sometimes called the Texas Ladies, makers of a collection of song vids known as the Texas Tape); Linda Brandt (who vidded both solo and as part of a collective called the Three Sisters); Jean C. aka Dargelos; and Pam Perry.[9] In fact, we can trace much of the genealogy of vidding from this first group of sixteen. For instance, Pam Perry inspired Mary Van Deusen, who is not only an immensely prolific vidder herself, having made nearly seven hundred vids since 1984, but also an influential teacher of others. So the fans who saw Hunter and

Barbour's first vids became vidders, and these vidders mentored other vidders, spreading the idea of the art form.

Hunter and Barbour's first vids are also a record of their aesthetic and technical experimentations. They can be seen as a catalog of early vidding techniques, such as freeze-frame, use of internal motion, and long clips. Some of these techniques were abandoned as audiovideo technology improved, while others were refined and formalized into a VCR-vidding practice.

Stilling the Image

Hunter and Barbour's first two vids were modest affairs; in fact, each used only a single, stilled frame. BEHIND BLUE EYES (1980), discussed at length in chapter 1, was a character vid about Starsky, and ALL THE TIME (1980) was a vid about Hutch. These early vids not only evoke the fannish slideshows of years past but also take advantage of one of the early video tape recorder's few features: it could still a moving image. "What VTRs could do was hold a freeze frame cleanly," vidder Flamingo explains in her 2001 essay on early *Starsky and Hutch* vids, "and this was used a great deal."[10] This feature was important because these early video machines couldn't cut cleanly; that is, a vidder couldn't make a clean, hard cut between two clips without leaving electronic garbage, sometimes termed "rainbow noise," on the frame or creating other visible or audible distortions. Some early vidders therefore used freeze-frame as an editing device. This permitted them to cleanly transition between one shot and another. Vidders discovered that they could intersperse frozen images between video clips more or less seamlessly. They could also use freeze-frames and stills to extend a particular video clip to a desired length, to fit with the music.[11]

We see all these techniques in THE BOY CAN'T HELP IT (1980) (Video 23   https://doi.org/10.3998/mpub.10069132.cmp.23), a vid whose credits (Producer: Kendra Hunter; Executive Producer: Diana Barbour; Conceived & Executed by Terry Adams; Thanks for the Songs and the Scenes to Melanie Rawn & Carol Huffman) clearly show the extent to which vidding was communal and collaborative. But these credits are just some of the vid's freeze-framed cards; others thank Paul Michael Glaser, who plays Starsky, the eponymous "boy" of the title ("The Boy Courtesy of PMG"), as well as the video recording machines themselves, which the vidders have nicknamed Peter, Charlie, and Saucy. But these inserted cards aren't just crediting all the *Starsky and Hutch* fans making the vid;

these freeze-framed cards are also being used as connective tissue to link the vid's clips without any audio or visual distortion. Kandy Fong wryly describes the making of THE BOY CAN'T HELP IT as "how they did it when the machine couldn't edit."[12]

But the device of freeze-frame also works with the vid's theme; it stops our gaze, literally. THE BOY CAN'T HELP IT is a love letter to Starsky—or, to be more accurate, a lust letter. The vid is scored to Bonnie Raitt's "The Boy Can't Help It" (1979), a gender-reversed blues cover of Little Richard's "The Girl Can't Help It" (1956). Raitt reverses the song lyrics as neatly as Hunter and Barbour et al. reverse the gaze. Now it's the boy who just can't help being so sexy that he demands our (female) attention. This reverses a common sexist trope of male songwriting: that women are to blame for attracting male attention, and men are only acting naturally in response. Here it's a man who just can't help being so damn attractive to the female spectator. The vid gives us various views of Starsky: wearing nothing but a towel, cavorting naked in a hot tub. There is a distinct focus throughout on Starsky's ass. "As he walks by, the women get engrossed," Raitt growls, low and sultry, as Starsky walks away, his short jacket emphasizing his butt. One of the vid's significant freeze-frames has Starsky face down on a bed, ass in the air, while Raitt sings, "He's got a lot of what they call the most." (See Image L. https://doi.org/10.3998/mpub.10069132.cmp.183) Gaze arrested; spectator engrossed.

The vidders have used freeze-frame to isolate a single image out of what is obviously a larger sequence to catch the characters in a compromising pose. This kind of spectatorship only became possible with the VCR, and so one cannot underestimate its importance, both to the history of fandom and to the development of a female gaze.[13] The VCR enabled women to stop the flow of filmic time in order to look, really look, at an image in the safety of domestic space. The VCR also allowed women to pick and choose among images and to repeat their experience of those images, to the point where a fan could tell another fan's favorite scenes because her repetitive viewing would have affected the quality of the VHS tape itself, stretching that section out and sometimes causing blurriness or other distortions.[14]

The ability to look frankly (safely, openly) at the bodies of others and to repeat that viewing experience as often as one likes recalls other historical moments of successful female spectatorship,[15] but these were as nothing to the pleasures of the VCR. The VCR gave fans the ability to pause and look, to repeat and rewind, to fast forward over unwanted material or skip to one's next favorite scene. These interventions can be seen as film editing in its most basic form. They alter time and the sequence of events, thus creating an individualized edit for the person in control of the VCR. You can have a version of the story in which your favorite scenes happen three times, and the boring bits happen fast or not at all. The next step, the one that leads to vidding, is to isolate and recombine these images into new montages. The frame of found kinkiness that is Starsky's ass is pulled out of the jumble of television images, given to us for prolonged examination (the freeze-frame is on screen for a full ten seconds, 0:31–0:41), and contextualized with other images of desirous looking, such as clips where the camera attends to Starsky's body.

Starsky and Hutch fans mastered this sort of close, not to say fetishized, looking. In fact, the fandom documented its discovery of what it calls the "Magnificent 7": seven frames from the *Starsky and Hutch* episode "The Fix" (1975)[16] that, "when shown slowly and advanced one at a time, made it look like the guys were kissing"[17] (Figure 14 https://doi.org/10.3998/mpub.10069132.cmp.150). *Starsky and Hutch*, which actor David Soul famously described as "a love story between two men who happen to be cops," was an early and influential slash fandom, and many fans created works that interpreted the visible affection between the two partners as gay romance. The greater history of slash fandom[18] is therefore closely tied up with the history of vidding, in that slash fans were particularly and intensely motivated to make visible—literally; they wanted to see on screen—their interpretation of certain stories and relationships. This was the case from the first: Hunter and Barbour built a vid called KISS YOU ALL OVER (early 1980s) around the famous seven frames and named their song tape *The Magnificent 7*. Today's digital vidders have tools that can not only isolate frames but create them, and, as I discuss in the final chapter, fans are beginning to piece together new movies by pulling and shaping still images and GIFs out of existing movies and linking them.

Discovering Musicality

Internal Motion

Freeze-frame wasn't the only technique in the early vidding arsenal; vidders also worked to discover and highlight the musicality in existing televisual footage. Hunter and Barbour's THE BOY CAN'T HELP IT features two sequences of Starsky dancing—scenes that exist purely as aesthetic

Fig. 14. The Magnificent 7.

appreciation of a body in motion. The first of these sequences, which takes place during the song's guitar solo, simply reproduces a dance sequence from the show, albeit a sexy one: Starsky, at a nightclub, not only shows off his moves but begins to strip. He takes off his jacket, which he theatrically flings away, then undoes his cuffs and begins to roll up his sleeves. Starsky literally seems to be dancing to Raitt's song, and this rhythmical striptease certainly exemplifies its meaning. Starsky is clearly framed as the object of sexual attention.

But the second, and far more glorious, dance sequence is manufactured by the vidders themselves. Raitt's song ends with an extended outro of male singers repeating, nearly chanting, "Can't help it / Just can't help it." The vidders create a new dance by extending—looping—a clip of Starsky leaning over the Torino's door and doing a little butt shimmy of excitement. As Starsky, Paul Michael Glaser rocks his hips from side to side, nearly twerking, then does a little step first to the right, then to the left. Hunter and Barbour et al. cut and loop this footage, synchronizing it with the rhythmic chant of the outro to create an almost hypnotic spectacle that lasts for over fifty seconds—an eternity in vidding time. (See Figure 15 https://doi.org/10.3998/mpub.10069132.cmp.151 and Clip 7. https://doi.org/10.3998/mpub.10069132.cmp.164)

The vidders have contrived not only to have Starsky do a striptease for us but also to shake his booty for us, showing off the slinkiness of Glaser's hips and synchronizing his steps to the beat. The vidders have

Fig. 15. Starsky shakes his groove thing.

made Starsky dance and have also made the footage dance. They have discovered the musicality in these movements and extended them into an erotic appreciation of Starsky's body that lasts for the whole rest of the vid. This is a homemade example of the narrative stilling that Laura Mulvey associates with the male gaze. Starsky's butt is literally showstopping.

Long Cuts

Hunter and Barbour made other vids simply by discovering and drawing out the underlying musicality and rhythm of television without doing any editing at all. This was another way of solving the problem of how to make clean cuts with primitive equipment: don't make any. Two of their most famous early *Starsky and Hutch* vids use this technique, though they are markedly different in tone: **BEEP BEEP** (Video 24 https://doi.org/10.3998/mpub.10069132.cmp.24) and **THE ROSE** (Video 25 https://doi.org/10.3998/mpub.10069132.cmp.25) (both c. 1980). BEEP BEEP is a comedy; the audio track, "Beep Beep (The Little Nash Rambler)," is a 1958 novelty song by the Playmates that tells the story of a big Cadillac racing a little Nash Rambler. The song's humor comes from it being an accelerando; that is, the song starts slow but gradually builds, with the music and the singing becoming comically fast, which reflects the narrative of a car chase. In BEEP BEEP, Hunter and Barbour set this song against one long opening scene[19] from *Starsky and Hutch*—which works perfectly, not only because the sequence is about the men comparing their cars but also because the visuals become part of the accelerando. Hunter and Barbour bring out the underlying musicality in the footage. For instance, the show's own cuts line up with the song's beats, and musical phrases end at significant visual moments. At the start of the vid, which is slow, Starsky lazily plays kick the can next to his Ford Torino, which the vid reframes almost as a soft shoe. Starsky is waiting for someone, and on cue—in fact, on the line "What to my surprise . . . / A little Nash Rambler was following me"—an actual Nash convertible comes around the bend, driven by Hutch. He gets out and introduces the new car with a flourish. The song speeds up as an argument blossoms: the men argue the merits of their cars, with Starsky, a muscle car owner, scoffing[20] at Hutch's little Nash: "A grown man doesn't drive a car like that, not a grown man." The conversation grows heated as they yell and gesticulate. The increasingly frenetic tempo of the song thus "scores" the argument, which ends—as does the vid—on the beat of a car door slamming. Again, these visuals are all from a single scene, unedited (though the vidders chose the starting point, which affects the sound–image conjunction throughout), but Hunter and Barbour use the song to create a new narrative. The comic competition of the song's car drivers is used to draw out and explicate the dynamic between the TV characters.

While BEEP BEEP is lighthearted, THE ROSE is melodrama in literal, nineteenth-century terms: It uses song to accompany and amplify drama. Like BEEP BEEP, THE ROSE is one unedited sequence from the show, this one scored to Bette Midler's 1979 recording of "The Rose." The scene is famous in *Starsky and Hutch* fandom; it is the tag to "Starsky's Lady" (1977). In this episode, Starsky's girlfriend, Terry, is shot by an enemy of Starsky's. Although she survives, a fragment of bullet is lodged in her brain, and we are told she won't live long. However, she lives long enough to make certain arrangements. In particular, she wraps two presents to be opened exactly two weeks after her death, one for Starsky and one for Hutch. THE ROSE shows them opening these presents. Starsky and Hutch are sitting on the kitchen floor, drunk and playing Monopoly, a game that Starsky used to play (badly) with Terry. When the clock chimes midnight, they unwrap their gifts. Starsky's present is a book called *How to Win at Monopoly*, which connects Terry to Hutch, who is Starsky's new partner in Monopoly. Terry's present to Hutch establishes another point of connection between them: she has bequeathed him her teddy bear, Ollie, which she used to sleep with. Terry's letter to Hutch, which he reads aloud, his voice breaking, says: "To dearest Hutch: to you I entrust Ollie and Dave [Starsky]. Please love them both. Don't let either one of them change." Both men are crying by the end of the scene.

To play this sequence over Midler's rendition of "The Rose" is to amplify the scene's overt themes of love and loss. The sequence also orchestrates the passing over of the beloved Starsky (as symbolized by the bear) from Terry to Hutch. An analogous switch occurs in the song, which starts by evoking the idea of love as pain and ends by arguing that pain is necessary for the blossoming of new love: the eponymous rose. Terry is posthumously trying to kindle a deeper bond between Starsky and Hutch. That much is straightforward in the scene, and whether you want to read more into it—a sexual meaning, a queer reading—is up to you.[21] But Terry's message couldn't be clearer. She instructs Hutch to love Starsky and take care of him in her absence. This unashamed love between the partners is what draws fans to the show.

Hunter and Barbour time their vid so that the three verses of "The

Rose" divide the tag scene into three distinct movements: the setup, the opening of Starsky's present, and the opening of Hutch's present. The first section, in which Midler sings about the pain of love (it is a river that drowns, a razor that cuts . . .), scores the setup: Starsky and Hutch sit on the kitchen floor, drowning their sorrows. The song's melancholy speaks to a context that is not visible: the two men are killing time while waiting to fulfill a promise to the dead. The song's second verse—which is about taking risks for love—provides the soundtrack for Starsky's determined, teary opening of his present. The song's climactic third stanza, which is the most intense and orchestrated, with Midler's voice multitracked, is reserved for Hutch. We see him unwrap and hold up the bear. Then, almost miraculously, on "Far beneath the bitter snow," the camera begins a slow push into a tight close-up of Hutch as he reads Terry's letter, the motion encouraging the same looking beneath that the lyrics suggest. We stay on Hutch as his mouth trembles and his eyes grow wet on the song's final lines: "Lies the seed / That with the sun's love, in the spring / Becomes the rose," whereupon we cut back to Starsky, who is smiling and crying.

It's a masterful use of image–music conjunction, with meaning that is both intentional and found. As Flamingo notes, "Even though it is only one scene played over a song, there is still timing involved." Flamingo gained this knowledge firsthand: she herself remastered the vid when the original, off-air *Starsky and Hutch* footage became unwatchable— remastering being the process of reduplicating a vid exactly with cleaner footage. So even though the vid is only one scene with no cuts, Flamingo notes, "It took me two hours to get the timing exactly right, so I know it was no coincidence how this vid plays out. It took timing and work to land the scene where it is so that it ends in the right place."[22] The fact that a fan takes the time and makes the effort to remaster an older vid is, of course, a sign of a vid's importance; it's relatively thankless work. But fans remaster vids that continue to be relevant to the community.

Flamingo believes that THE ROSE is "the best of the group of first vids Kendra and Diana brought to ZebraCon," noting that it "tells a story with an emotional impact that holds up today." That said, THE ROSE really does require context; otherwise the vid's shots of men playing Monopoly and giving each other teddy bears may come off as surreal rather than symbolic. Flamingo once had a bad experience showing THE ROSE to an unprepared audience: "The vid wasn't 'set up' or explained by the presenter and the audience had no idea what was going on and laughed inappropriately. That was not a fun experience."[23] As I discussed earlier, the experience of being laughed at by spectators who fail to understand the meaning of the melodrama was all too common in early vidding, and it's one of the reasons that vidders have historically kept close tabs on their work, controlling who is permitted to see it and the context within which it is shown. However, for the fans who do get it, THE ROSE remains a surprisingly effective (and affective) vid; it still has the power to bring entire rooms of fans to tears. The vid has also supercharged the song, which has become not only a *Starsky and Hutch* anthem, still often sung at the close of small slash conventions like ZebraCon, SHareCon, and Escapade, but an anthem for fandom itself.

In some convention contexts, it is appropriate to sing along with vids; in others, it is not. But THE ROSE is unusual in that fans sing it as a way of invoking the vid and its themes. In the 1993 ZCon program, thirteen years after THE ROSE was made, ZCon founder Karen B. wrote a note about the song next to its transcribed lyrics, provided for singing:

> Some people have asked why sing THE ROSE? . . . Back in the early years of ZCON, we began to sing along to this particular song after the Saturday night festivities . . . [as] a fitting way to end the evening. After a few years, it was a tradition. S&H is still the heart of ZCON and this song has so many memories of "good old days." Perhaps, most importantly, we believe fandom is a family. Our family. Despite irritations and problems, we love each other. That's what fandom's all about. THE ROSE is still appropriate after all these years.

THE ROSE now has its own afterlife: while still strongly associated with *Starsky and Hutch* and its fandom ("S&H is still the heart of ZCON"), it has transcended its immediate narrative context. Fans have taken Hunter and Barbour's vid, which tells the story of two men being instructed to love and take care of each other in the wake of a tragedy, and they have made it about themselves. THE ROSE is now a story that fandom tells about itself, and even more importantly, it is a story that fandoms sings about itself and to itself. Fans come together communally to sing THE ROSE. A fan of the British cop show *The Professionals* who attended ZCon in the late 1990s described what she called "a traditional group singing of 'The Rose,' which has some arcane S/H significance."[24] She hadn't seen the vid, but that doesn't matter; the group singing is what matters, and the vid survives in it. As fans recall:

My favorites memories of ZCon have been of leading the singing of "The Rose" on Saturday night. It felt so wonderful to be up there playing my guitar and hearing everyone sing along with me.

I think the thing I remember clearest is the entire con joining together to sing The Rose. . . . I might be a euphoric sentimentalist, but I think those moments bound the people in that room to each other as few other cons ever have. The last time I was there it brought tears to my eyes, because I was remembering many of the people who used to sing it with us who were no longer alive.

My eyes are never dry during the group singing of The Rose. There is no moment at any convention I have ever attended that can match that feeling . . . those precious moments of camaraderie with my fellow fans. It's one of those moments that writes itself down on the scrapbook pages inside your heart where it can never fade.[25]

These recollections show fans using THE ROSE to express grief as well as love, themes that are central to Hunter and Barbour's original vid. In this case, these feelings are expressed not just through song but actually through singing. While singing along with the vids in certain formal vid show settings is discouraged as discourteous to others, the reminders in vid show program books ("No talking, singing along, etc."[26]) suggest that fans need to be held back from doing so.

But fans find other places to sing. Fans sing at cons either formally (as in the traditional group singing of THE ROSE, or more recently in scheduled fan events like Vividcon's Club Vivid or Vid Karaoke) or informally (for example, during the first few years of Vividcon, fans went to the indoor swimming pool in the basement on the last night to swim and sing together in chorus, as the tiled pool room had good acoustics). More recently, conventions like CON.TXT have gone the other way, chiding people with "No shushing." While scholars such as Henry Jenkins, Melissa L. Tatum, and Mark Soderstrom have talked about the importance of singing in fan culture, the topic has been primarily addressed through the fannish folk songs of filk. The history of vidding is tied up with the history of filk. As I discussed in chapter 2, the first vid—Kandy Fong's WHAT DO YOU DO WITH A DRUNKEN VULCAN? —incorporated a filk sung by Fong and her friends, and Fong has vidded several others filk songs, including Leslie Fish's famous **BANNED FROM ARGO** (c. 1980). But filk, while wide-ranging, tends to be known for its witty parodies, bawdy tales, and repurposed sea shanties rather than for the expression of heartfelt emotion in song.

I don't want to draw too sharp a distinction here. Vidding has a strong comedy tradition, among which you can find bawdy, clever vids—the Clucking Belles' MEN (2003) (Video 26 https://doi.org/10.3998/mpub.10069132.cmp.26), a literal sea shanty, comes to mind—and filk certainly has its share of sentimental ballads (which filkers punningly call "ose," as in "more ose"). But strong emotion is popular in vidding—"Big Emotion,"[27] as one vid show has it. It's the sort of thing that in the nineteenth century might have been called "sensation" and that the kids of the twenty-first century sometimes call "feels." (See "Spotlight on: Big Emotion" in the online appendix.) Vidders and vid fans seek an embodied, cathartic reaction from stories that have musical as well as simply plot-based or spectacular values. By adding song to story, vidders make the mass media a site of collective feeling. In the recollections above, we see this collective feeling in one of its purest forms as fans ritually sing and cry together; they are happily overcome. Fifteen, twenty, twenty-five years later,[28] fans sing THE ROSE, a song made meaningful as one of the first vids made by the first VCR vidders.

Impact and Influence of Early VCR Vidding

The impact of Hunter and Barbour's video work was immediate and powerful; as I noted above, after seeing Hunter and Barbour's vids in 1980, sixteen fans brought vids to ZCon in 1981. These fans included the Texas Ladies, the Three Sisters, and Dargelos & Pam Perry, and as Kandy Fong and Sandy Herrold explained in their 2008 talk, we can see each of them solving the editing challenge in their own way.

Shorts

Many of Dargelos & Pam Perry's first vids were shorts; that is, the vids would use only a small portion of a song, just enough to establish the image–music conjunction, then get out, a technique that continues to be used for comedy vids. (See "Spotlight on Comedy Shorts" in the online appendix.) So they vidded twenty-seven seconds of SINGING IN THE RAIN (1981) (Video 27 https://doi.org/10.3998/mpub.10069132.cmp.27) over a scene where Starsky and Hutch climb, fully clothed and drenched, out of a swimming pool, and forty-eight seconds of YOU OUGHTA BE IN PICTURES (1981) over a sequence where Hutch goes undercover as an actor in a western. The short duration of the vids meant that cutting was either absent or kept to an absolute minimum. Dargelos & Pam Perry's early vids were made with Betamax machines and a turntable and were collected on a song tape called *Mondo Esoterica* (1985); this tape is also notable for having credits made by computer (likely an Osborne or Apple IIe). The vidders explicitly thank "Diana/Kendra for the original inspiration."

Fade to Black

Linda Brandt, who vidded both alone and collectively with Lucy Keifer and Donna Williams as the Three Sisters, was not only an early *Starsky and Hutch* vidder but also one of the first people to make multifandom vids, which use different fandoms in the same vid, tying the sources together via a thematic line. The Three Sisters made vids in a number of fandoms popular in the early 1980s, including *The Professionals* (1977–83), *Simon and Simon* (1981–89), *Remington Steele* (1982–87), *Hardcastle and McCormick* (1983–86), and *Scarecrow and Mrs. King* (1983–87). THAT'S WHAT FRIENDS ARE FOR (c. 1985) (Video 28 https://doi.org/10.3998/mpub.10069132.cmp.28) is an early multifandom vid that creates parallels between the buddy cop friendships/homoerotic relationships of four shows: *The Man from U.N.C.L.E.* (1964–68), *Riptide* (1984–86), *I Spy* (1965–68), and *Alias Smith and Jones* (1971–73). Some will remember that the song was a fund raiser for the American Foundation for AIDS Research.

THAT'S WHAT FRIENDS ARE FOR is also notable for its fade-to-black cuts. As Fong and Herrold noted, fade to black was a feature of the particular VTR Brandt used. On that machine, "[if] you twirled a knob, you could fade to black, then pause the recorder—change the scene on the playback machine—and twirl the knob back to go from black to the new scene."[29] These fades allowed the Three Sisters to create aesthetically pleasing transitions in the days when hard cuts caused rainbow noise and other jarring and ugly distortions; fade-to-black transitions were also useful for smoothing over the aesthetic differences between footage from different shows.

While fade-to-black transitions fell out of favor with the flying erase head (which I discuss in more detail below), they experienced a resurgence of popularity in the YouTube era. Many born-digital vidders cut to black in between clips or on the beat simply because they find it aesthetically pleasing to do so. Fade to black is just one of a million transitions offered by today's video editing software, a tool to deploy when artistically appropriate. But for many vidders with strong connections to the VCR era, the technique, now sometimes called fadebop, is judged negatively. For those vidders, it still has connotations of cheating, not technologically but aesthetically. Fade to black is seen by some as a crutch because it is less difficult than skilled continuity editing like match cuts or raccord.

Hard Cuts

In these very early days, the price you paid for cuts was distortion, both visual (rainbow noise and other visual artifacts) and auditory. In the *Starsky and Hutch* vid DESPERADO (c. 1983) (Video 29 https://doi.org/10.3998/mpub.10069132.cmp.29) by the Texas Ladies, you can tell when the cuts come without even watching. You can hear a noticeable bending and warping of Judy Collins's silvery soprano at every cut. The vid is more committed to montage than most of this period—there are more clips, and they are more intentionally placed to build story—but the vidders paid a severe aesthetic price.

"These are not things vidders could get away with today," Flamingo notes, "but even with the wobbling soundtracks, freeze frames, and very long clips, fans greeted these early vids with astonishment and appreciation."[30] In a December 1981 *Starsky and Hutch* letterzine, one fan appreciatively describes the 1981 ZCon where many of these new vids debuted: "Rooms filled with laughter and cigarette smoke. Wine flowed with love. Zines and stories and song tapes took our time . . . a song tape was born. The reward was given this year as we watch the results of your hours of hard work. 'What I Did for Love.' 'Another One Bites the Dust.' 'Just to Feel this Love.' 'Forget Your Troubles, C'mon Get Happy.' . . . Give yourself a hand, Ladies. Your work deserves more."[31]

WHAT I DID FOR LOVE and JUST TO FEEL THIS LOVE FROM YOU were by the Texas Ladies; FORGET YOUR TROUBLES, COME ON GET HAPPY was made by Dargelos & Pam Perry; ANOTHER ONE BITES THE DUST by Linda Brandt. These vidders and others collected their individual vids on song tapes, which they then copied and distributed to other fans, and in 1985, five of these song tapes were nominated for the first and only Encore awards at the tenth anniversary *Starsky and Hutch* convention, obscurely named the Paul Muni Special.[32] The five nominated tapes were *The Texas Tape* (The Texas Ladies), *Mondo Esoterica* (Dargelos & Pam Perry), *Dialogue & Songtape* (The Three Sisters), *Rebel Productions* (Carol

Huffman), and *The Magnificent 7* (Kendra Hunter, Diana Barbour, and Terry Adams). Fittingly, *Magnificent 7* won it.

From this small group of innovative *Starsky and Hutch* fans, we can trace a chain of influence that extends more than two decades. To be clear, this group represents only one small subset of vidders, and in the wake of vidding's explosion of the digital era, only a small number of contemporary vidders would or could claim Barbour, Hunter, Brandt, and so on as ancestors. But at the same time, the impact of this first group of vidders is extraordinarily visible considering the underground nature of the vidding world. In 2017, vidder and vid historian Morgan Dawn tried to visualize this impact in a diagram tracing the genealogy of about thirty-five vidders or vidding collectives. (See Image M. https:// doi.org/10.3998/mpub.10069132.cmp.184) This diagram, while partial and limited to her sphere of vidding, shows the kind of direct and personal connections vidders had before the Internet. VCR vidders had mentors: fans who showed them what vids were and how to make them.

Morgan Dawn describes her diagram as follows: "A sample relationship map showing connections between some of the vidders over the decades. These connections varied: some fans collaborated creatively or inspired others to take up vidding, others shared only the VCR equipment or jointly distributed their solo creations on shared songtapes." Other relationship maps are certainly possible, but this map is useful for tracing some early connections. It shows Hunter and Barbour's influence on other *Starsky and Hutch* fans; it also gives us a glimpse of the lost offshoot of *Dark Shadows* vidding, where a burgeoning community was stifled after being accused of copyright infringement. (See "Spotlight on: *Dark Shadows* Vidding" in the online appendix.) But it primarily shows a direct link from the innovators of the early 1980s (Fong, Hunter, Barbour) to many of the influential vidders of twenty years later.

Making a VCR Vid

By the late 1980s, home video technology and fan technical experimentation had developed to the point where there became a more or less definitive process for making fan music videos, even as VCRs varied from type to type and individual machines had their own idiosyncrasies that needed to be taken into account. Fans typically taught each other to vid directly, one on one, leading to influence chains like the one that Morgan Dawn documents, but fans also documented their process in mimeographed handouts and booklets. (See Image N. https://doi. org/10.3998/mpub.10069132.cmp.185)

Here's a quick overview, starting with the perhaps unnecessary reminder that video is not film. There is no celluloid image to work with, no literal cutting or splicing of frames. Consequently, editing a VCR vid requires recording a series of clips of the right length in the right order, one after another, on a blank VHS tape. That is to say, VCR vids were historically made in sequence. Vidders could not edit asynchronously, put down pieces, or swap out clips. Making a vid thus required at least two VCRs: one to play the clips and the other to record them. It also required an audio source (phonograph, tape player) wired into the recording machine.

The primary distinction to be made in VCR vidding was whether or not your recording machine had a video dub feature; only later, more expensive machines did.[33] If your machine had this feature, you could lay down your audio track on the vid master tape before building your visual track on top of it. However, if your machine didn't have video dub, then copying clips over would erase the audio you'd already laid on the tape. Consequently, you had to build the video layer of your vid first, without sound, and then—only at the end—add the audio track.

Either way, a vid needed to be carefully planned in advance. Vidders created elaborate storyboards. They diagrammed their songs on paper, writing out the lyrics and making charts that indicated what clip went where and how long it lasted. They used stopwatches to measure both the music and the length of the video clips they planned to use, counting seconds and beats, timing small movements and gestures. The VCRs of the era were of no help in this. Their simple mechanical counters (tiny rotating wheels of preprinted digits) were not only idiosyncratic and imprecise but also failed to correspond to anything in the real world, as they measured neither time nor frame rate. "We never did figure out what the little counter counted," Kendra Hunter mused.[34] She and Barbour simply called them UOMs, for units of measurement. This watching, measuring, and timing was much of the real work of making a vid. Only once the vid had been thoroughly planned out on paper would the actual laying down of clips begin.

Early VCR vids would be made in order, from first image to last, with one clip copied onto the destination tape, then the next, and then the next. But that makes it sound easier than it was. While VCRs improved over the 1980s and 1990s, they were still primarily designed for recording whole programs (including commercials), not for editing short sequences into a montage. Vidders continued to struggle to make clean, invisible cuts. A simple cut—by which I mean a straightforward hard cut, because there were no fades, wipes, dissolves, or other effects in early home video equipment—was difficult before the development of the fly-ing erase head, a technical innovation on later VCRs that erased the bit of tape between the erase head and the video recording head. Without a flying erase head, the little strip of tape between the two heads would produce flashes of color at each edit, termed rainbow noise. VCR vidders were so plagued by rainbow noise that they named their newsletter after it; Tashery Shannon's *Rainbow Noise* ran for several issues in 1993–94. (See Image O. https://doi.org/10.3998/mpub.10069132.cmp.186)

Clean edits were also made difficult by the phenomenon of rollback. When you pressed the Stop button after recording, the videotape would roll back a few seconds' worth of frames on the reels, so if you then con-tinued recording from that point, you would overwrite those seconds or frames. For this reason, vidders always tried to hit Pause rather than Stop while vidding, but pausing VHS tape stretched it out; moreover, a paused VCR was designed to turn off after a couple of minutes, so you were working to set up your next clip under tremendous time pres-sure. Vidders developed a work-around for rollback. They measured out clips that were a few seconds or frames longer than required, so their VCR would roll back to where they actually wanted to place the next edit. Notably, the amount of rollback wasn't standard from VCR to VCR, so each vidder had to determine and master the idiosyncrasies of her own machine. This meant vidders couldn't easily work on new or bor-rowed VCRs. Vidders consequently bonded with the machines they vid-ded on, rather like race car drivers and their cars. This metaphorical relationship between vidder and machine gives subtext to many fan vids about cars, planes, spaceships, and so on. Examples include AROUND THE BEND (Video 21 https://doi.org/10.3998/mpub.10069132.cmp.21), WALKING ON THE GROUND (2005) by Seah & Margie (Video 30 https:// doi.org/10.3998/mpub.10069132.cmp.30), GOD IS A DJ by Dualbunny (2006, *Battlestar Galactica*) (Video 44 https://doi.org/10.3998/ mpub.10069132.cmp.44), and STARSHIPS (2012) by bironic (Video 31 https://doi.org/10.3998/mpub.10069132.cmp.31).

Once rollback had been conquered and the clips finally laid down in order from start to finish, then, and only then, would music be imported onto the tape. In the early days of vidding, the audio track was the last element to be added, and only once it had been would the vidders see if they'd timed everything correctly, if their cuts had landed in the right places, if the vid moved with the proper musicality. Having begun this section with the reminder that video is not film, I now offer the reminder that video is not digital. There's no editing timeline in VHS vidding, no audio waveform to match clips to. Rather, a vidder had to be the mistress of her stopwatch. She had to measure everything precisely and hope that her machines cooperated—and even then, she had to hold her breath as she laid down the audio and hope that everything had gone right.

Pressure!

Vidders have made many metavids over the years—that is, vids about fandom and fan culture in general,[35] and about vidding in particular. (See "Spotlight on: Vids about Vidding" in the online appendix.) One of the most famous of these is PRESSURE (1990) (Video 32 https://doi.org/10.3998/mpub.10069132.cmp.32), by Sterling Eidolan and the Odd Woman Out, a subgroup of the vidding collective known as the California Crew.[36] (See "Spotlight on: The California Crew" in the online appendix.) PRESSURE is a rare live-action vid—meaning that the vidders themselves shot the footage used in the video—about making a VCR vid. While the vid purports to document the Herculean efforts of making a fan vid over a single weekend (which vidders sometimes did do, especially before conventions), PRESSURE was in fact a short film shot over months in 1990 and is a masterpiece both of editing and continuity. Many vidders associated with the larger California Crew studied film-making or were in some way attached to the film industry of Southern California. Vidder Lorry C., the primary architect of PRESSURE, minored in film at the University of Southern California, and PRESSURE's live-action footage shows the influence of her training.[37] Shots are interestingly framed, sequences are edited together naturally and effectively, and careful attention is paid to continuity in haircuts, props, and clothing, which contributes to the illusion that the action is happening over a single weekend.

"We wore the same clothes for months," Brenda Wagner (aka the Odd Woman Out, or sometimes the Odd Woman In) recalls.[38] She also remembers the risks they took to get the shots of her driving from her house to the house of her fellow vidders:

> I remember at the time we actually stopped on the side of a busy Orange County freeway, dropped off Kathy [C.] and the camera and the tripod, and then drove to the next exit, drove back to get on the previous entrance to drive by her, and then we were on, like, a walkie-talkie to tell her we were getting close, "Okay, here we come! Do you have the video?" "Yeah! It's recording!" "Okay! Here we come!"—

and then pull up, have her jump in, and—California freeways are not safe places![39]

PRESSURE tells the story of a frenzied weekend of vid making. It starts with the vidders preparing for the weekend at their own homes. Brenda selects videocassettes from an enormous VHS library; Kathy and Lorry put out snacks (crucial!) and set up the equipment. We follow Brenda in her car as she drives to spend the weekend with her fellow vidders. Once she gets there, the real work of making the vid begins. Brenda and Lorry listen to the vid's audio over and over, waving their hands like conductors; they also time the beats with a stopwatch and measure out the song's segments, mapping it with a calculator. Meanwhile, Kathy is framed as being engrossed in an enormous pile of fanfiction zines, though of course, this is just a cover story for why she's not visible. In fact, she's behind the camera.

The next morning, the vidders start looking for clips, rewinding and measuring various scenes. Their thumbs—up or down, or seesawing to show *mezze-mezze*—tell us their evaluations of the clip; they perform their own aesthetic judgments for us. We are shown the vidders spending all of Saturday doing this, from early morning until late at night. The mounting tension of Billy Joel's song is exacerbated by frequent cuts to a digital clock that tells us the both the day and the time. It shows time marching steadily: Friday at 7:29 p.m. becomes Friday at 7:30 p.m., Saturday 1:59 a.m. becomes Saturday at 2:00 a.m. Time is also measured by the subtle but creeping accumulation of soda cans in the frame, which leads to one of the vid's most delightful climaxes: a slow pullback revealing that the exhausted vidders have fallen asleep in front of the television, their work metaphorized and memorialized by a towering sculpture of empty cans. ("All those soda cans actually came from different weekends of making videos," Lorry noted wryly. "Many *many* hours."[40])

Sunday morning, they wake up and start again. Only at the end of this third day do they actually begin to edit footage into a vid. The vidders line up all the cued VHS tapes containing the clips they've decided to use, in order, and Kathy takes the hot seat to do the actual editing. They have to work fast: as noted above, a paused videocassette recorder will turn off in a few minutes, so the clips must be timed out and laid down quickly. Pressure!

At the end of the vid, we see the vidders confront the nerve-wracking moment where they must import the audio track; they are working before video dub, so their audio is copied over last. This is the moment of truth

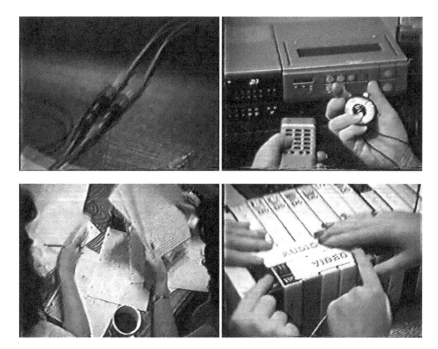

Fig. 16. PRESSURE: Making a VCR vid with two VCRs.

in vid making: seeing how well your meticulously timed clips line up with the actual audio track. Errors had an unfortunate tendency to cascade; a vid whose timing was off would likely get more and more out of sync. PRESSURE ends with nail-biting shots of snaking audio cable, and we see the vidders performing their worry—covering their faces, gnawing their lips—before finally collapsing in what I choose to believe is relief.

If "man versus technology" is a clichéd theme, then the story of woman versus technology is less well plumbed. PRESSURE makes it clear that tales of "vidding uphill, in the snow, both ways" are not hyperbole. These women filmmakers are actually making art with jerry-rigged equipment. PRESSURE itself was made by the same process being documented within the vid; it was shot on video, then edited together with stopwatches and VCRs. PRESSURE tells more than a technological story; it also tells a story of female teamwork and creativity, of collaboration and pleasure, of feasting the body and the eyes. "It used to be about having fun, getting together and making videos," Lorry recalls. "PRESSURE was the culmination of it all."[41] The VCR vids made in the 1980s and 1990s are incredible technological achievements, but they are also important artifacts of female community, with technologically minded women coming together to make themselves, and their perspectives, visible on screen.

The Three Great Houses of VCR Vidding

PRESSURE doesn't say this outright, but one of the vid's implied "pressures" was likely the deadline of an impending convention. In the case of Sterling Eidolan and the Odd Woman Out, that convention would have been MediaWest, aka MediaWest*Con. In the days before the widespread adoption of broadband Internet, there were only two ways to see vids: you could go to a convention where vids were shown, or you could get a copy of a VHS cassette to watch at home, presuming the vidders chose to make their works available in this way. Many did not, fearing piracy or wanting to keep control of a vid's image quality.

In terms of fan conventions, there were many kinds that showed vids: large, multifandom conventions like MediaWest; smaller multifannish conventions like EclecticCon; slash-specific conventions like Escapade, ConneXions, or FriscoN; fandom-specific conventions like Shore Leave (*Star Trek*), ZebraCon (*Starsky and Hutch*), or LeapCon (*Quantum Leap*); later, there were vidding-specific conventions such as Vividcon and VidUKon, which I discuss in more detail in chapter 4. These conventions had various kinds of video programming. A convention might have a video room with a television showing favorite TV episodes, blooper reels, and fan music videos, or it might have a formal vid show as part of the programming, with vids projected onto a screen. Some cons were known as venues for premiering and showcasing new work, while others curated vids related to a particular fandom or theme. Some cons just set up a television in the con suite—a convention's information center and food stop—and showed whatever people brought.

MediaWest*Con, founded in 1978 and held annually in Lansing, Michigan, became known as a locus of VCR vidding. But according to Rachael Sabotini of the Media Cannibals, it was just one of "the three great houses" of VCR vidding. In her 2005 talk, "The Genealogy of Vidding," Sabotini terms these houses the MediaWest Tradition, the Descendants of Mary Van Deusen, and the San Francisco School, and describes the characteristics and aesthetics of each.[42] While this is just one vidder's perspective—albeit that of a well-placed and influential vidder of the time—the distinctions she makes between the different schools and the kinds of vids they created are useful in shaping a picture of the VCR vidding scene and are supported by other vidders' observations. The subtitle of Sabotini's talk, "How Who You Know Affects What You Do," shows both its strengths and limitations. On the positive side, it shows the extent to which analog vidding was communicated from person to person. On the negative side, it forces us to acknowledge that we know considerably less about vidders who were unnetworked or whose networks did not overlap with public staging grounds like fan conventions or newsletters.

Great House 1: MediaWest

MediaWest*Con was founded as part of the general splitting off of what is now known as media fandom[43]—that is, fan activities centered around genre television and film, including the making of transformative works like fanfiction, art, and vids—from SFF fandom, which had its origins in *Amazing Stories* and the pulps, and which sees itself as rooted in the written word and original, professional publishing. SFF fandom originated much of the infrastructure of media fandom—including conventions, zines, and APAs (amateur press associations)—as well as much fannish jargon still in use, including terms like *BNF* (big-name fan), *con, fanboy, filk, gafiate* (get away from it all), and *mundane* (as a noun, meaning someone not in fandom and uninterested in fannish things). But whereas science fiction fandom tended to see fan work as training for professional work, media fans often made works never intended for the market. This had something to do with gender (science fiction fans tended to be male, media fans female),[44] but it also had something to do with the achievability of the professional goal. It was far more likely for a male science fiction fan to end up a science fiction magazine writer than it was for a female media fan to end up being a Hollywood screenwriter or director. The scale of the industry was totally different.

MediaWest, founded in 1978, aimed to welcome not only the Star Trek fans who had been marginalized by "serious" science fiction readers, but also fans of Star Wars, the Doctor Who franchise, *Battlestar Galactica, Blake's 7, The Hitchhiker's Guide to the Galaxy,* James Bond, buddy cop shows, and more. In the wake of *Star Wars* (1977), production of sci-fi TV and film went through the roof, and the next ten years brought not only more entries in the Star Wars franchise but also *Raiders of the Lost Ark* (1981), *Blade Runner* (1982), *E.T. the Extra Terrestrial* (1982), *The Adventures of Buckaroo Banzai* (1984), and even the long-desired return of Star Trek to the big screen. All of these blockbuster franchises became fandoms, as did 1980s TV shows like *Starsky and Hutch, Remington Steele* (1982–87), *Blackadder* (1983–89), *Scarecrow and Mrs. King* (1983–87), *The Equalizer* (1985–89), *Beauty and the Beast* (1987–90), the Grenada *Sherlock Holmes* starring Jeremy Brett (1984–94), *Wiseguy* (1987–90), and *Quantum Leap* (1989–93). As fandoms, they inspired fanfiction, fan art, cosplay, skits and plays, crafts, and vids.

In the 1980s and 1990s, MediaWest was the single most important place to buy and sell fanfiction zines (the con hosted a zine reading room), to buy fan art at dealers' tables and the con's auction, and to show and see vids. The con became famous for its song video contest, which gave a variety of awards in categories like "Song Interpretation" (how well the action interprets the title or lyrics of the song), "Constructed Reality" (how convincingly a vid uses existing clips to create entirely new stories), and "Humor." Vids were shown in the fan video room and were segregated into the genres of gen (nonsexual or heterosexual stories), mature, and slash, with the latter two categories only being shown late in the evening. This practice offended slash fans, queer fans, and their supporters, who experienced the segregation of vids that staged queer readings as a form of homophobia, and which led in part to the creation of the slash convention, Escapade, and its famed vid show, in 1991 (chapter 4).

MediaWest's vid shows were not curated by the convention programmers; rather, the moderators just played the tapes that vidders handed them. While some groups curated and sequenced their own collections—for instance, the California Crew's tapes were designed to be complete shows, with opening and closing credit sequences and vids carefully sequenced for fannish and thematic variety—others would just hand over tapes featuring many similar vids in the same fandom.

Because the vids shown at MediaWest were designed to be seen on the convention screen by a wide variety of fans—not only fans of many different films and shows but also fans with wildly varying experiences of vids in particular—successful MediaWest vids were built for broad appeal. They were designed first and foremost for narrative accessibility, with meanings intelligible to even a casual spectator. Humor was prized, as the MediaWest award category demonstrates. Multifandom vids, which use a broad variety of visual sources, also tended to connect with audiences, who would rejoice in the pleasure of seeing a favorite character or show appear in the vid, or simply enjoy surfing the media landscape. Meeting a television character unexpectedly can feel like running into old friend, an experience I had recently watching the California Crew's group vid to **WE NEED A LITTLE CHRISTMAS** (1990): Oh look, it's Mork!

Oh my god, it's Tom Hanks in drag in *Bosom Buddies*! Holy cow, Kenny Rogers! And Kermit the Frog! (They are all celebrating Christmas, of course—hanging ornaments, putting tinsel on trees, and so on.) Similarly, rather than perform an in-depth analysis of canon that might only resonate with highly knowledgeable fans, many MediaWest vidders told new stories; that is, they constructed realities from their libraries of existing footage. A good example of this is the still-admired California Crew's vid CENTERFIELD (1992) (Video 33 https://doi.org/10.3998/ mpub.10069132.cmp.33), which takes all the baseball episodes from various television shows and, through the magic of continuity editing, creates coherent teams of TV characters making coherent plays. For instance, Ralph Hinkley, the eponymous *Greatest American Hero*, pitches to Andy Travis of *WKRP in Cincinnati*, only to have the ball caught by *Remington Steele*'s Laura Holt, who is playing shortstop; Laura throws to first, and Andy is out. Characters from other shows can be seen pacing beside the bullpen, warming up, or cheering from the stands, with the vidders taking advantage of the relative sameness of the mise-en-scène when it comes to baseball episodes of television: sunny day, bleachers, grass, similar uniforms.

The California Crew are in many ways the paradigmatic MediaWest vidders. With their near industry-level professionalism, vidders associated with CaliCrew made clean, comprehensible vids that worked even for the most casual spectator. CaliCrew are to the MediaWest song video contest what Meryl Streep is to the Oscars: nearly always nominated, and frequent winners to this day, both under their group name and under their various subcollective identities. Other vidders and vidding collectives who made names for themselves at MediaWest include the Bunnies from Hell, Chris & Christina, P. R. Zed, the Central Consortium, the Vid Weasels, and Apocalypse West. Some later vidders would criticize vids made in the MediaWest aesthetic as being overly literal—that is, as having achieved clarity at the expense of the poetic, metaphorical, or analytical: "If something said 'blue eyes,' by god, there better be blue eyes on the screen,"[45] Rachael Sabotini notes. But the image–music conjunctions in MediaWest were designed to be clear and obvious to a broad audience of fan-spectators.

Great House 2: The Descendants of Mary Van Deusen

Henry Jenkins's chapter on vidding in *Textual Poachers* (1992), "'Layers of Meaning': Fan Music Video and the Poetics of Poaching," is an excellent overview of the VCR vidding culture of the era. Also of the era is the fact that the vidders he discusses are identified only by their initials. As Jenkins explains, "Several of them expressed concerns about possible legal prosecution for their appropriation of media images and copyrighted music." Jenkins discusses the work of individual vidders like K.F. (Kandy Fong) and L.B. (Linda Brandt), as well as the work of vid collectives like the Bunnies from Hell and the California Crew, but the central vidder of Jenkins's chapter is M.V.D., aka Mary Van Deusen.

Inspired by Pam Perry, Van Deusen began making her own vids as early as 1985, but even when Jenkins wrote about her in 1992, she was nowhere near the height of her influence. Like many female fans of the era, and vidders in particular, M.V.D. was technologically minded. As I've already noted, many female *Star Trek* and media fans had advanced degrees in science and engineering.[46] Early vidders also tended to have scientific expertise, interests, or careers; for instance, Sterling Eidolan and the Odd Woman Out were a film student, an analytical chemist, and an engineer. Van Deusen had an undergraduate degree in physics, graduate degrees in mathematics and computer science, and a career working for the research division of IBM specializing in computer language design.

Once bitten by the vidding bug, Van Deusen immediately invested in an advanced-model editing VCR, and later managed to get her bosses at IBM interested in her hobby. IBM asked her to use her vidding skills in service of the company and supplied her with broadcast-quality editing equipment so she could produce corporate videos for use in house. They also paid for her to have additional videographic training. As Van Deusen later recalled, "It was the most amazing few years you can possibly imagine."[47]

But Van Deusen didn't just learn; she also taught others, often offering to collaborate with new vidders on their first vids. Judy Chien remembers that M.V.D. was "very generous with her time with people who were interested in vids and she would . . . tell them about how to make vids, and sometimes have like little tutorials in her room at cons. And she invited me up to her house for one weekend, to see how she made a vid, and actually I'm credited on that vid. Although you know she totally made it, and I said, 'Maybe that scene?' [laughter]."[48] Caren Parnes agrees that Van Deusen encouraged vidders by collaborating with them, noting that when M.V.D. thought her collaborator was making the majority of the creative choices, she put that person's name on the vid, even if she herself was doing most or all of the technical work. "She did not put her name on it," Parnes remembers, "even though she was helping them actually produce the piece. . . . She wanted to give them the credit because she felt creatively [the vids] were their product, not hers."[49] Van Deusen also taught Patricia Fraser Lamb (aka P.F.L., a literature professor and one of the first aca-fans), Deejay Driscoll, Victoria Clark, and others. (See "Spotlight on: Mary Van Deusen and Her Descendants" in the online appendix.)

The vidders that Mary Van Deusen taught would go on to make vids by themselves, and also teach future generations of vidders. But while M.V.D. was technologically minded, the lessons she taught her descendants were not primarily technological; they were philosophical and conceptual. M.V.D. is notable for calling her vids literary music videos, which she characterizes as having "a point to make or a story to tell." Literary music videos do this "by either interpreting the lyrics in the context of the video, or by using the music intensity to create a coherent video story. And just as a short story can have flashbacks and points of view and timeline, so can a literary music video."[50] In a 1990 correspondence with Jenkins, M.V.D. elaborated on what she saw as the distinctively literary qualities of her vids: "Our videos wouldn't be classed under fine arts; they would be classed under literature. The structure that underlies my music videos is the identical structure that underlies a short story. You are analyzing a character through a music video in the same way that you analyze character through a story. It has a purpose. It has a conclusion. There is a change in a character you are drawing your reader through. You want to produce identification and emotional response."[51] It was this focus on character and story—on narrative, strong emotion, and poetic values like repetition with a difference—("Probably my favorite technique is to continuously change the meaning of some key word," M.V.D. noted)—that made her popular within fandom. Rachael Sabotini emphasizes that "character and story" were "the strongest overarching value[s]" in the aesthetic of M.V.D. and her descendants—"well, that and cutting to the beat," Sabotini adds. "I can't stress that enough. Cutting to the beat."

In an essay defining literary music videos, Van Deusen explained them almost entirely in terms of narrative lines rather visual qualities; in fact, she later published what she called her "music video plans" online.[52] These plans set episodes and shots against particular song lyrics (Box 1).

Box 1. Excerpt from Mary Van Deusen's song plan for a *House* vid set to Bob Dylan's "Hard Rain's Gonna Fall"

Oh, what did you see, my blue-eyed son?	
Oh, what did you see, my darling young one?	
I saw a newborn baby with wild wolves all around it	FOREVER—taking smothered baby away
I saw a highway of diamonds with nobody on it,	AUTOPSY—riding on his motorcycle
I saw a black branch with blood that kept drippin',	DADDYSBOY—pain and operation
I saw a room full of men with their hammers a-bleedin',	AUTOPSY—man with bloody pants
I saw a white ladder all covered with water,	HUMPTYDUMPTY—man falls off roof
I saw ten thousand talkers whose tongues were all broken,	CONTROL—mute can speak
I saw guns and sharp swords in the hands of young children,	MOBRULE—policeman from nose
And it's a hard, and it's a hard, it's a hard, it's a hard,	AUTOPSY—dying cancer girl hugs him
And it's a hard rain's a-gonna fall.	

The words in all caps are from *House* episodes, e.g., "Control" (season 1, episode 14, 2005) or "Daddy's Boy" (season 2, episode 5, 2005). From http://www.iment.com/maida/tv/songvids/plans/hardrain.htm

---

She also challenged and encouraged her readers to imagine their own song vids:

> Consider Frank Sinatra's "I Did It My Way" and, as you look at the words, free associate with *Star Trek*'s Captain Kirk.
>
> > And now the end is near
> > And so I face the final curtain.
> > My friends, I'll say it clear,
> > I'll state my case
> > Of which I'm certain.
> > I've lived a life that's full
> > I've traveled each and every highway.

And more, much more than this,
I did it my way.

There, you've just watched a literary song video.[53]

It's a reasonable objection to say that you haven't watched anything at all—or, to put it another way, that the aesthetic M.V.D. is articulating here isn't just literary but also anticinematic. After all, what is a movie without images? There's some truth to this objection, and it would be the primary dividing line between the descendants of M.V.D. and the San Francisco/West Coast school, who were more visual, but it's worth noting that vidders, as obsessive media fans, carry footage collectively in their minds; that's part of what media fandom is about. M.V.D.'s explanation is not aimed at just any reader but specifically at one whose mind is already full of *Star Trek*, a reader for whom these lyrics serve as prompts to filter images dancing in her head. These are living room vids designed to be watched multiple times by viewers who are very familiar with the source. Still, it is fair to say that M.V.D.'s description of a vid as "a random collage, with each piece of lyric appearing with video that helps the viewer/listener pay attention to those lyrics" privileges narrative content and musical intensity ("And so I face the final curtain") over visual elements like framing, color, or motion. While all vidding is dependent on song choice, M.V.D.'s vids tend to be driven by the lyrics to the song she's chosen, which is likely to be a ballad, whether it be a sentimental ballad, a comic ballad, or even a hard rock power ballad.

I don't think M.V.D. really means that the visuals are a random collage; rather, I think she means a personal collage, a crafted, individual curation of shared footage. Literary music videos are highly contextual, even as every vid is only one among many possibilities; a vid therefore is a personal take on a public canon. "You might find that you wouldn't have chosen the same scenes I did," M.V.D. writes. "One of the nice things about music videos is that each song maker interprets lyrics in the context of their own life—which makes for fascinating variations when people do the same song for the same fandom." For M.V.D., a vid is something like the external manifestation of a fan's internal psychological reaction to a show and its characters; it is expressive, allowing the vidder to put her own internal feelings about a character or show on the screen for others to see and share and bond over.

Perhaps this is why M.V.D.'s vids got such reactions from other fans; she was one of the first to make visible how others might have been feeling. Fandom has always been connected to strong emotion for Van Deusen; in a biographical statement, she describes becoming active in Star Trek fandom in 1984 after the death of her mother. "Grieving for her was too hard," Van Deusen writes. "Grieving for Kirk or Spock when they appeared to die . . . let some of the steam out of the teapot." Janice Radway's respondents in *Reading the Romance* (1984) use almost the same language of built-up pressure to explain why they like escapist literature:

> ANN: Those pressures build up.
> DOT: Yeah, it's pressures.
> ANN: You should be able to go to one of those good old—like the MGM musicals and just . . .
> DOT: True.
> ANN: Or one of those romantic stories and cry a little bit and relieve the pressure and—a legitimate excuse to cry and relieve some of the pressure build-up and not be laughed at.
> DOT: That's true.
> ANN: And you don't find that anymore. I've had to go to books for it.[54]

M.V.D. talks about letting steam out of the teapot; Ann and Dot want to "cry a little bit and relieve the pressure." But it's interesting that their first point of reference is not romance novels but good old MGM musicals. It's musical melodrama they're missing ("I've had to go to books for it"). These reactions seem akin to the queer experience of the musical, which is typically first experienced by gay and other kids through the Broadway cast album. A cast album, unlike the theatre experience, is neither live nor communal; in fact, like television watching, it is typically experienced by its audience at home, alone. David Halperin has described a gay man's collection of cast albums as a sign of "the isolating experience of unsharable sentimentality"[55] common to gay men's childhoods. We might think similarly of the female fan's collection of videotapes. Attending live musical theatre or opera as an adult is therefore its own kind of coming out. It makes a private experience public and marks the isolated spectator as part of a larger audience. Similarly, participation in media fandom turns television watching into a collective experience, and vidders like M.V.D., by projecting their free associations onto a screen, make previously isolating and "unsharable" feelings visible. They're making the mass media into musical theatre.

M.V.D. writes: "I don't understand the intensity of the reaction that comes from adding music to a psychological theme, but I do know the intensity is there." She describes "letters and calls from people who talk about the compulsion they have to watch these videos. People will break tapes or wear them out just playing them over and over again. They laugh to them, they cry to them. They seem to use them to work through emotional traumas." In this way vids belong in the category of melodrama, sentimental and romance novels, soap operas, musicals, torch songs, the blues, and other "ethnic" musical forms, which Sophie Mayer describes as "the places that women—as well as queer people, teenagers, black people, gypsies, Jews, and working class people—go to drown their sorrows."[56] *Melodrama*, of course, is literally music (*melos*) + drama.

Great House 3: The San Francisco School

Like the names of most artistic movements, the monicker "San Francisco School" was imposed on the group afterward and was not used by its members. Vidders self-identified and branded themselves through their vidding collectives, but finding large patterns and creating "schools" is an outsider's job. The vidding collective JKL—which stands for members Jill, Kay, Kathy, and Lynn—may have been seen by others as central to a "San Francisco" aesthetic, but as Lynn observes, "We definitely never talked about ourselves this way. Which doesn't mean other people didn't say it, I'm just saying we didn't! For one thing, only one of that list [of San Francisco School vidders] lived in SF proper, so if anything we felt we were 'Bay Area.' As for the genealogy side of this: Tash [Tashery Shannon] and Gayle [Gayle F.] had old tapes of M.V.D.'s and Kandy's and the other early vidders, so I'd say this was more an M.V.D. offshoot than anything else."[57] M.V.D. did in fact either influence many Bay Area vidders, both directly (M.V.D. taught Patricia Frazer Lamb, who taught Tashery Shannon the technical basics of making a VCR vid) or indirectly (M.V.D.'s vids were the first that many vidders saw). But at the same time, claims of a new aesthetic seem justified because the Bay Area group showed considerably more interest in the visual side of vidding than did the "literary" vidders. Many had studied film and filmmaking directly,[58] and several were artists or graphic designers. They were more affected by MTV[59] and commercial music videos, which, drawing from the avant-garde, tended to be more about striking images, sensation, and color than storytelling or narrative sense. By marrying M.V.D. to MTV, vidders like Tashery, Gayle, Jill, Kay, Kathy, Lynn, and Morgan Dawn brought a renewed focus on cinematic values like framing, color, and movement. (See "Spotlight on: The San Francisco School" in the online appendix.)

"Tashery and I were movie buffs," Gayle remembers, "and had studied directing, cinematography, etc." Tashery confirms this:

> While I'm more musically oriented than Gayle, we'd both studied film. I took filmmaking in college, lumbered around with a huge 16 mm camera and film in metal cans. Editing? Ha, a machine with reels and a cutting board, and glue for the splices! That was in the '70s. When I began vidding, VCR editing seemed amazingly clean and futuristic to me! While Gayle didn't make films, she'd also studied film and of course was an experienced visual artist—paint, pen and ink. We came to vidding with a background in editing. We didn't have to learn why you usually don't want to make jump cuts, or foul up the continuity of actors' sight-lines from one edit to the next, or about how motion carries through, or else opposes the direction of, the actors' or camera's motion from the previous shot. A lot of editing technique was already there for both of us, and came out naturally, we took it for granted when critiquing and discussing our edits. In fact, maybe the fact that we did critique and discuss our edits so intensely is also part of the background we came to it with.
>
> Jill also is an editor with practical training. If there's such a thing as a "Bay Area style," these are probably what set it apart? Because as it happens, Kay, Lynn, Kathy, all have a strong sense of rhythm that each brings to vidding, along with differing degrees of editing background but a strong eye for it. All of them have sensitivity to these things, and did before we ever got together.[60]

As with the California Crew, this visual sensitivity is evident in the work. Where M.V.D. tended to vid lyrical ballads that told a story, vidders Gayle and Tashery (working together as Shadow Songs) made their most famous vid, **DATA'S DREAM** (1993, digitally remastered with additional sources added in 2004) to Enya's ethereal new age song "Orinoco Flow," with its haunting refrain of "Sail away, sail away, sail away . . ." (See Video 34. https://doi.org/10.3998/mpub.10069132.cmp.34)

The song's few lyrics are mostly a list of exotic place-names ("From Bissau to Palau in the shade of Avalon / From Fiji to Tiree and the isles of Ebony"), which Gayle and Tashery use to orchestrate a sumptuous and sensual journey through forty years of cinematic fantasy. The vidders use footage from everything from *Clash of the Titans* to *Fantasia* to *Peter*

Pan to *E.T. the Extra Terrestrial* to *Flash Gordon*, emphasizing scenes of flight. Characters soar through mystical worlds under their own power, ride magical cars or bicycles, or cling to the necks of magical creatures like unicorns, winged horses, or Dumbo. This literal flight of fancy is framed as the dream of Data, the popular android from *Star Trek: The Next Generation* who aspires to achieve full humanity. The first (silent) clips of the vid are from an episode in which Data is implanted with a chip that allows him to dream. Data conjures up the image of a black raven, which takes flight and escapes through a window—and it is clear that the rest of the vid, with its fantastical images, is Data's/the raven's dream. This fantastic Technicolor voyage represents the android's liberation from soullessness: It is the dream of flight that makes us human. DATA'S DREAM is therefore less a story than a powerfully felt imaginative experience, a poetic visual montage of color and motion. Data's raven becomes a golden bird becomes a soaring eagle becomes a Pegasus with huge, outstretched wings, soaring over montages of golden castles and pink seas shining with moonlight.

Vids like these were hugely influential. Morgan Dawn remembers that Gayle was "the first person to talk to me as a video editor about color, and color flow, and color complementarity. Which is something that nowadays, with digital editing, people can . . . manipulate all the time. But it was a brand-new concept that you would pick clips, not just based on content and movement and context, but also color."[61] Morgan Dawn cites DATA'S DREAM as the vid that made her want to become a vidder herself, and years later, she took on the task of remastering it with cleaner, sharper DVD footage, substituting appropriate clips from newer fantasy fandoms like Harry Potter, Lord of the Rings, and *Farscape* for older footage that had not been digitized.

Vids from the San Francisco School continue to be admired by vidders, who like their combination of aesthetics and storytelling; many have been used as teaching tools in panels at Vividcon (chapter 4). Moreover, many Bay Area VCR vidders made the switch to computers and still make first-rate work.

Vids in a Fandom versus Vidding as a Fandom

For most people, then and now, vids are just one way of expressing their engagement with a particular fandom. Kandy Fong made new *Star Trek* out of slides because she wanted more *Star Trek* at a time when there wasn't any; *Starsky and Hutch* fans innovated with their VCRs to express their feelings about *Starsky and Hutch* and showed the results to other *Starsky and Hutch* fans at *Starsky and Hutch* conventions. The vid room at MediaWest and other multifannish cons showed vids all day and night with the understanding that people would drift in and out, their attention grabbed by a vid in a favorite fandom or by a multimedia vid that celebrated some televisual theme or aspect of television in general.

Today it's the same. Most fans only watch and enjoy vids in their (current) fandom: Harry Potter fans made MARCHIN' ON (see Video 2 https://doi.org/10.3998/mpub.10069132.cmp.2) a sensation on YouTube; Marvel Cinematic Universe fans have racked up millions of hits for vids like Grable424 and djcprod's GLITTER AND GOLD (2016) (Video 35 https://doi.org/10.3998/mpub.10069132.cmp.35) or voordeel's BATTLE ROYALE (2017) (Video 36 https://doi.org/10.3998/mpub.10069132.cmp.36). There are also vids for wildly popular shows that have not been taken up by the culture of media fandom or by the particular subculture of vidding I have been describing, including vids for soap operas like *Days of Our Lives* (1965–), sitcoms like *New Girl* (2011–18), dramas like *This Is Us* (2016–), or the Shonda Rimes show *Scandal* (2012–18).[62] Today, thanks to social media, millions of people might watch a vid or two—or even make a vid or two—without being connected to organized media fandom, with its conventions, cosplay, fan art, and fanfiction, and certainly without being connected to any vidding house or self-conscious vidding tradition.

But in the late 1980s and early 1990s, a group of fans emerged that was not just interested in making vids about their favorite fandoms but also was interested in vidding itself as an art. As I will discuss in the next chapter, this group had significant overlap with fans who were interested in slash as an interpretive strategy above and beyond their interest in any one particular fandom. These fans, as well as vidders associated with all three of the so-called great houses, converged at the Escapade slash convention in Santa Barbara, California, bringing a new level of attention to vids and vid practice.

FOUR | Conventions, Computers, and
Collective Action (1991–2007)

Vidding as a fandom in itself—by which I mean vidding not just as a tool used to express love for some other story world or universe but also as an art form with its own developmental trajectory, canon of influential work, and critical language—was codified in and around two fan conventions: Escapade (1991–) and Vividcon (2002–18). The heyday of these two conventions coincides with fandom's rapid expansion onto the Internet. As early adopters of technology, media fans organized online in the early 1990s on Usenet and in IRC; on topic-specific mailing lists, on web rings, forums, and blogs; and eventually on the nascent social networks. Analog media and distribution methods were supplanted by their digital counterparts as letterzines gave way to e-mail lists and discussion forums, and as fanfiction zines were superseded by online archives. However, vidding remained primarily analog through the 1990s and an off-line phenomenon well into the aughts. For most fans during those years, seeing new vids meant physically going to where vids were shown; secondarily, it might mean getting a nonattending membership at a convention with a vid show and having them mail you a VHS tape or DVD of premiering vids.

But conventions were where the conversations were happening and where an artistic community—contentious, invested—was forming. Fans came together annually in places like Santa Barbara, Los Angeles, and Chicago to watch vids and talk about them. These conventions became a place not only to hammer out a language for articulating different vidding aesthetics (and thus a kind of grassroots film school) but also to provide a context within which fans could collectively grapple with the technological, legal, and political issues of the digital revolution. These included the practical problems having to do with creating and sharing vids in the digital age, like building sufficiently powerful computers; learning new software; obtaining footage; getting online; and negotiating the advantages and disadvantages of different modes of digital distribution, including their technological difficulty, artistic presentation, and legal terms of service. However, they also included a host of issues that have turned out to be crucial in this brave new digital world: questions of copyright and sampling; of spreadability, context, and artistic control; of privacy, publicity, and pseudonymity; of credit and profit; and of the vast constellation of problems that form the field of what we now call technical ethics.[1]

These issues are part of our current international conversation about the Internet, but fans in general, and vidders in particular, were talking through them years before most people. The vidding community of 1991–2007 was both tightly connected and well informed, and therefore easily mobilized as activists when digital concerns became higher profile in the second half of the aughts. Vidders helped to found the Organization for Transformative Works, the fan advocacy nonprofit that created the Archive of Our Own to house fanfiction, and that has done much political lobbying and other work on behalf of fans and remixers. Vidders also formed coalitions, joining forces with anime vidders, political remixers, vloggers, machinima makers, and others. And vidders organized testimony and collaborated in various ways with Internet advocacy organizations, such as the Electronic Frontier Foundation, Public Knowledge, MediaCommons, Critical Commons, and the Institute for Multimedia Literacy to fight for the digital rights of ordinary people. Vidders were ultimately instrumental in securing the 2009 DMCA exemption for noncommercial remixing, as well as its renewals and expansions in 2012, 2015, and 2018. But all these accomplishments were built on organizational and community work that vidders and other fans had done two decades earlier, starting at a California fan convention called Escapade.

Fan Vidders and Conventions

Escapade: California's Slash Slumber Party

Escapade is a convention dedicated to slash—that is, to creating and enjoying interpretations of pop culture texts that imagine same-sex romance or sexual intimacy between characters. Historically, slash was used to refer almost exclusively to fan works (fiction, art, vids) that foregrounded or created male/male romances (Kirk/Spock, Starsky/Hutch), at least partly because male characters tended to take center stage[2] in the stories that fans liked, though there were femslash vids featuring pairings like Xena/Gabrielle, Janeway/Seven of Nine, and Buffy/Faith. Much as MediaWest offered a collective home to fans of many individual science fiction and fantasy media universes, Escapade was an outgrowth of the single-fandom conventions of the 1980s dedicated to slash-heavy fandoms like *Starsky and Hutch* and *Blake's 7*. Founded by slash fans Charlotte C. Hill and Megan Kent, Escapade was designed to appeal to what they saw as a younger, hipper audience. These were fans of particular slash pairings, but they were also fans for whom slash itself was the attraction. For such fans, "slash" was not just a noun but also a verb indicating an interpretive strategy and a shared activity. Being a slasher was thus both an identity and a practice. Slash fans did something active: they slashed the television they watched, creating homoerotic readings that they shared in conversation or through art. Because they watched television with their so-called slash goggles on, we shouldn't be surprised that Escapade became a center for vidding and vid culture. Being a slash fan was already correlated with a particular way of seeing, a distinct and active mode of spectatorship.

Slash fans have had an outsize impact on fandom and on the discourse about fandom. Slash is certainly overrepresented in the scholarly literature, probably because as a phenomenon, women coming together to make homoerotic art seems to demand explanation. But I would argue that slash fans have earned their oversized footprint. They have been unusually productive and innovative, mostly because they were forced to be. The kinds of stories slash fans liked were simply not available in the mass media,[3] so they had to write their own. Then, having written the stories, slash fans had to create an infrastructure to share and distribute them, which required negotiating with other fans' desires not to see queer or erotic material. This was easy enough when it was just a matter of separating gen from slash zines in the dealers' room (slash zines were kept under the table), but things got complicated online, when different kinds of fans were attracted to the same groups, mailing lists, and forums. Fandom's solution was to design and build elaborate tagging systems for their work, creating labels to tell readers what's in the tin. These came into use as story headers and found their apogee in the curated folksonomy of the Archive of Our Own. This metadata has subsequently attracted the attention of computer scientists, librarians, web developers, and other information specialists[4] who admire fandom's organizational creativity. For instance, Maciej Ceglowski, the owner of Pinboard, was surprised when his new bookmarking site was suddenly "filled with slash fiction." However, he eventually concluded, "The fans are all right." Better than all right, in fact; Ceglowski realized that fans

> had constructed an edifice of incredibly elaborate tagging conventions, plugins, and scripts to organize their output along a bewildering number of dimensions. If you wanted to read a 3000 word fic where Picard forces Gandalf into sexual bondage, and it seems unconsensual but secretly both want it, and it's R-explicit but not NC-17 explicit, all you had to do was search along the appropriate combination of tags (and if you couldn't find it, someone would probably write it for you). By 2008 a whole suite of theoretical ideas about folksonomy, crowdsourcing, faceted information retrieval, collaborative editing and emergent ontology had been implemented by a bunch of friendly people so that they could read about Kirk drilling Spock.[5]

This is the sort of thing that gives slash fandom its reputation: the combination of cheerful female depravity and an unbelievably obsessive commitment to information technology. But slash fans had to work hard to make and distribute the kind of stories they wanted to see. They also had to carve out and defend spaces for themselves, often against the will of more mainstream fans.

For instance, in "Fandom and Male Privilege: Seven Years Later," Rebecca Lucy Busker talks about her experience with the Batman LiveJournal community site Scans_daily in 2005:

> [Scans_daily] had been founded by women fans to be friendly, but not exclusive, to slashy interpretations and discussions of these comics panels and pages. Many of the fans who initially came to post and discuss comics there approached comics as part of their larger media fandom, and also as a part of their larger *slash* fandom. However . . . the community began attracting more mainstream comics fans, whose background was in the broader realms of geekdom, and for whom slash was either unknown or at least a very strange thing (slash being at least slightly less mainstream at the time). Not surprisingly, most of these fans were men. Also perhaps not surprisingly, many of them missed the community information that said "slash-friendly" on the way in.[6]

According to Busker, it wasn't enough that female fans had created this community and let male fans join if they wanted; the men wanted to control (in this case limit) what was talked about. This kind of community building and defense draws people together—another reason why slash fandom is so coherent and organized. Moreover, many slash fans have made long-term commitments to fandom, building projects over many years (archives, challenges, forums) and sticking around to administer or maintain them. Fans of gen aren't confined to fandom the same way. They have the whole commercial art world to choose from.[7]

For these and other reasons, slash fans in general, and the slash fans who congregated around Escapade in particular, have had an outsize impact on fandom, including vidding and vid culture. (This is not even to mention fan studies: Henry Jenkins, Constance Penley,[8] and Camille Bacon-Smith all went to Escapade.) Their collectivity was key. Fans who didn't come to multifannish conventions did not make the same sort of impact, and it's fair to fear that consolidated slash fandom may have run roughshod over or otherwise obscured the work of smaller, less organized, or more marginalized groups of fans. For example, fans of *Xena: Warrior Princess* made VHS vids and showed them at weekly "Xena nights" at Meow Mix,[9] a famous lesbian bar on New York's Lower East Side. Vids were also shown at commercial *Xena* conventions. But most of those vids never made it out of their specific community; they weren't shared via song tapes or digitized and put on the Internet. But the fans who came together at Escapade were from many fandoms and so created multifandom structures and institutions that became influential.

All vidding—and indeed all filmmaking—is about getting others to see through the filmmaker's eyes. Slash fans had a particular interpretation of the world that they wanted to literally make visible to spectators, with the goal both of pleasing the converted and converting the uninitiated. According to Sandy Herrold of the Media Cannibals, "Sometimes a vid can be a fight—a fannish fight set to music," where fans argue for particular versions of canon by foregrounding their competing interpretations in their vids. In slash and femslash vidding, these interpretations are often about a character's sexuality. As fellow Cannibal Rachael Sabotini elaborates:

> We have been fighting it out visually and in fiction for—you know, since everything was founded. Since fandom was first kicked out of science fiction fandom. We have vids that present a character's bisexuality . . . because everyone's argued this character is always straight. Well, if you take and synthesize the three minutes of clips of the way

he looks at other men, perhaps when you put all three of those three minutes together—set to good music—you come away with the idea that maybe he's not so straight after all.[10]

Successful slash and femslash vidding could make fans see the romantic possibilities of same-sex pairings. More broadly, it was a way of making queer sexuality visible in the world. Sandy Herrold talks passionately about the power of slash vidding:

> The first time I made a *Highlander* vid and showed it to a guy who I had explained about slash to, he was like, "Eh, as if. It's not there. There's no way that you can convince me that they would ever do that." By "they," he admitted later, he meant both of them, both the producers and the characters. Neither of them would do that, whatever *that* is. And then he watched a *Highlander* vid that I had made with the group and said, "Oh my God. Oh my God! I think—Ohhh! You put it in my head! You put it in my head!" And I was like, "Yeah! That's what I'm doing here! I'm putting pictures in your head—they're not even my pictures, but by putting them together in this way I have changed your picture of the whole universe."[11]

The desire to seize the means of production, to subvert the meanings of mainstream television and film for politics and pleasure, obviously has important feminist and queer implications. These were not lost on the fans who congregated at Escapade in the 1990s. The Media Cannibals, a "semi-autonomous Media Fan Collective" based in the progressive Pacific Northwest, chose a rainbow for their credit logo, "because even that point in time [c. 1992], we were about queer awareness."[12] Katherine Scarritt, a longtime fan, con organizer, and vidder who ran the Escapade vid show in the late '90s, is typical of media fans in recognizing the feminist implications of participation in fandom's female art world:

> You know, one thing people with [Camille Bacon-Smith's 1991 book] *Enterprising Women* and all that stuff got right is: this is something particularly about women, and women's feelings and issues and all that. Even though there are some men here and there in the fandom . . . I know one thing Sandy [Herrold] has talked about is how she really didn't want men to come to Escapade because women tended to defer to men, and it just ends up as an inhibiting factor. Because we're automatically trained to do that, and especially, any of

us, again, over thirty: that is in us, whether we like it or not. I don't want to be that way, but I find myself doing it too, sometimes. And so, if they're looking for the key to it [fandom] or whatever, that's where it's going to be found. But it's women saying things the way they want it to be, not the way they are told it ought to be, even by the women's movement.[13]

Vidding was a chance for women to put their desires on screen without any thought for the male spectator. As Media Cannibal Gwyneth put it, "But what I *really* want to do is direct!"[14]

To direct this way, to use vidding to subvert mass media texts, vidders had to learn the language of television and film. Vid fans got increasingly serious about their art form at Escapade; they began to look at the media as makers, not just spectators. Sandy Herrold says:

In trying to learn how to tell my story visually, I have learned the visual vocabulary that they use, that I'd never realized was there. So the ability of television and movies to manipulate me visually is still there, I still react to it, but now I notice what they're doing: *oh, this is how they're making this one more important than this one, this is how they're setting things up for us to react to later*. I've learned to notice their language in trying to subvert their language.[15]

Vidders like the Media Cannibals were not just interested in learning the language of film; they also wanted to develop a language for vidding. Because both Charlotte C. Hill and Megan Kent were vidders—Kent in particular was known for vids such as the *Starsky and Hutch* comedy **DON'T USE YOUR PENIS FOR A BRAIN** (1988) (see Video 99 https://doi.org/10.3998/mpub.10069132.cmp.99 and "Spotlight on: Phallic Critique" in the online appendix)—they wanted Escapade to have a formal vid show. Kandy Fong was tapped to run it. The MediaWest vid show had segregated slash from gen and showed slash vids only at night, which was the vidding equivalent of keeping slash zines under the table. But Escapade's vid show was oriented around slash and femslash. Escapade also eliminated MediaWest's vidding contests. There were no competitions at Escapade, other than the contested interpretations of the vids themselves. The first year, Fong curated a show from existing vids, but the next year, the show featured premieres, and for the next decade, Escapade was *the* place to debut new work. Escapade became a meeting ground for the many different cultures of VCR vidding, be they old-school *Star Trek* and *Starsky and Hutch* vidders, the aggrieved slash vidders of MediaWest, literary vidders who'd been inspired by Mary Van Deusen, or members of the San Francisco School. It also created a community for new vidders from all around the United States: the Media Cannibals from the Pacific Northwest, the Chicago Loop, the East Coast Consortium, JAM, Cybel Harper, T'Rhys (notable for being the first known computer vidder), and many others. Vidders asked each other, "What are you bringing to Escapade?"

But Escapade's most important contribution to vidding was arguably the creation of Vid Review, a space given to reviewing and discussing premiering vids modeled on the group critiques of art school. Sandy Herrold claims that this influenced vidding in a way that changed vidding forever, because, as she notes wryly, "That's when we start to talk about vids in large, painful groups." "Before Escapade," Rachael Sabotini remembers, "you'd go to a con, you'd show your vids, but there was nothing afterwards." Vid Review started off as a postpremiere show vid discussion, except everyone quickly realized that they didn't have the language for a good discussion. As one fan said, "It was like trying to discuss poetry without a common understanding of grammar or spelling."[16] They couldn't even explain why some vids had gone over better than others. Sabotini remembers, "Some people would show their vid and it would not get a good reaction, and other vids would get a *great* reaction. So there was a lot of pissiness about 'Why did your vid get such a great reaction and ours didn't, because ours is better quality and more technically competent than yours is.'" Later vidders might have said that the "quality" vid wasn't received as well in the con setting because it was a living room vid that required great canon familiarity and multiple watches to get all the layers. However, as Herrold points out, "We didn't have the vocabulary to say that. So what were we saying? 'Your vid is too . . . small? Your vid wasn't . . . caught?'" This lack of precise terminology led to arguments—what Herrold describes as "five years of learning to talk about vids in ways that didn't end friendships." Sabotini remembers early Vid Reviews as "incredibly fraught, because one of the things we were interested in was honesty about our reactions to things. And we had people from lots of different disciplines, that were attending . . . but things that were important to one group were not necessarily important to another group, and we fought. Like. Crazy."[17]

Vid Review was where these arguments happened, and where a common language was eventually hammered out. A public critique that went vid by vid, Vid Review soon expanded from one to two hours. It was

---

Box 2. Panels and roundtables on vidding at Escapade

Panel Title	Program Description
"Song Video Roundtable" (1994), led by Kandy Fong and Deejay Driscoll	"Bring works in progress or finished works you're having difficulty with for a quick jump-start."
"Songvid Editing" (1994), led by Megan Kent and Sandy Herrold	"Authors get edited and usually have to do at least one rewrite of a story. Artists have erasers. What stops songvid makers from doing drafts and re-edits of their work? Let's talk about editing style (what cuts to use for best emphasis) and technique (how to physically do the inserts)."
"Music Video Critique and Workshop" (1996), led by the Media Cannibals	"Roundtable critique of videos, how to tell/recognize story, POV, rhythm. Also, tricks of the trade."
"Con Vids vs. Living Room Vids" (1998), led by Jill and Stacy	"What are the elements that make a music vid accessible to a large crowd, or more appropriate to an intimate setting?

---

hosted each year by a different vidder so as to air different perspectives and philosophies. Escapade also began to distribute Vid Comment forms during the premiere show so fans could write down their responses or give anonymous feedback. Panels and roundtables on vidding became part of Escapade's regular programming, as the examples in Box 2 demonstrate.

The Media Cannibals in particular pushed for these discursive innovations. As a large group themselves, they were used to talking about vids, and they wanted more and better discussion with others. Compared to fanfiction culture, which had, and indeed still has, a strong tradition of writing detailed feedback to authors, vidding was a relative black hole. In the VCR era, vids were either shown at cons, where people might clap with more or less enthusiasm, then move on to the next panel or the bar, or distributed via VHS tapes, which you had no idea if the audience even watched. It was hard to get quality responses. Escapade tried to change that.

By the end of the 1990s, conversation had gotten to a point that discussions could be summarized and codified on handouts or online. Mary Schmidt's "Making Fannish Music Videos" (See Image N. https://doi.org/10.3998/mpub.10069132.cmp.185) came out in its third edition in August 1997, but that was just one of any number of booklets and essays: "Structuring Your Vid: Knowing Your Audience" by Sandy Herrold (1995), "Vidding 101" by Stacy Doyle and Carol Stoneburner (2000), "Creating Mood" by Laura Shapiro (2004), "How to Do Music Videos" by Stacy Doyle, "The Language of Vidding" by here's luck (2004), "The Craft of Vidding" by Killa and Carol S. (2003), "Editing Techniques and Vidding" by P. R. Zed and Carol S. (2004), and "The Life Cycle of Vid and Vidder" by Luminosity (2002). Other meta was posted to the web, like Sandy Herrold's "Don't Touch the 3rd Rail! or Vidding *Suggestions for Serious Vids*" (1999, Box 3).

Vidders now distinguished not just between con vids and living room vids but also between action vids, character studies, comedy vids, constructed reality vids, catharsis vids, ensemble vids, lyric vids, mimic vids, mood vids, narrative vids, persuasive (or argument) vids, recruiter (or promoter) vids, relationship vids, and universe vids.[18] Vidders had learned how cinematic techniques could be used to create a mood; they compiled lists of shots (long shot, medium shot, close-up, two-shot, rack focus, handheld) and kinds of motion (internal vs. external motion; pans, whip pans, pushes and pulls, dolly and zoom shots); they also tried to learn how those shots could be deployed to create certain effects (Box 4). Similarly, vidders formulated and disseminated definitions of musical terms: lyrics, mood, tempo, instrumentation, musical movement, verse, chorus, bridge, climax. Whole panels at conventions were devoted to song choice: what makes a good vid song?

These analytical conversations—what fans call meta—also took place on the VIDDER mailing list started by Chicago Loop member tzikeh in July 1997. One hundred vidders and vid fans from all over joined the list, which invited "vidders, vidders-in-training, or vidder-groupies" to "focus on all aspects of vidding, from song choice to technical questions to finding the right clips and anything in between."[19] The list was explicitly for "both slash and gen vidders," and it hosted a few male vidders as well. VIDDER list members debated aesthetics, reported on vid shows they'd seen, swapped tapes with each other, and reviewed them. Together, they confronted the future that was looming: computers and the Internet. "Care to join me on the bleeding edge?" list member Randy Reed asked in a February 1998 post.

Box 3. Don't Touch the 3rd Rail! *or* **"Vidding** *Suggestions* **for Serious Vids"**

On Vidder (*a mailing list for people who make and enjoy songvids*), we've discussed whether vids have a grammar or not; a set of rules that people agree on to make communication easier. Whoo-boy! Not an easy question, and one that evokes a rather emotional response.

After some conversation, we agreed that there aren't a lot of **rules** that make sense in vidding. But we were able to compile a list of techniques that in **serious** vids, tend to be *misused* more often than not.

So, vidding techniques to use sparingly, or think seriously before using:

Blooper reel clips in serious vids
But, it can work if it isn't an obviously 'blooperish' clip or it is the **perfect** clip or the serious song has a more humorous section.
Jump cuts
Can work if the show itself has a fairly jerky style or if you use three or four in a row . . .
Use of credits
But here's some counter-examples. I don't know if any of you have had a chance to see the UK vid . . . I *think* it's called "So Long." It's a vid that says goodbye to the characters of Kes from Voyager and Ivanova from B5 that uses the credits to establish the actors/characters— both clips say "Character as Actor's Name" and then we get a shot of the character disappearing and then we get credit shots of Jeri Ryan as Seven of Nine and Tracy Scoggins as Captain Lochley . . . introducing the replacement characters. I thought this was an excellent use of credits.The Chicago Loop showed a Buffy video recently that used the Buffy credits in an interesting way—I guess it can be done!
Songs with illegible lyrics
But there are some beautiful vids to instrumentals with no lyrics at all . . . Maybe this one should just say, "if your lyrics can't/don't carry the narrative, you'll have to work harder to make sure the clips do."
Black, or fade to black, within the body of the vid
But black can add drama, and fading to black can end a verse or a chorus, or even change POV if it's done very carefully.
Single cuts longer than 8 seconds
Except that once in a while a really long clip is just what you need; what the whole vid has been leading up to.
Clips (with internal cuts) longer than 15–20 seconds.
Again, there are rare times when letting the scene run (especially if the camera work in the scene is really well shot) can work.

Box 3—*continued*

Unusual versions of well-known songs

Many fans will hate a new version of a song, at least until they've heard it a few times; on the other hand, the new version may give you the gender change you need, or speed up the song enough to be useful, or have much clearer lyrics than the better-known version of the song.

POV changes

They can be very powerful—especially when you're making some sort of compare and contrast of two characters' situation, or their feelings for each other. But, done sloppily or casually, they utterly confuse your audience. (*Personally*, I don't think you can change POV in all songs—you need either a song that has a mood change, or a bridge or in the middle, *or* a song with some strong "I" statements right after the place you want to change, to reorient your audience. *Even more personally*, I think you only get to change POV once—or maybe twice, if the music *really* supported you, perhaps in a duet—and after that, there's almost no chance that the audience will understand what you're trying to say. There are vidders with twice my experience and skill that disagree with me on this one, though.)

These are harder to defend—can someone find examples of these that work?

- Many cuts in a row all the same length (i.e., vary your clip length)
- Many cuts in a row all of head shots (i.e., vary your clip type)
- Doing a whole vid to one show, but including just one clip of the actor from a different show
- Freeze frames
- Speeding up the clip

And this last one isn't really negotiable:

NEVER, EVER, leave any patches of lost signal or gunk between the clips. To quote Methos, "Cut clean."

My latest video is available as a real video file at [URL] its 1.8 mb file so it takes about 20 minutes at 28.8 (less at 56k) assuming the server doesn't stall. The video itself is not exactly crystal clear, it plays at a little over 10fps so its not particularly smooth and the song sounds like its being filtered through a tin can. I can solve some of these problems by making the file bigger but my isp will only let my web

---

Box 4. Excerpt from "Creating Mood," a handout by Laura Shapiro distributed at Escapade 2004

Cutting Tempo/Clip Length

- Fast (Short Clips)—Hectic, pressure, stress, excitement, unsettling, chaotic, acceleration, rising tension, anger, sexiness
- Slow (Long Clips)—Mellow, relaxed, sadness, romance, sensuality, release, peaceful, thoughtful, denouement

Organizing Shots in a Sequence

- Alternating Close-ups of Two Characters—Intimacy, shared connection, shared emotion
- Moving In—Cutting from a long shot to a medium shot to a close-up creates a sense of focusing in, heightened interest and tension, specificity
- Moving Out—Cutting from a close-up to a medium shot to a long shot creates a sense of distance, space, generality
- Jump Cuts—Disorientation, erratic

---

page be 2mb so at 1.8 i'm too close to the limit to do more. If someone knew an isp that actually had a real video server that they would license access to cheap, we wouldn't even have to download it.

But whatever you may think of quality issues, i think its good enough that you can see what I'm doing with the vid and give me some feed back. To those of you who despise Jewel a priori I do humbly apologize but I just thought it expressed the angst of Mulder bereft of Scully.

A more '90s post can hardly be imagined. But online distribution *was* the bleeding edge in the age of dial-up Internet: it took twenty minutes to download a postage-stamp-size video file.[20] Reed was also an early proselytizer of digital vidding, putting up an information page on the now-defunct Angelfire web hosting site. DIGITAL VIDEO IS THE FUTURE, it announced. "In the next five years (maybe less) vidding will be done on computers and completely (or at least mostly) digital. Do you want to be left behind?"[21] Vidders most certainly did not want to be left behind, but in this era, vidding on a computer meant building your own system from scratch. Nothing out of the box had enough memory or storage space, or the right capture card. So the VIDDER list became a place to trade information about systems, software, and peripherals, leading to endless threads sharing technical advice.

> Q: I've got a Miro Motion DC20 . . . , but I don't think my drive is fast enough. Where can I find the specs—do I have to open the machine?
>
> A: Depends. <PC advice> If you have a mass-market machine (like a Packard Hell or Compaq), you should be able to find out the specs from documentation that came with your machine. If you had a machine custom-built, then it should say somewhere on the invoice or you could call the place you got it from. Alternately, if you know enough, you can check out what it says when the machine starts and in the bios. </PC advice>
>
> Q: Also, can I purchase an external EIDE?
>
> A: Not as far as I know. However, it's not hard to add a hard drive to your system (if your motherboard supports EIDE). The other option is to add a good SCSI card and get an external SCSI drive, but that's the more expensive route. You can get a good 8.4 gig EIDE drive (Quantum Fireball) for about $350 at the moment, and prices are only going down.[22]

What these vidders are trying to do is to build a computer system that will allow them to capture, digitize, edit, and export their VHS footage. This is what computer vidding was from the mid-1990s to the mid-aughts—the era of dial-up—and it's a distinction that might not be immediately obvious from Randy Reed's information page. Digital video was the future (meaning digital footage via DVD; Internet video distribution is further off), but the present avant-garde thing was computer vidding: the use of hardware and software to import and edit VHS clips on a computer. In 1998, most movies and TV were not yet on DVD, let alone the relatively niche genre television shows—*Blake's 7*, *The Professionals*, *Quantum Leap*—beloved by fandom. *Star Trek* was released on DVD from 1999 to 2000, *Starsky and Hutch* from 2004 to 2006. Other shows that fans wanted to vid—*The X-Files*, *Buffy the Vampire Slayer*, *The Sentinel*—were still running and so being taped onto VHS while airing. Cutting-edge vidders used capture devices like the Miro DC20 to digitize their VHS clips, assembled them with software like Media Studio or Premiere, and then exported them back onto VHS for distribution through the usual channels: convention showings or song tapes. Vidding with DVD footage didn't come until later, and sharing video online required the widespread adoption of broadband Internet. Broadband users didn't break 50 percent until 2007.[23]

While vidding with computers was gathering steam in the late 1990s, the first computer vid that we know of had been made a few years earlier: T'Rhys's **IN THE AIR TONIGHT** (1994). (See Video 37. https://doi. org/10.3998/mpub.10069132.cmp.37) This vid was also notable for being a *Star Trek/Blake's 7* crossover. T'Rhys not only edited using a computer but also used a computer to create effects, so the *Blake's 7* ship, the *Liberator*, appeared on the *Enterprise's* viewscreen, creating the first blended clips and thus creating an encounter (in this case a hostile one) between characters right in front of our eyes.

The vid was shown at Virgule, a slash con in Seattle. Fans were blown away:

> The best thing happened at the Virgule music vids. I was watching "In the Air Tonight" done for TOS [*Star Trek: The Original Series*], and realizing that the almost slo-mo like jerkiness in the images wasn't a special effect of a video machine, but that it was DIGITIZED, that the images had COME THRU A COMPUTER . . . not video tape to video tape. I was impressed. And then, on the old Enterprise's view screen, right there in space and time, WAS THE LIBERATOR. AND IT MOVED. My heart nearly stopped.

It's perhaps not surprising that this first computer vid was slash; it was in many ways a fanfiction story come to life. Sandy Herrold posted to the VIDDER list: "All of the technical wizardry was placed in support of a fabulously over-the-top slash narrative: Avon shoots and kills Spock, and Kirk, driven mad through his pain, presses the self-destruct on the Enterprise and kills them all"[24] (Figure 17 https://doi.org/10.3998/ mpub.10069132.cmp.153). Where else were you going to get a story like this? In terms of quality melodrama, it was the best of *Star Trek II: The Wrath of Khan* and *Star Trek III: The Search for Spock* combined. It was the sort of story that fans of genre TV had to make for themselves.

In 1994, IN THE AIR TONIGHT was considered a rarity and T'Rhys was hailed as a visionary, but by the end of the century, computer vidding was well on its way to disrupting the VHS vidding world. Hardware and software that had only been available to industry professionals was suddenly within the reach of (obsessed, dedicated, technically minded) consumers, so a new generation of vidders—including the many vidders associated with groups such as the WOAD Society, the Chicago Loop,

Fig. 17. The art of montage: Blake fires, Spock is hit.

and the East Coast Consortium—went immediately to editing VHS foot-age via computer, eschewing methods that VCR vidders had collectively hacked into being over two decades. Computer editing software, having been designed for the purpose, easily did all the things that vidders had tortured VCRs into doing. Clean cuts were no longer difficult, and you could sequence and resequence clips with ease. You no longer had only a few chances at an edit; unlike tape, digitized footage didn't stretch, blur, or break. Moreover, computer editing brought new powers that VCR vid-ders had only dreamed of. You could change a clip's speed or color, crop the frame, use transitions beyond hard cuts, though the really transfor-mative effects would have to wait until digital footage became standard. There was only so much manipulation that digitized VHS footage would take.

Between the coalescing of aesthetic expertise and the new accessi-bility of digital editing software, vids suddenly took an enormous aes-thetic leap. The late 1990s and early 2000s produced a run of vids at and around Escapade that have become canonical to the community, includ-ing many already featured in this book or its online appendix, including DANTE'S PRAYER (Video 5 https://doi.org/10.3998/mpub.10069132.cmp.5), WOULDN'T IT BE NICE? (Video 9 https://doi.org/10.3998/mpub.10069132.cmp.9), and DATA'S DREAM (Video 34 https://doi.org/10.3998/mpub.10069132.cmp.34). It's important to note that some of these are VCR vids by VCR vidders working at the top of their game, while others are by computer vidders who are expressing old community aesthetics with new tools. But there was an explosion of energy and cre-ativity all around.

VCR vidders like Katherine Scarritt and Gwyneth Rhys experimented with analog tools like mixing boards to get fades and other effects on

VHS. Scarritt took advantage of the coming digital revolution to purchase used analog equipment on what was then a brand-new site: eBay. Scarritt remembers, "Equipment that had previously only been available to professionals, price-wise, was now available on eBay for something reasonable. . . . I was able to buy a mixer, for seven hundred dollars at the time, and it would mix two video streams together."[25] Scarritt used this mixer to make SCARBOROUGH FAIR (1997) (Video 38 https://doi.org/10.3998/mpub.10069132.cmp.38), a *Highlander* vid about Duncan McLeod set to Simon and Garfunkle's "Scarborough Fair/Canticle." Scarritt had a specific artistic goal for the vid, noting that the song "is actually two songs that are layered together. And the voices are layered. It's beautifully done. One of them's about war, and one of them's about love. And so . . . I want[ed] to be able to layer the video together about Duncan, war and love, same kind of thing." The mixing board allowed her to do that. However, it had to be done live: you had to have two complete video streams to mix together. "So basically, I had to make one whole vid to the one song, and another whole vid for the other," Scarritt remembers. "And then I played them, and I mixed as I went." The result is a visually textured reading of Duncan's life. As a man who's lived many hundreds of years, Duncan moves through the song's repetitive cycles of impossible love, always in the past tense or, improbably, the future ("she *once was* a true love . . . then *she'll be* a true love . . ."), fighting a never-ending war (soldiers fighting "for a cause they have long ago forgotten"). The vid, which fades dreamily between Duncan's romantic and military narratives, conveys the sense of swirling history that fans loved about the show.

A year later, Gwyneth borrowed Scarritt's mixing board to make her first VCR vid, THERE'S NO WAY OUT OF HERE (1998) (Video 39 https://doi.org/10.3998/mpub.10069132.cmp.39), a vid paralleling the experiences of three heroic female protagonists: Buffy (*Buffy the Vampire Slayer*), Scully (*The X-Files*), and Nikita (*La Femme Nikita*). Gwyneth introduces each of the characters at the start, then devotes a section of Gilmour's song to each protagonist—three repetitions, three heroines—using the numbing, almost trippy repetition of the music to enforce the sense of claustrophobia. She also uses the board to enforce the parallels between the characters using fades and dissolve: "I knew that all three women enter a room in the series pilots and I wanted to start drawing their parallel lines immediately." Like many of the best Media Cannibals vids, THERE'S NO WAY OUT OF HERE gains power through close analytical observation of the visual text. Rhys herself describes this as "a refinement of something the Cannibals were doing in a way that other vidders weren't then," which was "finding similar shots, similar ideas in different shows, and really bringing them out."[26] Rhys pulls out shots that visually echo each other: "I was inspired by all the parallel imagery to make this: the shots of their own gravestones, coming into mysterious rooms, etc." Stitched together, those shots create a tapestry of female heroism that gives emotional weight to their struggles and angst. The vid was received rapturously at Escapade and has been shown many times since. Like many influential VCR vids, it's been remastered with digital footage and thus dragged forward into the digital age.

But it was computer vidding that was really changing the landscape. Many of the computer vidders who attended Escapade had met in and around *Highlander* fandom, which may explain why they released their vids under the collective banner of the WOAD Society, with "woad" referring to the plant that yields the blue dye that is used to color the warriors' faces in the show. However, the vidders associated with the WOAD Society—which included such influencers as Luminosity, Killa, T. Jonesy, and Carol S., and which later came to include sisabet, Destina, and Melina—vidded in most of the popular fandoms of the day. Their first collection, *It Came from Outer Space* (2002), featured three VHS tapes of vids from *The X-Files, Stargate SG-1, Star Wars, Blake's 7*, and of course *Star Trek* (both Original Series and Next Generation). But computer vidders like these began showing work at Escapade that was truly visual art as well as fannish storytelling and media criticism.

Consider a vid like Carol S.'s LANGUAGE (2002, *Stargate SG-1*). (See Video 40. https://doi.org/10.3998/mpub.10069132.cmp.40) The vid was described as "bizarrely experimental" in a review on the VIDDER list: "The source is heavily digitally modified—I have no idea of the technical term for what's been done, but the images end up violently stylized." The images were posturized—that is, processed so that the image consists of distinct, flat areas of color. In addition, Carol S. had a scroll of calligraphic text rise up over the images as the song progressed, creating an aesthetic composition more like a painting than a frame of Hollywood film. (See Image P. https://doi.org/10.3998/mpub.10069132.cmp.187)

In a vid about language and the impossibility of communication, this vid shows as well as tells: language is a tangible thing that stands between us and the images. The text, composed for the vid by another fan named Quinn, begins, *"If I reach for you, will you reach back? Will you meet me half-way, or will you turn your back, walking away? I want to find the words to tell you what you mean to me, what I want to mean to you, but I can't."* But fans trained to read vids whose every shot carried recognizable context were flummoxed: "The clips are strongly decontextualized. . . . The text that scrolled up the screen was an interesting idea, but I think ultimately I'd have to call it a failure. It was impossible to read—were we supposed to be able to read it? What's the effect of a vid called LANGUAGE filled with language that cannot be deciphered?"[27] But of course that frustration with words is the point of the vid. Similarly, decontextualization is a theme of the song. Suzanne Vega sings, "I'd like to meet you / in a timeless placeless place / Somewhere out of context." But this was a new aesthetic for vidding, which had historically valued visual clarity (partly because quality footage was so hard to obtain) and meanings built out of fandom's shared narrative contexts. LANGUAGE is not Mary Van Deusen's idea of a literary music video; ironically, Carol S.'s LANGUAGE is painterly and poetic. In Vid Review, one fan noted that the vid reminded her of Peter Greenaway's *The Pillow Book* (1996), not traditionally thought of as a fannish text.

Vidding was at this point an art form on full boil. Like the California Crew before them, many of the Escapade vidders had a strong sense of auteurship. This expressed itself not only in the range of work that was getting made—which showed that vidders were only now beginning to see what was possible—but also in credit sequences, song tape boxes, liner notes, T-shirts, and other identarian branding (Figure 18 https://doi.org/10.3998/mpub.10069132.cmp.154). As tzikeh puts it in her trademark signature line: "VENI, VIDI, VIDDED: I showed up, I watched TV, I made something of it." The bold assertion "I made something of it" was an identity-creating move for the vidder as artist.[28]

Ironically, this explosion of creative energy brought vidders into conflict with Escapade, the convention that had enabled all this development, because not all of the new work was slash, and Escapade was first and foremost a slash con. Where some fans had once said "slash is my fandom," others were now saying "vidding is my fandom." Some were beginning to ask whether Escapade's vid show was fully meeting the needs of its slash-oriented audience.

Discussion broke out on the VIDDER list, with Shoshanna Green opening her (pro-vidding) post with "Escapade is not only a great slash con, it's also a great vid con" before going on to discuss the incipient conflict that was brewing:

There's been some talk, both last year and this, that the Escapade vid show is "too het." I could not disagree more. As I said above, one of

Fig. 18. Branded VHS song tape collections, c. 2000.

the attractions of the con for me is the great vid show, and I don't discriminate among slash, gen, and het vids, the way I do in fiction. . . .
I'm just there to see *vids*. Both vidders and non-vidder viewers, in various groupings, have been talking since the con (and probably since
before it) about whether a significant number of people (whatever
that means) dislike seeing het vids in the show and, if so, whether
anything should "be done" about it. My sense is (certainly my hope
is) that nobody on the con com is going to ban or even officially dis-
courage "het vids" (how could they even be defined?)[29]

Ironically, among the proposals that had been raised was the creation
of a "het ghetto" at Escapade to mirror the segregation of slash vids at
MediaWest. In the ensuing discussion, vidders articulated how important
Escapade had become to vidding as an art form. LynnC defended the
importance of Escapade as a forum for artists regardless of audience:
"Vid shows aren't strictly put together as entertainment for the con go-
ers. They are a forum for vidders to show artwork done in the last year—

yes, most of the vidders are slashfen, or they wouldn't be there, but art is inspired by many things on the screen, including het relationships. If the audience has expectations that aren't met by the show, the audience needs educating. NOT the vidders."[30] Lynn further elaborated that she went to Escapade "to see the state of the art and what my friends are thinking about." Carol S. also noted the importance of Escapade as a venue for all her vids, slash and otherwise: "The Escapade main show is the only place I *ever* get a wide range of feedback (if you corner your friends and make them watch your vids they are unlikely to be truly negative no matter how they feel). It's not just that Escapade is the only con I consistently attend that has a vid show at all, it's also that the main show at Escapade is the only place that hands out feedback forms."[31]

But not everyone at Escapade wanted an art scene. One VIDDER list member articulated the case for the other side, claiming that vidders had turned Escapade into a captive audience for their artistic explorations. That fan claimed that vidders were taking advantage, ventriloquizing their thoughts as, "I want 100 people in a room to watch this, even though I know better than anyone that it's a vid that most people won't get, and it's not appropriate for this venue"—because it requires multiple rewatches, for instance. The fan asked vidders to consider whether their vids were appropriate for Escapade: "Maybe because it's got major het cooties, or because it's a combo of a very obscure show and very context driven clips and an obscure and inaccessible song."[32] To be fair, the 2001 show had featured thirty-four vids and was three hours long.

Although this explosion of new and experimental vids exhausted some, it energized others—and inspired them to vid. Vividcon founder astolat saw DANTE'S PRAYER at Escapade in 2001 and made her own first vid a month later. Others were similarly inspired, and the 2002 Escapade vid show was, if anything, even stronger. Reviews from that year were gleeful: "Oh my GOD, what fantastic vid shows."[33] "It was amazing, and my mind is still awhirl."[34] "Best. Fucking. Show. Ever."[35] Fan and fan critic Eliade attributed the strength of the 2002 show to the impact of computers: "Digital computer vidding is beginning to solidify into the revolution it is—the source for most vids was shockingly clean and the cumulative effect of seeing that much vidding technique just blows me away."[36]

At this point, it was clear that there was enough interest in vidding, not to mention enough vids, to sustain an entire convention. Shortly after the end of Escapade 2002, astolat sent out the first announcement of a new con, Vividcon, to the VIDDER list:

> Vividcon is currently in the planning stages. Our goal is to provide a
> con dedicated to fannish vidding, for people who like to make vids
> and people who like to watch them.
>
> Think continuous vid shows throughout the weekend, fandom-
> specific vid shows, panels to discuss vids, panels on novice and ad-
> vanced vidding techniques (both for digital and VCR-to-VCR vid-
> ding), a try-it-yourself room with vidding systems you can play around
> with, collaborative vidding sessions, and <insert your idea here>.[37]

Because the new convention was dedicated to vidding itself, all kinds of
vids of would be welcome. There would be no more arguments about
whether this or that kind of vid was appropriate, as had happened at
MediaWest and Escapade. As astolat quickly clarified in response to
questions, Vividcon was to be "an equal opportunity con," by which she
meant, "We do not discriminate against vids for genre, sexual orienta-
tion, fandom, age, technique, or anything else. That means, among
other things, that gen, het, slash, and adult (for violence, e.g.) vids are
all welcome and will all be given equal opportunity to be shown and
discussed."[38]

The first Vividcon was put together quickly and took place in Chicago
on August 16–18, 2002. That first con had only two days of programming, though it expanded the next year to three days. However, even at
that first Vividcon, a fan could watch an astonishing fifteen hours of vids
on a big screen in a theatre setting; as astolat later recollected, "Vividcon
was designed to give vid fans a massive fix to hold them for the entire
year and to give vidders a great showcase for their vids."[39]

Vividcon: Vivid Constructed Realities

For no reason than anyone can remember, the mascot of Vividcon is a
llama with its foot resting on a videocassette.[40] (See Image Q. https://
doi.org/10.3998/mpub.10069132.cmp.188) In fact, the 2002 Vividcon
premiere show would be the only one ever released on VHS, which was
on its way out; future Vividcon shows were distributed on DVD. But by
then, both the llama and its VHS cassette had become iconic. The first
Vividcon llama was tinted with rainbow colors to evoke the rainbow
noise that had so plagued vidders of the past. In subsequent years, the
llama would be dressed to evoke a theme that reflected that year in fandom, with a subtitle to match. For instance, 2003's Pirate!Llama ("Vids
Ahoy!") evoked the popular *Pirates of the Caribbean* fandom of that year;

2007 gave us a bespectacled Harry Potter llama ("Accio Vids!"), 2009 a Star Trek llama ("To Boldly Vid!"), and 2014 a Captain America llama ("Even When I Had Nothing, I Had Vids").

The VHS cassette under the llama's foot was only one way in which the history of vidding was evoked by the branding around the con. As I noted in the introduction, the word "vid" was itself embedded in the name "Vividcon," and the limited liability company that astolat and her crew formed to administer the convention was called Vivid Constructed Realities, a name that both alluded to the genre of the "constructed reality" vid and was also easily shortened to VCR.

Vividcon adopted many aspects of vidding practices and culture that had developed at Escapade. This included a Vid Review of the entire premiere show as well as an in-depth review of only one or two vids. Vids were shown in a theatre-like setting, in the dark, without talking or singing. At the 2001 Escapade, the audience had been instructed to sit down and be quiet because the year before, there had been "problems with people talking and walking around during the vids."[41] The next year, vidders addressed the problem creatively by means of an "intro vid." They created a genre of fan video analogous to the short videos that run before the feature at the movies to establish etiquette. Made by tzikeh of the Chicago Loop, Escapade's **INTRO VID 2002** (Video 41 https:// doi.org/10.3998/mpub.10069132.cmp.41) instructed the audience to follow four simple rules: don't talk, don't walk around, don't sing along with the vids, and turn off all cellphones and beepers (yes, beepers were still a thing). These rules applied to all of Vividcon's vid shows. They were enforced not only with a series of increasingly meta intro vids but also through the convention's infrastructure. The first year, the doors to the screening room were locked, with audience members not allowed to enter once the show started or to reenter if they left. When this proved to be too draconian, the con committee rigged the main door with a button that triggered a discreet light manned by a volunteer, who would quickly let people in and out between vids. To make the room as dark as possible, blackout curtains were drawn and the hotel's emergency light bulbs were removed. A surround-sound system was brought into the hotel. All of this is to say that Vividcon took vidding seriously as filmic art and worked hard to create what they considered to be the best atmosphere possible for spectatorship. Vidders responded accordingly and upped their game.

That said, Vividcon also made space for people who wanted (or needed, for disability or other reasons) to view vids differently. An overflow room was set up for premieres that permitted talking and moving around, like at the convention vid shows of old. Vividcon also established a vid library that stocked a large collection of VHS tapes (and later DVDs), which members of the convention could check out and watch in their rooms, just in case fifteen, twenty, or twenty-five hours of theatre-style shows were not enough. The Springhill Suites in Chicago had been chosen partly because each suite had a living area with TV and VHS (later DVD) players, so congoers could have a living room vid experience with friends as well as more formal theatre-style vid viewing. Vividcon also innovated new vid-watching experiences, like Vid Karaoke, a late-night event in which fans, mostly properly lubricated, did karaoke to vids subtitled for the purpose. This allowed singing back into the vid-watching experience, albeit in this highly structured way.

But the chief alternative vid-watching experience was Club Vivid, a dance party during which vids were projected on large screens on both sides of the dance floor. Club Vivid was initially intended simply as fun convention programming—a night of dancing and drinking and canapés set to a curated playlist of danceable vids. But after the first year, the Club Vivid VJs, having learned which vids were good to dance to and which ones weren't, put out a call for new vids to be made specifically for Club Vivid. Club Vivid thus became a space for debuting new work.

As a result, vidders began making what I will call dance vids, which are arguably a different genre than the con vids or living room vids of old. Dance vids are designed to be danced to, so they're particularly rhythmic and fast paced in their cutting as well as in their song choice. Dance vids are also designed to be viewed while the spectator is moving and may also be partly obscured by the crowd of other dancers, so they tend to be particularly colorful and spectacular. In *Keeping Together in Time: Dance and Drill in Human History* (2008), William H. McNeill describes the pleasure humans take in synchronized motion and argues for the importance of dance in creating emotional bonds. In a Club Vivid vid, those pleasures can triple: not only do the clips dance through raccord and rhythmic editing, but characters are made to dance on screen, their choreography emphasized, and the fans dance with them and with each other.

Club Vivid always began with what was essentially a found vid, which fans call THE JOXER DANCE (2003). (See Video 13. https://doi.org/10.3998/mpub.10069132.cmp.13) THE JOXER DANCE is an untouched sequence from *Xena: Warrior Princess* in which the ancient Greek characters perform a hilariously over-the-top rendition of the 1972 pop-rock hit "Dancing in the Moonlight," complete with conga line, as part of an anachronistic "Battle of the Bands." The original idea, according to Melina, who cut the clip, was simply to play the footage as the first "vid" of Club Vivid so as to draw people into the room. The first year, people just watched it and laughed. But afterward, spurred on by vidder F1renze, some fans began trying to learn the sequence's complicated choreography and to perform it along with the characters on screen. Each year, more fans joined in the choreography, but everyone could participate in the conga line, which saw fans snaking around the room and dancing, just as Xena, Gabrielle, and the other characters were doing on screen. THE JOXER DANCE became a Club Vivid signature event, a happy start to the night. Club Vivid's closing vid, the colorful anime spectacular STOP THE ROCK (2003) by Nappy (Video 42 https://doi.org/10.3998/mpub.10069132.cmp.42), was ritualized into an event as well. It's no accident that the night's final vid is an anime music video. Because it's the last vid after a multihour dance party with an open bar, few people have seen STOP THE ROCK while sober, which makes it great for a final, sweaty blowout. It's not a story or an interpretation; it's a sensation.

Many of the vids already discussed were made for Club Vivid: A FANNISH TAXONOMY OF HOTNESS (HOT HOT HOT) (Video 20 https://doi.org/10.3998/mpub.10069132.cmp.20), SNAKES ON A PLANE (Video 10 https://doi.org/10.3998/mpub.10069132.cmp.10), STARSHIPS (Video 31 https://doi.org/10.3998/mpub.10069132.cmp.31). However, notable dance vids also include fan favorites like astolat's **DROP DEAD GORGEOUS** (2003, *Smallville*) (Video 43 https://doi.org/10.3998/mpub.10069132.cmp.43), Dualbunny's GOD IS A DJ (2006, *Battlestar Galactica*) (Video 44 https://doi.org/10.3998/mpub.10069132.cmp.44) and **RAISE YOUR GLASS** (2013, *Community*) (Video 45 https://doi.org/10.3998/mpub.10069132.cmp.45), jarrow's **PAUL MCCARTNEY** (2007, *Will & Grace*) (Video 46 https://doi.org/10.3998/mpub.10069132.cmp.46) and, perhaps most famously, Luminosity's *300* vid **VOGUE** (2007) (Video 47 https://doi.org/10.3998/mpub.10069132.cmp.47), which was recognized by *New York Magazine* and which has had one of the most fascinating afterlives of all vids. (See "Spotlight on: VOGUE" in the online appendix.) I justify my designation of "fan favorite" by how immediately and how long the vid stayed in Club Vivid's rotation. Many of these vids were repeated year after year because fans would be disappointed not to see them and dance to them. Several were sequenced into a climatic segment near the party's feverish end.

Most Club Vivid vids literally make their stories or analysis dance:

DROP DEAD GORGEOUS sets its analysis of Clark's Kent's character (he lies about everything, but he's drop dead gorgeous) in the context of shots of Club Zero, a fictional nightclub on the show, and scenes of gyrating bodies; in GOD IS A DJ, the song tells us that life is a dance floor, and the vidders tells us that *Battlestar Galactica*'s Starbuck dances when she moves, fights, or pilots a spaceship. A FANNISH TAXONOMY OF HOTNESS constructs a montage that puts characters from a variety of party scenes across television shows onto a single dance floor. "People at the party, hot hot hot!" Buster Poindexter sings, providing the voice of the vidders; the vid takes on new meaning when you realize that it was made for a context in which fans are dancing alongside the characters. Fandom is not just *at* this giant televisual party; this is *our* party. And in vids like RAISE YOUR GLASS and PAUL MCCARTNEY, vidders continue a tradition that goes all the way back to THE BOY CAN'T HELP IT: editing comic choreography to emphasize its continuities with dance. In PAUL MCCARTNEY, jarrow edits footage from *Will & Grace* so that the characters bounce and gyrate, gesticulate, snap, and boogie together.

There is joy in creating and observing these kinds of patterns. As jarrow recollects, "I decided to start by grouping similar clips together (fainting, victorious arm pumps, hugs and kisses, gasping in shock, dances, etc.) and see if I could make sense of it. . . . When I was rewatching the episodes, I grabbed interesting motion-y bits with absolutely no idea that they would be paralleled later (by other characters or themselves). It was such a delightful surprise to end up with something like twenty different clumps of paralleled motion."[42]

If the atmosphere of Club Vivid tends to favor vids with a celebratory aspect, then this celebration is not only of the shows or the characters— though certainly many do celebrate shows and characters. Consider Gwyneth's **BRICK HOUSE** (2010) (Video 48 https://doi.org/10.3998/mpub.10069132.cmp.48), which asks its spectators to admire magnificent fan-favorite actress Gina Torres. However, many Club Vivid vids have a meta aspect. In vids like FANNISH TAXONOMY OF HOTNESS, GOD IS A DJ, RAISE YOUR GLASS, and VOGUE, it's fandom's own creative power that's being celebrated. God is not the DJ here. Fandom is; the vidders are.

In this meta aspect, Club Vivid vids exemplify the vids of Vividcon generally. Many Vividcon vids celebrate vidding or vidding's history. From the first, Vividcon kicked off with a recitation of that history. In 2002, the congoers gathered on the first morning of the convention for a combination vid show/panel called "Retrospective: How on Earth Did We Get Here?" where one version of vidding history was rehearsed. That first year, tzikeh gave a talk and showed older vids, including BOTH SIDES NOW (Video 22 https://doi.org/10.3998/mpub.10069132.cmp.22), THE ROSE (Video 25 https://doi.org/10.3998/mpub.10069132.cmp.25), PRESSURE (Video 32 https://doi.org/10.3998/mpub.10069132. cmp.32), and SCARBOROUGH FAIR (Video 38 https://doi.org/10.3998/ mpub.10069132.cmp.38). That genealogy was itself later made into a vid by Seah & Margie: WALKING ON THE GROUND (2005) (Video 30 https:// doi.org/10.3998/mpub.10069132.cmp.30), which tells the story of vidding's evolving technological and cultural practices. (See "Spotlight on: WALKING ON THE GROUND" in the online appendix.) In subsequent years, Vividcon's history panel/show was called "The Wayback Machine," "Genealogy of Vidding," or simply "Vidding History," and other moderators rehearsed a variety of subhistories, all of which have informed this book. No other programming was ever scheduled against this annual history lesson. These panels, in conjunction with Vividcon's vid library, demonstrated the con's commitment to establishing an artistic history of the form.

But Vividcon also wanted to be forward looking. Attendees came not only from the vidding communities of the past but also from the new online communities. Vividcon attracted vidders from groups like Nummy Treat (2002), a mailing list dedicated to Buffyverse vids, and from online communities like the Fourth Wall (2007). The con also attracted a few interested anime vidders as the increased visibility of user-generated video online opened doors between the worlds of AMV and live-action vidding. These vidders shared aesthetics and tips in panels with titles like "Topics in Craft: POV," "Timing Is Everything," "The Language of Music," "Typography in Vids," "Literalism vs. Metaphor" and "Curse You, After Effects!" These panels were often paired with vid shows that illustrated the point; other vid shows were curated by theme (for instance, "You're My Best Friend," "End of the World," "Spies Like Us") or technique ("Unreliable Narrators," "Constructed Reality," "No Source? No Problem").

The moment of Vividcon—a moment defined by this combination of artistic cross-pollination, rapidly accelerating technology, and the regular opportunity to present new work—produced an explosion of high-quality vids, with many vidders consciously trying to top themselves from year to year. Many of the vids I discuss in this book were Vividcon premieres. But Vividcon arguably established its own canon. For example, in the 2011 vid show "Ten Years of Vividcon," the moderators chose a premiering vid representing each of the con's first ten years, and chose

vids like sisabet's *Farscape* vid **BE SO GLAD** (2006) (Video 49 https://doi.
org/10.3998/mpub.10069132.cmp.49), AbsoluteDestiny's *Firefly* and
Serenity vid **RODEOHEAD** (2007) (Video 50 https://doi.org/10.3998/
mpub.10069132.cmp.50), and hollywoodgrrl's *Fringe* vid **BOOM BOOM
POW** (2010) (Video 51 https://doi.org/10.3998/mpub.10069132.
cmp.51). This list not only tells you about the vids that were valued
within the community but also illustrates the diversification of the vidding community in the aughts. Sisabet came out of online *Buffy* vidding;
AbsoluteDestiny is an anime turned live-action vidder; hollywoodgrrl is a
multiple winner at the Fourth Wall.

Luminosity and Melina's 2010 intro vid **PREVIOUSLY . . .** (Video 52
https://doi.org/10.3998/mpub.10069132.cmp.52) creates another
canon. It is a parody of the "Previously on . . ." voice-overs that bring
the viewer up to date on the plot of a serialized television show. The
vidders got a male narrator with a broadcaster voice to solemnly intone,
"Previously, at the Vividcon Premiere show . . ." to tell you what vids you
missed; at the same time, the list assumes the spectator's familiarity with
the twenty-six vids that are name checked or, even more interestingly,
only alluded to.

> Previously, at the Vividcon Premiere show: Aeryn and John danced
> **THE MASOCHISM TANGO** [1], Connor and Murphy were **REBELS OF THE
> SACRED HEART** [2], Hannibal Lecter was **UNINVITED** [3], Iron Man
> had no **HANDLEBARS** [4], Frodo and Aragorn Climbed a **MOUNTAIN**
> [5], *Stargate Atlantis* Built Its City on Rock and Roll [6], Duncan had
> **TROUBLE WITH POETS** [7], *Farscape* was an **ECSTATIC DRUM TRIP** [8],
> Jaye had a **BRIGHT FUTURE IN SALES** [9], The Doctor explored **THE
> MOONS OF JUPITER** [10], Jason Bourne visited a **STREET CAFÉ** [11],
> Joan Built a **BIG RED BOAT** [12], Skies were Blue for Everyone [13],
> Starbuck was a **JOKER** [14], Charlie Jade Remembered [15], Faith
> was a **SUPERSTAR** [16], Kirk had **RAZZLE DAZZLE** [17], Jeremiah
> went to **WOODSTOCK** [18], Cylons want to **FIX YOU** [19], Girls were
> **SUPERSMART** [20], Sam Tyler was **CRAZY** [21], We Put Giles There
> [22], War was Hell [23], Astronauts Soared [24], Penguins Marched
> [25], and then the Earth Exploded [26]! And that's what you missed
> at Vividcon Premieres.

By the end of this recitation, the allusions are coming fast. "We Put Giles
There" at least echoes the title of Laura Shapiro and Lithium Doll's
vid, **I PUT YOU THERE** (2006)[43] (Video 122 https://doi.org/10.3998/

mpub.10069132.cmp.122), but you have to know that "War was Hell" refers to a comment made about Feochadn's *Band of Brothers* vid, **EBBEN? NE ANDRO LONTANA** (2002). (Video 123 https://doi.org/10.3998/ mpub.10069132.cmp.123). You also have to know in which vids astronauts soared, penguins marched, and the earth exploded. (For the answer to these and other questions, see "Spotlight on: PREVIOUSLY . . ." in the online appendix.) This is not just a canon of vids but a rehearsal of collective experience within a community.

The Collapse of Context

However, even as Vividcon was becoming a hub for vidding, vidding was breaking out of old-school fannish spaces thanks to the digital revolution, Web 2.0, and the Internet. As I noted in the introduction, 2005 marked the thirty-year anniversary of vidding, the third year of Vividcon, and the debut of YouTube. Online video was only made possible by the spread of broadband Internet, which in 2005 was only at 37 percent in the United States, but growing fast. Broadband enabled the development of video streaming sites like Imeem, Blip, Vimeo, Bam Vid Vault, and YouTube, and these sites made user-generated videos like fan vids visible.

The vidders of the early aughts didn't like YouTube. Many of them didn't like the loss of control over one's work that streaming represented, but even those who were willing to trade control for ease of spectatorship preferred Imeem to YouTube. Imeem had social networking features that fans liked, but more importantly, it offered better visual quality and sync. Vidders complained that "YouTube's conversion process throws the video and audio out of sync by a half second,"[44] which might not have mattered to most people but was crazy making to vidders who had timed their videos to the frame. Images were also often pixelated. (Later iterations of YouTube improved both image quality and synchronization.)

However, the real problem with YouTube was that it created a culture of indiscriminate uploading, which YouTubers framed as sharing but which vidders experienced as theft. One vidder bluntly described "the people on YouTube" as thieves: "Many vidders have had their work stolen, myself included, and put up by users who claim it as their own."[45] This did happen, and sometimes still happens, not only with vids but also with fanfiction and fan art; vidding credits or artists' signatures are cut off, or characters' names are changed. But in addition to outright theft, there was also the problem of—well, fannish behavior. Someone who saw your vid and really, really liked it might feel compelled to share it with the wider public, regardless of whether the vidder wanted that kind of exposure. YouTube made this easy to do.

Typical of vidding history, the clash of cultures started with *Star Trek*. Killa and T. Jonesy's *Star Trek* comedy vid, **KNIGHTS OF THE ROUND TABLE** (2005) (Video 53 https://doi.org/10.3998/mpub.10069132.cmp.53), which closed that year's Vividcon premiere show, went viral on YouTube almost as soon as such a thing was possible. The vid was put up by someone not the vidders in July 2006. A masterpiece of timing and lip synching, KNIGHTS OF THE ROUND TABLE was called "the best-edited fanvid ever in the history of YouTube" in 2011, and the claim remains credible today.[46] The *Star Trek* footage is impeccably matched to music from *Monty Python and the Holy Grail*; even the song's opening dialogue ("Look, my liege!" "Camelot!" "Camelot!" "Camelot!" "It's only a model." "Shh!") is matched to the position and affect of the *Star Trek* characters as well as to the movement of their lips. The characters' stylized gestures perfectly match the beats of the song, and while the vid is easily understood and accessible to novice vid watchers, it also provides contextual and canon-based pleasures for hard-core fans. For example, for the climactic phrase "I have to push the pram a lot," we see Spock pushing the futuristic wheelchair of previous *Enterprise* captain Christopher Pike—a meaningful scene for fans.

The self-declared nerds of the Internet went wild for the *Python/Trek* crossover, posting on blogs, lists, and forums urging others to check out this little bit of "geek heaven."[47] The vid even jumped from the Internet to television: I remember seeing a clip from KNIGHTS OF THE ROUND TABLE presented as a humorous outro at the end of a local news broadcast in New York City. Some might see this intense attention as success, but as noted previously, vidders at this time feared exposure. They worried that vidding would be seen as piracy and they'd be seen as copyright violators. Killa and T. Jonesy contacted the user who'd put the vid up on YouTube and requested that it be removed. What happened next can be gleaned by reading between the lines of a MetaFilter thread, "I have to push the pram a lot" (July 18, 2006):

> "This video has been removed by the user.": (
>   —posted by potsmokinghippieoverlord at 1:44 PM on July 19, 2006
> Please tell me there's another source! I tried to show the hilarity to someone else, and now it is gone!
>   —posted by piratebowling at 1:27 PM on July 19, 2006

The Youtube poster says he was asked by the creator to remove the video from YouTube. (*The* Creator . . . ?)
—posted by Snerd at 1:28 PM on July 19, 2006
Is this it listed on this page? Scroll a little over half way down in the page, or search for "Knights of the Round Table" http://seacouver.slashcity.net/vidland/vids.html
—posted by BillsR100 at 1:23 PM on July 19, 2006
Holy Dilithium Crystals! Check out the other stuff on that creator page—FIFTEEN Trek music video remixes and much MUCH more.
—posted by mwhybark at 1:29 PM on July 19, 2006
That site is going to get hit with the Slashdot effect, but you can't stop the YouTube.
—posted by etoile at 1:28 PM on July 19, 2006

Here we can see, almost in real time, the discovery of vidding by the larger Internet. In searching for "another source," these MetaFilter users discover Killa's own small fannish website, "Vids by Killa and Friends," on which she offers her vids for download to other fans in the old-school manner. "Holy Dilithium Crystals! Check out the other stuff on that creator page," one user yells, driving eyeballs to a fan site that had been made with a smaller, more insular audience in mind.

The MetaFilter fans are aware that driving traffic to Killa's site could have huge negative repercussions for her. The "Slashdot effect" is a sudden and huge increase in traffic, of the kind that would typically bring a website down back in the days when bandwidth caps were small and owners paid out of pocket for web hosting. At this moment of Internet history, before social media, most websites were personal and not ad supported, so there was no upside to getting more clicks or views. Increased traffic, particularly if you were hosting large files like videos, meant only more bandwidth and a bigger bill, which most people couldn't afford. Your site would go down, or a savvy webmaster would quickly take it down to avoid running up costs.

While some sites would try to get back up again as soon as possible, Killa instead chose to take her page down for good, not wanting to expose her fan works to the gaze of outsiders, copyright holders, and network TV stations. But as MetaFilter user etoile predicted, that didn't stop the YouTube: copies of KNIGHTS OF THE ROUND TABLE continued to pop up on YouTube, racking up millions of hits. A month later, another of T. Jonesy and Killa's collaborations, CLOSER (2003)

(Video 54 https://doi.org/10.3998/mpub.10069132.cmp.54), became perhaps the most famous example of a fan vid gone viral and taken out of context. (See "Spotlight on: CLOSER" in the online appendix.) A slash vid that told a disturbing story of a Vulcan *pon farr*—a mating ritual—gone wrong, CLOSER garnered intense and baffled admiration from people who didn't really understand what they were seeing. While the vid's editing was admired, many mistook it for parody[48] and left comments like "too funny," "hilarious," "the best spoof . . . that I've seen in a long time," apparently assuming that anything having to do with male/male desire ("lol @ gay star trek") or rape ("Vulcan rape lol")[49] must be meant mockingly, as a kind of slam (in the same vein as "George Lucas raped my childhood," or, as Julie Levin Russo argues, homophobic *Brokeback Mountain* parody trailers[50]). Accordingly, most YouTube comments assumed the vidder was male: "Dude knows his Star Trek," "That's the sickest thing I've seen in a while . . . LOL! Good job man," "Dude, ew."[51] The vid got millions of hits and was even brought to the attention of Shatner and Nimoy—not what the vidders intended, and definitely not the vidder's intended audience.

While CLOSER was perhaps the most famous case of a vid wrenched out of context, it was hardly the only one. The years after YouTube's debut saw many vidders complaining about unauthorized uploads as well as worrying about the repercussions of this unintended exposure. In one thread, "Stolen vids on YouTube," vidder StarCrossedGirl discovered that one of her *Star Trek* vids had been put up by multiple users, some claiming it as their own work. When she contacted them, some apologized and took it down, but one replied, in a public comment: "If anyone is a thief on You Tube, it's you StarCrossedGirl! I have a gut feeling that you never thought about breaking copyright laws concerning Star Trek, Jefferson Airplane & Led Zeppelin owners rights. The You Tube executives have been sent and informed of your nasty letter. If any videos are to be taken down, it will be yours! !!"[52] Talk about adding insult to injury! The vidder wondered, would her vids be taken down? Could she get into real trouble? Other vidders had similar experiences— and similar fears: "Don't post at YouTube," "Don't post in the open," "Bottom line—vidders create and host illegal downloads, plain and simple. Don't be stupid about it."[53] Ironically, however, fan vids soon came to typify YouTube's culture of remix and user-generated content, even as they sent individual vidders scurrying for cover, afraid of piracy, bankruptcy, and humiliation.

The Move to Collective Action

But even in this moment of fear and panic, other perspectives began to emerge. Laura Shapiro, an early and influential voice, wrote an essay for the LiveJournal Vidding community called "You Can't Stop the Signal" (December 4, 2006) in which she argued that vidders ought to seize the moment and step into greater public visibility. Shapiro described a vidding community torn between controlling their work and claiming their place in the emerging narrative of remix video. But, Shapiro argued, the moment of control had already passed:

> However legitimate a vidder's fears may be, the fact is that the vids are already out there. The minute we put our vids online, we expose ourselves to the world. . . . We can't stop people from finding and watching vids, especially since the advent of YouTube and similar sites. We can't stop people from sharing our vids without our consent or even our knowledge. We can't control the distribution of our own work in a viral medium.
>
> We also can't control other people's attitudes. New vidders arrive on the scene every day, without any historical context or legal fears, and plunk their vids onto YouTube without a second thought. They post publicly and promote themselves enthusiastically, and why not? That's what everybody does on the Internet, from the AMV creators to machinima makers to Brokeback Mountain parodists to political remixers. All of these works are potentially infringing, but these creators don't hide, and they are drawing attention. Lots of it. Bloggers and news sites are writing about independent media and the rise of user-generated content, and academics are writing books about fannish creations of all kinds. Almost nobody is talking about us yet, but it's only a matter of time. If we aren't there to represent our points of view, what do you think they will say about vidders?[54]

Shapiro's views were no doubt affected by the fact that the month before, she had been asked by Henry Jenkins to participate in the planning of what would become the 2008 24/7 DIY Video Summit at the University of Southern California. Jenkins, then the rare aca-fan who had both attended Escapade and published about vidding, contacted Laura Shapiro so that she could bring the perspective of live-action vidders to the table. The 24/7 DIY festival, put together by Steve Anderson and Mimi Ito, was intended "to bring together DIY video creators, activists, policymakers, Internet companies, and media industries to celebrate new forms of creative practice, debate competing visions of the future, and craft shared agenda."[55] Shapiro, a vidder from the tech-central Bay Area and a political activist, was intrigued by the conference's goals, which included bringing digital video communities together and creating alliances between them. She joined the 24/7 DIY Video Summit planning committee and began to publicize the festival to vidders.

These and other issues were pressing enough that Vividcon 2007 organized a Town Hall on Vidding and Visibility to discuss these questions within the community—or at least as much of it as could be gotten together in person at one time. Almost all of the convention's 150 or so members crowded into the main panel room to discuss the "question of should vidding be more or less visible, and how do we control it, assuming we can or should control it."[56] Various postconvention reports summarized the discussion, which turned into a debate about personal privacy versus normalizing fan works, particularly women's fan works. Vidders shared stories about engaging the broader world outside of fandom. For example, Luminosity described showing vids at 2003's Slayage, an academic *Buffy the Vampire Slayer* convention, and getting only condescension in the panel that followed, with one male scholar referring to "your little movies" and a woman academic asking where the male vidders were, implying that if men weren't doing it, it was only a hobby, not art. Another example: Jackie K. Jono discussed an interaction she'd had on the academic media site In Media Res, where a male media critic had uploaded a fan vid as a prompt for discussion, which he described as "a generic YouTube redaction of scenes from *Bleak House* under a soundtrack of Andain's 'Beautiful Things,' a song apparently about teenage suicide. It is classic DIY self-made creative content, using television (without regard to IP law) to produce a personal 'trance' or reverie about *watching television with thoughts in your head*."[57] The critic thought that the vid had failed to explicate the source text's Marxist critique, but Jono took offense at the critic's dismissive tone. Replying "I am a vidder," Jono explained in a comment what she thought the vid was doing and why it might matter:

> The vidder has taken this story and pulled out of it a theme I find more interesting. She is exploring what it means to be beautiful in the context of this society. The woman who is the main character of the vid has a beautiful soul but has been disfigured by smallpox. . . . The

social status of women in this world is based primarily on their appearance and the context of their character is completely irrelevant. That theme goes right to the heart of the psychological, social, and philosophical issues of self worth, jealousy, and identity that I have to deal with every day. . . . The fact that the vidder chose to focus on that theme rather than the more directly economic one that is central to the story is, in a way, quite political.[58]

Jono concluded: "Fan fiction and fan vids have a very long history. Historically, they have been made by women for other women about stuff women tend to like and men often scoff at." Jono told the Town Hall that she had felt compelled to defend this random vid, which had been pulled from YouTube and made by a fan she didn't know.

Vidders SDWolfpup and Rowena discovered that their vids, respectively COIN OPERATED BOY (2004) (Video 55 https://doi.org/10.3998/mpub.10069132.cmp.55) and BUFFY, ABRIDGED (2004) (Video 56 https://doi.org/10.3998/mpub.10069132.cmp.56), were being shown in theatres around the United States as part of the sing-along screenings of *Buffy the Vampire Slayer*'s musical episode, "Once More, With Feeling." The sing-along people had gotten permission from Fox, the program's owner, to show the episode in theatres (though Fox revoked those permissions a year later), but nobody asked the vidders for permission to show their work as part of the entertainment, though *Buffy* creator Joss Whedon had posted a "shout-out to our video making peeps" on the Whedonesque blog after attending a showing of the sing-along in Los Angeles.[59]

Laura Shapiro told the room about the coming 24/7 DIY Video Summit, and I told the story I told at the start of this book: that I had attended Signal/Noise 2k5: Creative Revolution at Harvard with fellow fans Naomi Novik and Rebecca Tushnet, only to hear that people started making cool remix videos in the '90s. Six months before Vividcon's Town Hall, in December 2006, *Time* had decided that You—the You who makes videos for YouTube—was the person of the year. Now vidders at the Town Hall asked each other, "Are we Time Magazine's 'Person of the Year' or are we criminals?"[60]

After listening and talking, fandom came to a number of conclusions: "People are finding us whether we want it or not. We can't hide in plain sight anymore. We could choose to require passwords again, or we could explain." The suggestion was made that "those who can afford to be public about their involvement in vidding, *and who are willing to take that step*, should do what they can to be a normalizing presence in the world, whether that be publishing academically, or talking about one's vids at work or at home, or whatever else people might be comfortable doing. Those who can't afford to be public can be supportive in other ways."[61] Vidders' decision to raise their profile—to normalize, to explain, to be "out" as a vidder if you could be—aligned with decisions that were being made in other parts of fandom. Naomi Novik, Rebecca Tushnet, and I, along with seventy other volunteers, had founded the nonprofit Organization for Transformative Works three months earlier, in May 2007. The OTW was also dedicated to creating a fan-controlled, public-facing side of fandom. Its very name articulated and promulgated a legal theory of fan works: that they are transformative, and thus a fair use of copyrighted material. The women who built the OTW feared that unless grassroots fandom became more visible, venture capitalists would create the front doors that new fans would walk through—and then buy and sell fans and fandom as a product. People were still joining the Internet in droves. When new fans searched online for "Buffy fanfiction" or "Star Trek vids" what would they find? What sites would they be sent to?

As I write this, we're more aware of the damaging effects of commercial social media: Cambridge Analytica hacking Facebook, Russian bots on Twitter, YouTube's algorithms steering spectators to ever more extreme videos, including those of white supremacists, to boost "engagement." But the fan communities that I come from, which included many early adopters of technology and scientifically minded women, were worried about the damaging effects of capitalism on their online networks almost as soon as social media arrived. It wasn't just prescience, though fans were indeed prescient; it was also that they were more fully online than most people and thus able to witness negative effects as they happened. Many Web 2.0 startups wrote terms of service (TOS) that clearly or implicitly excluded fans. Other social networks seemed more fan friendly, but then they would be sold—or more precisely, they would sell their large "user base" of "highly engaged content creators" (aka fans) for huge amounts of money, whereupon, like as not, the new owners would rewrite the TOS. (Fans, like other early Internet denizens, had a fear of being TOSed, or removed for violating the terms of service.) Each time that happened, fandom's network would be disrupted and its fan works—fanfiction, art, vids—put at risk.

The OTW was an attempt to take some control in that Wild West environment. Fans wanted a stable environment, a homestead. There was a lot of focus in the early OTW on ownership. Fans wanted to own the servers that housed their works; they wanted to own the means of production when it came to making fan works; they wanted their labor to benefit them, not some venture capitalist who wanted to scoop them up cheap and sell them or their data at a profit. In this spirit, the OTW's flagship project was called the Archive of Our Own (AO3), invoking both a Marxist ownership of the means of production and Virginia Woolf's dictum that "A woman must have money and a room of her own if she is to write fiction." The OTW also launched an academic journal (*Transformative Works and Cultures*), a community wiki (Fanlore), and a project for rescuing at-risk fan works, including analog works like zines and VHS vids (Open Doors). The OTW also launched a legal advocacy project and a vidding committee (later renamed "fan video and multimedia"). Many of the attendees of the 2007 Vividcon Town Hall on Vidding and Visibility were already involved with the nascent OTW, but more got involved afterward. Other vidders chose different forms of advocacy.

The vidders who had chosen visibility went at it with gusto. To the surprise of the organizers, a bloc of vidders showed up at the 24/7 DIY Video Summit, revealing themselves to be more highly organized (and more opinionated) than video makers in other genres. As the first chair of the OTW's vidding committee, I collaborated with Laura Shapiro on the 24/7 DIY showcase and gave a talk drawn from Vividcon's many history panels. (Notably, I was one of only three female speakers out of seventeen; remix culture was still heavily male dominated.) The summit was hugely influential, creating connections that later produced many positive outcomes, as I discuss below. The vidders who attended intermingled with other online video creators—AMV makers, political remixers, vloggers, machinima creators, activist media makers, and documentarians—as well as with media activists and scholars like Lawrence Lessig, Yochai Benkler, Henry Jenkins, Howard Rheingold, Michael Wesch, and John Seeley Brown. They also engaged policy makers from institutions like the Electronic Frontier Foundation (EFF), Critical Commons, and the Participatory Culture Foundation. Laura Shapiro and I filmed interviews with many of the vidders who attend the summit, and we used these and other interviews to make *Vidding* (2008),[62] a series of short videos for MIT's New Media Literacies project.[63] Topics included "What is Vidding?" (1:28), "Technology and Tools" (1:29), "Good Vids, Bad Vids" (1:28), "I Like to Watch" (1:29), "Collaboration and Community" (1:23), and "Why We Vid" (1:20).

OTW's communications team also became a hub for public relations and journalistic inquiry about fandom, giving quotes to journalists or connecting them to knowledgeable sources or people to inter-view. In 2007, Luminosity's VOGUE (Video 47 https://doi.org/10.3998/mpub.10069132.cmp.47) went viral and was picked by *New York Magazine* as one of "The Twenty (Intentionally) Funniest Web Videos of 2007."[64] This time, however, the aftermath of exposure was very different. Luminosity contacted the OTW, who helped her negotiate inquiries from the press. The result was "The Vidder," by Logan Hill,[65] a profile of Luminosity that, according to Henry Jenkins, "is respectful of her accomplishments and seeks to reclaim a place for women's creative work in the larger history of online video."[66] It begins, "Luminosity is the best fan that shows like *Friday Night Lights, Highlander, Farscape*, and *Buffy* ever had—but she can't use her real name in this interview for fear that their producers will sue her. As a vidder—a director of pas-sionate tributes and critiques of her favorite shows—Luminosity samples video in order to remix and reinterpret it, bending source material to her own purposes."[67] Rather than treat Luminosity as someone doing something weird or laughable, Hill asked her about her body of work and her visual influences.[68] Luminosity was subsequently asked by the magazine to judge "The Best Fan Vids of 2008": "Last year, we raved about underground fan vidder Luminosity's brilliant video riffs on *300* and *Supernatural*. So this year, we asked *her* to pick the best fan vids of the year. 'Vidders are becoming more comfortable with their tech, which allows some daring creativity, and it really shows,' says Luminosity, who doesn't use her real name owing to copyright issues."[69] Luminosity was also asked to be one of the judges of Total Recut's video remix challenge of 2008; other judges that year included media scholars and fair use advocates such as Lawrence Lessig, Henry Jenkins, Patricia Aufderheide, J. D. Lasica, Kembrew McLeod, and Mark Hosler—an excellent group, but again, note the skewed gender breakdown. Still, this was a marked difference from Killa and T. Jonesy's experience of going viral in 2006.

The vidding activism of this period culminated with the successful campaign to get a Digital Millennium Copyright Act exemption for non-commercial remixers like vidders. The DMCA posed a legal obstacle to vidders in that it protected DVD encryption technology and made the breaking of those encryptions illegal; in other words, even though it was technologically possible to do so, it was illegal for vidders to rip their own, legally purchased DVDs to get source clips for vidding. The prohibi-tion against ripping was meant to prevent piracy, not remix; legal scholar Rebecca Tushnet often uses the metaphor of fans as dolphins caught in nets meant for tuna. For vidders, DMCA's prohibition of decryption was particularly bitter in that they believed that the vids they were making were textbook fair use: vids are noncommercial, they use only short clips, and they're transformative in meaning and message, creating new interpretations and making analytical arguments. Whether as transformative art or protected speech, vidding ought to be a fair use. But because ripping DVDs was prohibited by the DMCA, vidders, like other remixers, were guilty on a technicality before they could even argue. As Michael Wesch explained in his "anthropological introduction to YouTube," "The simple act of ripping a DVD is actually illegal, which makes virtually everything we do illegal."[70]

The proposal for a DMCA exemption aligned vidders with other remix artists as well as with documentary filmmakers, who also wanted to incorporate short clips into their work. A coalition formed, with many of the key players having met at the 24/7 DIY Video Summit. The EFF proposed the exemption to the Library of Congress, and the OTW submitted a reply comment in support. The OTW also marshaled exhibits and testimony specific to vidding, both live at the open hearings and in writing. Vidders testified about vidding as a practice and about the ways they had been adversely affected by the DMCA. I talked about vidding history and rehearsed many of the arguments of this book. Vidder and vid scholar Tisha Turk gave more practical testimony, explaining why the Motion Picture Association of America (MPAA)'s remedy for remixers—getting clips by filming their screens with a camcorder (which ironically doesn't violate the DMCA)—wouldn't work for vidders, who need high-quality, information-dense images that can be manipulated without degradation.

The OTW also created and posted an online Test Suite of Fair Use Vids, a group of contextualized vids offered in support of arguments like the following:

> Vidding is a legitimate artistic and culturally valuable pursuit that represents an established and growing community.
> Vidding promotes both technical ability and creativity.
> Vids are forms of legitimate cultural criticism.
> Vids propose alternate readings and realities.[71]

The original Test Suite comprised four vids: Luminosity and sisabet's **WOMEN'S WORK** (2007) (Video 57 https://doi.org/10.3998/mpub.10069132.cmp.57), lim's **THIS IS HOW IT WORKS** (2006) (Video 58 https://doi.org/10.3998/mpub.10069132.cmp.58), **HANDLEBARS**

(2008) (Video 59 https://doi.org/10.3998/mpub.10069132.cmp.59) by Seah & Margie, and CLOSER, by T. Jonesy and Killa (Video 54 https://doi.org/10.3998/mpub.10069132.cmp.54). (See "Spotlight on: The OTW's Test Suite of Fair Use Vids" in the online appendix.) It was expanded in 2012 to include THE PRICE by thingswithwings (discussed in the introduction), PIECE OF ME (2008) (Video 60 https://doi.org/10.3998/mpub.10069132.cmp.60) by Obsessive24, IT DEPENDS ON WHAT YOU PAY (2009) (Video 61 https://doi.org/10.3998/mpub.10069132.cmp.61) by Gianduja Kiss, "WHITE" AND NERDY (2009) (Video 62 https://doi.org/10.3998/mpub.10069132.cmp.62) by talitha78, THE TEST (2010) (Video 63 https://doi.org/10.3998/mpub.10069132.cmp.63) by here's luck, and also BUFFY VS. EDWARD (2009), a non-musical *Buffy/Twilight* remix video by political remixer Jonathan McIntosh in which the feminist Buffy meets, rejects, and then kills Edward Cullen, *Twilight*'s stalkery vampire. In making BUFFY VS. EDWARD, McIntosh "was influenced by vidding and vidders like Laura Shapiro."[72] Political remixers and vidders had begun to intermingle and exchange ideas in the wake of the 24/7 DIY Video Summit.

The DMCA exemption for noncommercial remixers was granted in 2009 (and was renewed and expanded in 2012, 2015, and 2018. The 2021 renewal is in process as this book goes to press). "We won!" Turk crowed in her LiveJournal. "I am so happy, and also possibly a little overwhelmed." She added in a comment: "I have to say, the vidders in the OTW test suite are my superheroes; their work is cited all over the Register's recommendations. Vidders make art; once we made the copyright office look closely at that art and understand how and why it gets made, they had to acknowledge that the DMCA was restricting fair uses of copyrighted material."[73] This was true. In the recommendation, the register of copyrights recognized vidding as an art and understood and accepted the arguments about what vidders need to make them: "Noncommercial, transformative users have also sufficiently demonstrated that certain uses require high quality in order for the purpose of the use to be sufficiently expressed and communicated. For instance, where focus on background material in a motion picture is essential to the transformative purpose, as exemplified in the situation of bringing the background to the foreground, the use of decrypted DVDs is necessary to make the point."[74]

The register cited as an example Lierdumoa's HOW MUCH IS THAT GEISHA IN THE WINDOW (2008) (Video 64 https://doi.org/10.3998/mpub.10069132.cmp.64), a vid that was made in order to construct an absence—that is, to show how few Asian characters exist in a show, *Firefly*, that ostensibly describes a future in which the United States and China now form a single superpower. All of the characters can and often do speak Chinese, but, as the register noted, "the vid demonstrates that almost no Asian characters are featured and that they appear only in the background. The vid concludes with a text screen that states: 'There is only one Asian actor with English dialogue in all of *Firefly*' and in the next screen states, 'She plays a whore.'"[75] This was understood as a transformative use, and the register further understood Lierdumoa's focus on the background of the show meant that she needed high-quality footage, concluding that "if a transformative user begins with a work of degraded quality, the further degradation that will likely occur in rendering the work to the public can completely obscure the purpose of the use." The register then rehearsed others examples from vidding:

> For instance, WOMEN'S WORK, by Luminosity and sisabet, assembles short clips from the television series *Supernatural* depicting images of women who are "shown only as eroticized, suffering or demonized." In a number of the clips, the images are difficult to see and had this video been made using pixilated video capture, it is reasonably likely that the point of many scenes' inclusion would not be perceptible. Several vids cited in the record reveal that extensive editing is often performed on the clips reproduced from motion pictures. For instance, in Luminosity's VOGUE (using clips from the motion picture *300* to cast the violence in scenes from the movie in an aesthetically modified manner), not only are clips often rendered side-by-side and synchronized, but there is also color and timing modification of the clips used. Other vids also modify the original clips and images, saturating them with color and morphing images into others. For instance, lim's THIS IS HOW IT WORKS (using clips from the series *Stargate: Atlantis*) and US (with clips from a long list of movies) both morph and colorize clips to serve the messages of the vids. Although some vids cited do not significantly alter the actual images, the pace of the clips or the focus on a particular part of the clip by the vidder tend to demand clarity of the clips in order to perceive the purpose for inclusion. For instance, in CLOSER, by T. Jonesy and Killa, the vidders present an alternative interpretation of an episode from *Star Trek* in order to hypothesize about the relationship between Captain Kirk and Spock. In HANDLEBARS, by Seah and Margie, the vidders examine the Doctor character in the series *Dr. Who* [*sic*], extracting a multitude

of short clips from the series to demonstrate the development of the character while also choosing scenes that fit the lyrics of the song that accompanies the clips. In the course of the character development, the vidders begin whimsically, and then reveal how the smaller exercises of power lead to violence and destruction at the Doctor's hands. This vid criticizes the "moral blind spots by recontextualizing events viewers have already seen." Although some may question the significance of the comment or criticism at issue in these vids, some comment or criticism is involved that either requires or significantly benefits from the use of high quality reproductions of the clips from motion pictures.[76]

This validation was heady; in fact, this entire period of organization, visibility, and activism was exciting. In a very short period, vidders went from being completely underground artists to being profiled in national publications and formally recognized by the Library of Congress. "We are amazing and enormous—more than we realize," one vidder said at the Town Hall. "We have secret strengths as a community that we don't know about because we hide."[77] Now that vidding had come out of hiding, vidders felt suddenly energized, powerful, jubilant.

Being vidders, of course they vidded it. In the midst of what felt like a movement, Counteragent made **DESTINY CALLING: A TRIBUTE TO VIDDING** (2008) (Video 65 https://doi.org/10.3998/mpub.10069132.cmp.65) for More Joy Day, an annual online festival dedicated to spreading joy. "I was giddy with the flush of infatuation with the craft, the vids, and the vidders," Counteragent later told Henry Jenkins. "I was shouting my love from the mountaintops.[78] A metavid made from other (properly credited) vids, DESTINY CALLING has the same swelling pride as the Oscars montage of the year's best films. It is a joyful boast, a triumphant showing off of the art.

"So we may be gorgeous / So we may be famous," the song begins, cutting to instantly recognizable shots from lim's US and Luminosity's VOGUE before going on to name check and celebrate a host of other vids. The song's chorus runs, "This is our destiny calling / We're freaks / Unique / This is our destiny calling now," which nicely encapsulates both vidding's heroic public triumphs and the residual sense of being part of a freakish geek culture. In "Nothing but Net: When Cultures Collide," Cathy Cupitt describes DESTINY CALLING as "a snapshot of the fannish zeitgeist of that moment," noting that it not only alludes to the

Fig. 19. History of vids from Counteragent's DESTINY CALLING: A TRIBUTE TO VIDDING (2008).

formation of "a recognizable canon" but also references current events in vidding culture.[79] In DESTINY CALLING, Counteragent includes shots of Luminosity's *New York Magazine* profile, OTW's website, video editing software, and vids on YouTube. She also imagines a leather-bound *History of Vids* on the shelf of a library (Figure 19 https://doi.org/10.3998/mpub.10069132.cmp.155)—a book very like this one.

FIVE | Re/evolutions

Vidding Culture(s) Online

In 2007, lim made US (Video 12 https://doi.org/10.3998/mpub.10 069132.cmp.12), a vid about fandom. Like all her work, US is visually extraordinary; not for nothing does Counteragent associate the word "gorgeous" with US in her 2008 vid DESTINY CALLING (Video 65 https:// doi.org/10.3998/mpub.10069132.cmp.65), a tribute to vidding. Lim's aesthetic is painterly, and in US, she works over each frame (at twelve frames per second) to create the effect that footage (from *Star Trek*, *The X-Files*, *Doctor Who*, and other shows) has been sketched in pencil and then watercolored. Lim thus turns industrial entertainment into art, showing us the movement of an invisible hand coloring, scribbling, and otherwise embellishing the televisual images. That's what fans do. We remake the mass media so that it's personal, customized, handworked.

In lim's hands, Regina Spektor's song is made to tell the story of fandom in 2007, in the wake of the first shock of visibility. "They made a statue of us / And put it on a mountaintop," it begins, as lim shows us Kirk and Spock, the granddaddy of all slash pairings and the first fandom of the modern age. "Now tourists come and stare at us." Here lim cuts from Kirk and Spock turning away from some nosy old ladies to a clip of Henry Jenkins lecturing at MIT's Future of Entertainment conference in 2006. The outsiders had arrived—scholars, journalists, lawyers—to stare and gape. But US became popular because it captured not only how it felt to be seen as a fan but also how to see like a fan. US captures the fannish gaze, so to speak, with lim's invisible paintbrush adding pops of color to details of the televisual frame that one might not expect. Fans (and vidders in particular) see TV and movies differently. They look at backgrounds that aren't narratively important; they focus on details that others think irrelevant; they make extratextual connections across and between shows and story worlds and so make new things.

Lim frames this fannish art making process both as joyful and subversive. "We're living in a den of thieves," a later lyric goes as a cheerful Jack Sparrow sails past a sign reading "Pirates Ye Be Warned." While some fans in 2007 were challenging the idea that vidding was piracy, lim takes a more defiant stance. As Alexis Lothian notes in "Living in a Den of Thieves: Fan Video and Digital Challenges to Ownership," us stakes out a position that could unite vidders with other culture thieves like file sharers, whose work is not transformative.[1] us gives us not only a literal pirate but also Batman, a vigilante, staring up at a copyright symbol instead of a Bat-Signal. Other clips also make arguments about copying and the law. For instance, we see Tom Baker, the Fourth Doctor, unveiling multiple copies of the *Mona Lisa*.[2] This clip comes from the *Doctor Who* episode "City of Death" (1979), in which Leonardo da Vinci is forced by a villain to paint multiple copies of the *Mona Lisa* for the villain's profit. At the end of the episode, the original painting and all copies save one have been destroyed. But the Doctor claims that there's no real distinction between original and copy in this context; each of the new paintings Leonardo has made is a fake, an original, and a masterpiece, all at the same time. The Doctor suggests of the remaining *Mona Lisa*, "If they have to X-ray it to find out whether it's good or not,"[3] they've missed the point of art. At the end of the episode, the Doctor buys a postcard of the painting.

us also suggests that making fan works is a profoundly human activity and one that is, in Spektor's choice of words, contagious. This is a prescient observation. Starting about 2007, with broadband use hitting 50 percent of American adults, online fandom, already growing by leaps and bounds, exploded yet again. us ends with images of floods, of avalanches, and of uprising, culminating with a clip of the unmasking of vigilantes at the end of the 2005 film *V for Vendetta* and concluding with the image of a geeky girl with glasses, the fangirl.

This image graced the summer 2009 issue of *Cinema Journal*, and it remains the journal's most popular cover (Figure 20 https://doi.org/10.3998/mpub.10069132.cmp.156). Despite being a vid that, as Kristina Busse notes, aggressively questions outsiders' interest in fandom,[4] us was immediately taken up by outsiders. It was showcased at the 2008 24/7 DIY Video Summit held at the University of Southern California, shown at the 2007 Anime Weekend in Atlanta, and cited in the EFF/OTW's legal filings for the DMCA exemption.[5] By 2009, us was

Fig. 20. The final frame of lim's vid us on the cover of *Cinema Journal*, Summer 2009.

on display at the California Museum of Photography[6] and was being discussed on NPR's *All Things Considered.*[7]

us was also given a central role in Michael Wesch's "Anthropological Introduction to YouTube," which he presented at the Library of Congress on June 23, 2008, and which has since been seen by some two million people online.[8] Wesch describes us as "a powerful, poetic statement" of the value of remix, where "we can remix this culture that's being thrown at us, we can take it, re-appropriate it, and throw it back." In his speech, Wesch twice describes us as "poetic," and in fact he himself appropriates the poetic values of vidding for his own purposes, using the meanings that lim has created in us to underlie and heighten a speech about decriminalizing remix made by Lawrence Lessig. Wesch performs a close reading of the section of us where Spektor sings, "We're living in a den of thieves / Rummaging for answers in the pages," seeing it, as everyone who sees US does, as a poignant statement of what it feels like to be an artist searching for meaning in the vast detritus of culture when the very act of doing so is illegal. Wesch says:

> And this is one of the most poetic statements of this, this is by blimvisible [then lim's YouTube handle]. And you hear the Regina Spektor lyrics there—where she says *even though our parts are slightly used*, and then goes on and says—these are all clips from different films—and she's saying, *we're living in a den of thieves, rummaging for answers in the pages.* It's really a powerful, poetic statement, because most of what we do is actually illegal. Any remixing is basically illegal, and I could talk more about the parameters of that. We have fair use laws that should protect it, but the simple act of ripping a DVD is actually illegal, which makes virtually everything we do illegal. So here we are in this state. Here's Lawrence Lessig talking about this.

At this point, Wesch cuts to the climax of Lessig's 2007 TED talk, "Laws that Choke Creativity," but he keeps lim's US running underneath, so that the climax of the talk and the climax of the vid crest together. Lessig says some (but only some) of the things that lim is saying via her vid:

> We need to recognize that you can't kill the instinct that the technology produces, we can only criminalize it. We can't stop our kids from using it, we can only drive it underground. We can't make our kids passive again, we can only make them "pirates" and is that good? We live in this weird time, this kind of age of prohibitions, where many areas of our life we live life constantly against the law, ordinary people live life against the law and that's what we're doing to our kids. They live life knowing they live it against the law. That realization is extraordinarily corrosive, extraordinarily corrupting, and in a democracy we ought to be able to do better.[9]

Spektor's voice scaffolds most of this speech like the voice of the vidder, of all vidders. As Lessig's speech builds—"In a democracy we ought to be able to do better!"—the song also hits its peak: "They built a statue of us / They built a statue of us / Our noses have begun to rust!" with Spektor hitting the song's high note on "rust." The vid punches up Lessig's speech. Together, they create emotional impact. Wesch cuts back to

US in time for its ending: the uprising of the masses, including the fangirl with glasses, scored to forceful piano chords.

In other words, Wesch vidded Lessig to lim. He used US's messaging and musicality to draw out the revolutionary fervor of Lessig's arguments. While it may be obvious that the vid's visual meaning is lim's (that is, it's lim who gives us the unmasking vigilantes, the pseudonymous denizens of the Internet rising up to assert their right to copy and remix), and even that the vid's lyrical meaning is lim's (after all, it's lim who has made "living in a den of thieves" be about digital piracy; who knows what Regina Spektor meant by that line?), the musical meaning of Us is lim's too, because lim altered the song for increased impact.

Regina Spektor's "Us" is 4:48 minutes long; the radio edit is 4:02. But lim's version is 3:36, with the time mostly removed from the song's third repetition of the chorus and extended outro. Lim restructures the song so that it ends on the high note of "rust," followed by a concluding piano flourish. By contrast, Spektor's version goes around for another chorus after that climax, then fades out, presumably to let a DJ talk over those last few bars or use them to transition to another song. Lim makes "Us" a vidding song—one that builds emotionally to an epic finish. And it's lim's epic finish that Wesch draws on to vid Lessig's speech. At the end of the segment, he reads one of US's many YouTube comments: "My God! Are you doing that for a living? I never saw anything like this! You're an artist!"[10]

The Machine Is Us/ing Us

Before his introductory lecture on YouTube, Michael Wesch was famous for another video, "The Machine Is Us/ing Us," an introduction of sorts to Web 2.0 in which Wesch concludes that as more people start creating, tagging, and linking content online, we will teach the Internet how to make connections between things. In other words, Wesch was one of the first people to recognize that the Web 2.0 was going to be shaped by algorithms based on user habits and activity—if you liked this, you'll like that; people who bought this also bought that—though he never uses the word "algorithm." Instead, Wesch talks about the machine and what we today call machine learning, which he frames more or less positively—the Internet is us, and we are creating and organizing information together!—although his title reveals a dark undertone.

Now, more than ten years later, we understand that companies are using us, their users, to train their algorithms. Google used ReCaptcha to get us to collectively transcribe and digitize the Google Books archive, a project it finished in 2011.[11] Now it's using us to build machine learning data sets, like recognizing objects in images: "Click on all the boxes with stop signs in them," or "click on the boxes that have cars in them." In a 2019 article for *Wired*, Kate O'Neill records her sarcastic response to a meme inviting people to post then-and-now profile pictures:

> Me 10 years ago: probably would have played along with the profile picture aging meme going around on Facebook and Instagram
> Me now: ponders how all this data could be mined to train facial recognition algorithms on age progression and age recognition[12]

Zeynep Tufeki has talked about the ways in which YouTube's algorithms shape what people watch on the site—that is, what kind of videos are easy to find on YouTube and what kinds are not. In *Twitter and Tear Gas*, Tufeki explains, "Social media platforms increasingly use algorithms— complex software— to sift through content and decide what to surface, prioritize, and publicize and what to bury."[13] Tufeki has also warned about the dangers of network effects (or network externalities), the fact that, when it comes to social networks, the more people on them, the more useful they are to people, so for instance you have to be on Facebook because everyone you know is on Facebook. This not only leads to a winner-take-all state for platforms but also makes it hard for users to quit big sites even if they're actively bad. It also makes it difficult for alternatives to emerge or thrive, even if they have superior features or policies. As Tufeki puts it, "A perfect social media platform without users is worthless."[14]

Tufeki's fear is about what the combination of black box algorithms (so called because we don't actually understand how they work) and network effects are doing to our democracy. She's worried that proprietary, data-crunching algorithms are being used to make crucial human decisions about whom to hire, whom to insure, and—perhaps most crucially—whom to vote for.[15] Regarding YouTube, Tufeki argues that it has become "one of the most powerful radicalizing instruments of the 20th century,"[16] with its autoplay feature steering people toward ever more extreme content: right-wingers toward white supremacy, left-wingers toward government conspiracy, vegetarians toward veganism, and so on.

While Tufeki's research is about how these trends are affecting the political and social spheres, algorithms and network effects also affect the artistic and aesthetic choices we make—or that are made for us. This is true both in the mainstream world of art and entertainment and in subcultural arts like vidding. As I write this, Netflix is fighting it out with Amazon Prime, Hulu, HBO Max, Disney+, CBS Open Access, Apple TV+, Peacock, and others in an attempt to rule streaming TV before the winners take all.[17] This fight affects what kind of television is getting made as each service tries to develop their own must-see TV, aided by the slew of "second-to-second data about viewing habits, sign-ups and subscription loss"[18] that their algorithms provide. The fight to rule streaming TV is also a fight against user-generated content. The entertainment industry wants to take our attention back from YouTube and from "all the gaming videos, makeup tutorials and alt-right primers that millions of people spend millions of minutes watching on their phones every day."[19] That fight also affects what's getting made, from expensive event television with production values that YouTube can't match (for example, *Game of Thrones*) to professional, short-form content meant to compete directly with video for mobile devices like TikTok (for example, the now-defunct Quibi or SerialBox).

Vidders have already experienced much of the disorientation of network effects. As John Hondros details in his chapter on vidding in *Ecologies of Internet Video*, the decade after 2007 was characterized by a cascade of platform failures.[20] As I noted in chapter 4, many early digital vidders initially opted for Imeem, a streaming service that had better visual quality and audiovisual synchronization than YouTube at the time. Imeem also had strong social networking features, allowing fans to friend each other and to create forums, technical support groups, and thematic video playlists. But even as vidders moved to Imeem en masse, the service worsened. Banner ads were splashed over the videos, taking up a full third of the screen, a situation intolerable to aesthetically sensitive vidders. Finally, Imeem announced on June 25, 2009, that it was making "a few changes" to simplify the site: It was eliminating user-generated content entirely in order to focus on professionally produced content. Their post, which enraged vidders, explained, "Simply put, here's no ROI [return on investment] for us in UGV [user-generated video]."[21] With a single stroke, a strong fan network was disrupted and an online archive of vids destroyed. On July 6, 2009, Elisa Kreisinger wrote about the story for the Political Remix Video blog:

Last week fannish vidders found themselves caught in the midst of yet another online video massacre. . . . The end of the vidding community on imeem does not just stop with the loss of the vids but also a deletion of all comments and playlists, loss of the cumulative hit counts and vidding network disruptions. To add insult to injury, imeem continues to prohibit users from downloading their own content. . . . What this means for our blog is that many of our favorite vids will be offline until they can be relocated to other sites.[22]

Vidders scrambled to find other hosting sites. Many opted for Blip.tv, whose posted fair use policy had heard of transformative use.[23] But in 2013, Blip.tv was bought by a YouTube network, Maker Studios, and it too turned away from user-generated video in favor of branded original content. Again there was damage to the vidding community. Not only was the fan network disrupted but there was also a host of dead links throughout the various proposals, comments, and replies made to the Library of Congress in support of the DMCA exemption for noncommercial remix. A historian or lawyer who wants to see what works were offered in support of the exemption is sadly out of luck. Over the past decade, vidders tried many (failed) alternatives to YouTube, not just Blip.tv and Imeem, but Stage6, Bam Video Vault, Viddler, and others.

The process of building a place for your work and then losing it, over and over, was demoralizing after the giddy years of success. In 2014, as a former chair of the OTW vidding/fan video committee, I got an e-mail from an exhausted Luminosity asking for help:

Hey! My own vid site has been gone since January 2012. Youtube has taken down/blocked about 40% of my stuff last time I looked. Viddler is gone. Blip.tv is gone. I was TOS'd from Vimeo. . . .

In my own never-ending self analysis, I realize that this feeling of being a man without a country has really had an impact on my creativity. The only place my vids rest right now are on my own hard drives. . . .

I need to find a place to archive my vids, and I have no idea where to look! What I want and what I need are two different things, so I'd settle for a place to put my vids up for posterity's sake. Maybe it doesn't mean anything and all of this digital stuff is destined to fade away, but I feel that I should at least make the effort to preserve it.

Could you give me a starting point? Someone to talk to in order to find someone to talk to? To find a place where I can archive the work, where people could download it occasionally? I have over 120 pieces of work that are just languishing.[24]

At the time, the best I could suggest to Luminosity was Critical Commons, an online repository of user-generated media started by the University of Southern California in 2008. While Critical Commons was really designed for film and media professors, Steve Anderson explicitly invited vidders to use the site in the wake of the 24/7 DIY Video Summit. However, as is so often the case with academic projects, the site is not regularly kept up to spec in either technical or security terms. This makes it a lot less useful to fans.

Today, most vidders have their vids archived in more than one place, because if vidders have learned one thing over the years, it's the value of redundancy. Some vidders use Vidders.net and VidderTube, which are small and privately owned fan-run sites; others use more mainstream YouTube alternatives like Dailymotion and Vimeo. Vimeo in particular has been popular with vidders as well as with independent filmmakers, as it is ad-free and has high-definition playback. While many vidders post openly to Vimeo, others, in a move that evokes the protected download sites of the past, post their vids to the site locked under a password, which they post alongside the vids in fan-friendly spaces like Dreamwidth, LiveJournal, Tumblr, or the Archive of Our Own. Some vidders are working to get their vids hosted in a collection at the Internet Archive, while others are building and maintaining their own streaming sites— for example, Luminosity now houses all her vids at Luminosity's Vids at lumsvids.com. Others are trying out nascent peer-to-peer solutions like PeerTube.

Then, of course, there is YouTube, the behemoth, the Godzilla of the video world. The fact that, for many, YouTube is the only real game in town means that YouTube's policies and algorithms have enormous power to shape the kind of vids that get made today.

Broadcast Yourself

There are millions of fan vids on YouTube. Possibly the first thing that needs to be said is that most of the vidders on YouTube came to vidding through YouTube. For them, this book of history may be an interesting backstory to their hobby, or possibly vastly irrelevant. As Katherina Freund showed in her ethnographic research, by 2009, most vidders had come to vidding online; they simply "stumbled across a vid by accident on the Internet while looking for information on a favorite television show."[25] In the aughts, that stumbling might have been on Imeem, Blip. tv, or MySpace; they might even have downloaded a vid via an app like Kazaa or by torrenting. But today, it's probably YouTube. Network effects have left YouTube as more or less the only open place for video, whether professional or user generated. This includes fan vids, but it is by no means limited to vids, which is a large part of the problem. Even with millions of vids out there, vidding is now a tiny subculture lost in an enormous sea.

Much recent scholarly work on YouTube and user-generated video has been concerned with creating taxonomies of content. As I note in the introduction, Owen Gallagher, in *Reclaiming Critical Remix: The Role of Sampling in Transformative Works*, lists "vids/fanvids/songvids" as one of sixteen subgenres of remix videos, which include political remixes, movie trailers, supercuts, machinima, AMVs, fan dubs/lip sync, auto-tuned clips, subtitle videos, and other kinds of music video.[26] And that's just remix video. Beyond remix, there are other user-generated video genres. Patricia Lange argues in *Kids on YouTube* that geek girls rarely limit themselves to one genre of video. Instead, they create many different kinds, including blogs, sketch comedy, lip synching, personal event videos, hanging-out-at-home videos, media review videos, animation, machinima, promotional videos, documentaries, how-tos (such as painting or putting on makeup), technology experimentation videos, and videos for class projects.[27] Beyond this amateur content, there are the professional (or wannabe professional) YouTubers. Matt Gielen, a so-called YouTube growth strategist, has created a taxonomy of original formats, which he divides into eight categories: listicle, explainer, commentary, interview, music video, challenge, reaction, and narrative. Gielen argues that the most successful YouTube videos are hybrids, like a listicle that is also an explainer ("The 16 Best Life Hacks") or an interview that is also a challenge ("Hot Ones," in which celebrities are interviewed as they eat increasingly spicy wings).[28] Then there's mainstream industry entertainment, uploaded officially or unofficially: movie trailers, concert footage, commercial music videos, clips from movies and TV, theatre, news, sports.

YouTube's algorithms have to cope with sorting and serving all these videos to viewers; moreover, YouTube also has to cope with people lying and mislabeling what they're posting, because labels translate to clicks, and clicks translate to cash. YouTube's constantly evolving algorithms and policies have never been made with fan vids in mind, but vidders on

YouTube still have to work with, or around, them. Although YouTube has algorithms and policies that deal with a whole host of issues, I am interested in two main categories: those dealing with what can be uploaded and hosted, and those dealing with what is findable—that is, what is surfaced and served to users.

The Upload Algorithm

In the first years of YouTube, vidders and other remix artists were primarily concerned with the first of these categories: what YouTube allowed to be uploaded and hosted. From the first, YouTube videos were subject to takedowns that were based on claims of copyright infringement, with little apparent regard for legal fair use. On February 4, 2008, YouTube announced that they were working on Video Identification, the algorithm that was the precursor to Content ID. Video Identification was a match engine aimed at "establishing ownership" of a video for the purpose of clearing rights for advertising. "The beauty of this system is: machines did all the work!" the explanatory video's narrator boasted.[29] However, the machine wasn't able to detect fair uses of copyrighted material, and by March 8, 2008, MIT's Students for Free Culture had established its YouTomb project, which tracked takedowns looking for fair use and other violations. As the site explained, "MIT Free Culture became especially interested in the issue after YouTube announced that it would begin using filtering technology to scan users' video and audio for near-matches with copyrighted material. While automating the takedown process may make enforcement easier, it also means that content falling under fair-use exceptions and even totally innocuous videos may receive some of the collateral damage."[30] YouTomb noted that "the sampling and remixing of non-original material have often led to great cultural accomplishments,"[31] making it an early advocate for the value of remix art. Content ID, Video Identification's next iteration, gives "rights holders" more "fine-grained controls for managing their content if someone uploads it to YouTube,"[32] offering those rights holders the option to block, monetize, or track the data analytics associated with videos. That is, Content ID offers movie and television studios, as well as the music and record companies, the chance to "claim" the raw materials that fan vids are made of, then block, monetize, or track them.

While a transformative use should give remixers the right to monetize their own work, fan vidders not only don't seek to monetize, they also typically don't care whether their vids are monetized by the underlying "rights holders" of media or music via Content ID. (By contrast, political remixers do mind, as they tend to make works more forcefully critical of source texts.[33]) However, often these purported rights holders are not actually the true rights holders; as I noted earlier, people lie to YouTube all the time. Content ID has created incentives for copyright trolls to claim all kinds of content as theirs for the express purpose of monetizing it,[34] which can be frustrating. It's one thing not to profit from your works, but it's something else to see random trolls making money from you by falsely claiming to own music or video they don't actually own. Moreover, some trolls are extortionists; having (falsely) claimed a piece of your vid, they, like the real rights holders, have the power not only to monetize your work but to block it.

Blocking is the bigger problem. Vidders are mostly happy to let rights holders monetize their vids in exchanged for being allowed to show their work, yet they're often not allowed, even if their use of copyrighted material is legal and fair. Ideally, a real person would review contested videos and make a judgment about whether a use is fair, but people are expensive. Instead, YouTube put in a system in which users are presumptively guilty and get three strikes: three DMCA takedowns and you lose your account. YouTube also forced those who'd gotten a takedown notice to attend YouTube Copyright School; they had to watch and be tested about a video in which a (presumptively guilty) squirrel in a pirate hat gets lectured about copyright law. In addition to framing users as pirates, YouTube Copyright School discourages its students from asserting a claim of fair use or from using the DMCA dispute process, warning, "Be careful! If you misuse the process, you could end up in court, and then you would get in *a lot of trouble!*"[35] As the EFF noted, the video is particularly biased against remixers; it celebrates "making your own video," but "it is clear that 'your own video' does not include mashups and remixes."[36] And as Public Knowledge noted, there is no corresponding copyright education provided to copyright owners who make false or fraudulent infringement claims.[37]

Despite these warnings, many vidders and other remixers learned to negotiate YouTube's complicated and ever-changing dispute process. Some reached out to the OTW for help, or they used the EFF's "Guide to YouTube Removals."[38] Others sought help from other vidders, or they just muddled through on their own. Of course, most vidders don't fight their takedown notices. They just go away, or they post their vids elsewhere. There is no way to measure the chilling effects that this has on vidders and other video makers.

In a *Frontline* interview, Zeynep Tufeki talks about how she became a point person for political activists who had their web pages removed:

> I found myself spending an enormous amount of time going to these companies, to people I know, and saying: "Can you take a look at this? Can you take a look at this? Can you take a look at this?" (Laughs.) There were days I would be spending hours because there are so many cases like this, where people would just be coming to me and saying, "My page that is followed by hundreds of thousands of people is gone without an explanation, and Google won't respond"; "My YouTube video, gone without explanation"; "My Facebook page, gone without an explanation." I appealed to the degree—sometimes there's no way to appeal.[39]

As the founding board members of the OTW most associated with vidding and the law, Rebecca Tushnet and I have sometimes served this function for vidders. However, your right to artistic expression shouldn't depend on who you know, and the dispute process shouldn't be so complicated that it requires the help of experts. John Hondros has chronicled lim's extensive dispute with YouTube and the BBC over the blocking of her *Peaky Blinders* vid **HORSE** (2016) (Video 66 https://doi.org/10.3998/mpub.10069132.cmp.66),[40] which Rebecca Tushnet and I consulted on. Hondros describes the extent to which YouTube acted "as an ally of the copyright holders by making lim go through a long, convoluted, and, as she described it, 'scary' process that was no doubt designed to deter users."[41] This included escalating beyond YouTube's normal review process to a formal legal counter-notification, which required lim to provide her real name and address, and to make a sworn statement under penalty of perjury. Even then, she didn't really win; the BBC and its agents simply never responded, at which point, YouTube restored the video. As lim explains in her own essay about the experience, "This is Not Legal Advice: YouTube, Endemol, & The BBC vs. . . . Me," "You don't win, is the thing to understand. You just don't lose. To go any further they have to sue you. It's a game of chicken. Until one day it isn't, I guess."[42]

The difficulty that celebrated and connected vidders like lim and Luminosity have had negotiating the YouTube takedown process only illustrates the incredible unfairness of the process. What of the woman making her first vid? Even if you're a seasoned vidder, who wants to go through this, even with the support of fair use advocates? Fighting the machine is exhausting and demoralizing.

The Recommendation Algorithm

All of this is just to get your work hosted on YouTube; the second category of algorithm concerns what is findable.[43] It's this second algorithm that most YouTubers—who are not remix artists, who are producing "original" content—are looking to hack so they can get viewers, clicks, and cash. Seventy percent of the time people spend on YouTube is spent watching videos recommended by the site.[44] It is this algorithm that Zeynep Tufeki refers to when she calls YouTube "the great radicalizer" for its recommendation of ever more extreme content. But the recommendation algorithm produces a different set of problems for vidders and vid fans.

Vidders—even vidders who use YouTube—often complain that they don't like "YouTube vids." On the face of it, this is a nonsensical claim. There are millions of vids on YouTube, made in various styles. Many vidders from the old-school traditions whose history I've outlined here now host at least some of their vids on YouTube—those that YouTube allows, anyway—and YouTube has also been a site of community formation for new vidding groups and cross-pollination between groups. YouTube hosts (and blocks) AMV makers and live-action/AMV crossover vidders, K-pop vidders, soap opera vidders, and sports vidders as well as various communities of international vidders (notably Russian, Brazilian, and Chinese vidders). There are kids vidding on YouTube today who grew up with the entire archive of moving images in their bedrooms and with video editing tools as ubiquitous as crayons. These kids write using moving pictures as their native language.

So what does it mean when vidders say they don't like "YouTube vids"? They tend to mean either "I can't find the vids I like" or "the vids that I can find don't feel fannish to me." In other words, the vids they find seem to have a very mainstream sensibility. Both these things are likely to be true, and for the same reason: the YouTube algorithms, which decide what gets hosted, what gets surfaced, and what gets buried. So the vids that you are likely to see on YouTube are, first and foremost, the vids that have survived Content ID and the takedown algorithm, because you can't watch a vid that isn't hosted, and you can't watch a vid created by a vidder who didn't appeal her takedown notice or who lost her appeal. Second, the vids that are served are broadly popular among YouTube viewers, most of whom are not vid fans. So if there are two vids, one that appeals to, say, a highly engaged fan of the BBC's *Sherlock* and one that appeals to the millions of casual fans of the show, then it's the second of those two vids that's going to get millions of hits and be served up to *Sherlock*-interested fans. Also, vids based on mainstream network TV shows and blockbuster films will both outnumber and get more hits in the aggregate than those made from the cult, often niche TV shows that media fans have historically liked, so *Star Wars* will trump *Stargate: Atlantis* every time. Moreover, the YouTube algorithm wants you to keep watching YouTube, so it is going to queue up a variety of videos that it thinks that the vid watcher will want to see. Most of these videos won't be fan vids; YouTube might follow up a *Sherlock* vid with an interview with Benedict Cumberbatch or a panel about *Doctor Strange* (2016) filmed at Comic-Con. Or they might include videos about politics or beauty or comedy or something else that the viewer is interested in aside from *Sherlock* fan vids, because even vidders are likely to be using YouTube to watch a variety of things: cooking tips, concert footage, last night's Stephen Colbert monologue.

While we don't know exactly how YouTube's (ever-changing and proprietary) algorithm works, we do know some things about it. We know it highly values videos that cause a person to start a YouTube viewership session. We know that YouTube measures how long your content keeps viewers on the platform and how long they stay on after they leave your channel. We also know that the algorithm downgrades you if someone stops watching YouTube after one of your videos.[45] We know that the algorithm prefers longer videos, videos that people watch all the way through, and videos that get viewers to like, comment, subscribe, or otherwise engage with the site. We know that YouTube prefers you to watch videos directly on YouTube's site rather than as embedded in other sites like Facebook or Tumblr. We know that YouTube prefers users who upload videos regularly and consistently, like a television network. The algorithm also prefers to recommend new content to viewers. Getting a lot of views right after upload is key.[46]

None of these factors privileges vids, which are short in duration and irregularly posted. Many vidders will link or embed their vids on the social network they use to communicate with other fans (Twitter, Tumblr, Dreamwidth, Discord, AO3), and comments, likes, and feedback will consequently happen on that site and not YouTube. The vid watcher who watches an embedded video will probably not go to YouTube and be seduced into watching other videos on the sidebar. Vid watchers are also unlikely to immediately watch other vids by the same vidder (though they might follow the career of a vidder across fandoms). All these factors disadvantage vids, and this disadvantage can be further exacerbated by takedowns. Even if a vid is restored to a viewer's channel after a dispute, it's no longer considered new content. That's enough to bury a vid.

As Sophie Bishop notes in "Anxiety, Panic and Self-Optimization: Inequalities and the YouTube Algorithm," "The mobilization of viewing session algorithmic signals suggest that YouTubers who do not fit within an existing genre will be punished."[47] This punishment will happen unless you strategize assiduously to avoid it, as professionals and wannabe professionals do—and vidders, being nonprofit artists, overwhelmingly don't.[48] Tony Zhou, one of the creators of the excellent film-essay channel, Every Frame a Painting, confesses,

> Nearly every stylistic decision you see about the channel [Every Frame a Painting]—the length of the clips, the number of examples, which studios' films we chose, the way narration and clip audio weave together, the reordering and flipping of shots, the remixing of 5.1 audio, the rhythm and pacing of the overall video—all of that was reverse-engineered from YouTube's Copyright ID [*sic*]. I spent about a week doing brute force trial-and-error. I would privately upload several different essay clips, then see which got flagged and which didn't. This gave me a rough idea what the system could detect, and I edited the videos to avoid those potholes. So something that was designed to restrict us ended up becoming our style.[49]

Most vidders have not engaged in this sort of trial and error; many have never even considered such a thing. And yet. The style of fan vidding that developed after YouTube—the so-called YouTube vid—was also designed in the context of Content ID. YouTube fan vids tend to be flashy and fast cut; they tend to feature textures, overlays, distortions, and speed changes, sometimes to the point of parody. These are all things that will help the vid survive, even if an individual vidder doesn't realize the technological implications of these choices. In her satirical video, **HOW TO BE A PERFECT VIDDER** (2015) (Video 67 https://doi.org/10.3998/mpub.10069132.cmp.67), pingvi, a highly regarded Ukrainian YouTube vidder, mocks the unthinking or poor use of these elements by outlining six rules of vidding using the highly apropos Ken Ashcorp song "20 Percent Cooler": "Yeah, I own this beat / You can call me the king or the ruler. . . . / We're getting 20 percent cooler":

Rule 1: Use as much effects as possible.
Rule 2: Don't forget to use silly fonts, especially when they don't go with the video.

Rule 3: Low quality clips are cool. Good quality is for suckers.

Rule 4: If you make a funny video, with quotes, change the text as fast as you only can so you can't actually read anything.

Rule 5: Overlays are very important. Put an overlay over an overlay and an overlay on top.

Rule 6: Right cropping? Who fucking cares.[50]

Many YouTube vids fade to black between clips, a technique known as fadebop, though predigital vidders and their aesthetic descendants can be derisive about fadebop, which they see as a way of cheating the difficulty of raccord and the hard cut. YouTube vids are also notable for their audio mixing and sound work; they often include snatches of significant dialogue from the source visuals layered over the music. Audio editing was more or less impossible in the VHS era, and it was sufficiently difficult as to be rare in early computer vidding—although for an exception, see Luminosity's ECSTATIC DRUM TRIP (2005) (Video 68 https://doi.org/10.3998/mpub.10069132.cmp.68), which features an audio track of her own creation. But sound work is now increasingly common, and in talented hands, the resultant soundscapes are artworks in themselves. A work like KatrinDepp's **THE GAME IS SOMETHING** (2014) turns the BBC's *Sherlock* into a percussive symphony, using handclaps, ticking clocks, clattering teacups, fizzing Alka-Seltzer, and other noises from the show to add beats to Fatboy Slim's "Funk Soul Brother," bringing out the musicality in the mise-en-scène. (See excerpt, Clip 8. https://doi.org/10.3998/mpub.10069132.cmp.165)

In the case of Grable424 and djcprod's GLITTER AND GOLD (2016) (Video 35 https://doi.org/10.3998/mpub.10069132.cmp.35), the soundscape itself becomes an argument. Grable424 and djcprod use grunts and panting to make the comic book fighting of the Marvel Cinematic Universe (MCU) feel visceral, further emphasizing the song lyrics' insistence ("I am flesh and I am bone") on the fragile humanity of these superheroes.[51] The vid breaks up all the big fights and power shots to let the characters gasp for breath, literally giving them a moment to stop and collect themselves. Fan works often construct this sort of space for the human (often the physical, the sexual, the domestic) in the narrative, but GLITTER AND GOLD makes that physicality aural as well as visual. As Loki wryly says, early on in the vid, to cue us: "I'm listening!"

These features and techniques obviously have aesthetic value to vidders, and they are also made possible by the affordances of contemporary video editing and motion graphics software. Such software drives vidding even as it drives the aesthetics of mainstream entertainment, which this style of vidding mirrors. (Television footage is both shot and edited a lot more beautifully than it used to be.) Crucially, however, fast-cut vids with overlays, colorings, and sound work are more likely to survive on YouTube, which means that they can be seen, admired, and imitated. This can create a feedback loop, where more and more vids get made in this (obviously successful) style.

YouTube is changing vidding aesthetics because what gets seen affects what gets made. This doesn't mean that other vids and styles don't exist on or off YouTube; they do, and in greater numbers than ever before.

Tactics and Strategies in the Age of YouTube

Different fan communities have adopted different strategies in the age of YouTube and so have formed, to use Tisha Turk and Joshua Johnson's term, different vidding ecologies, or social worlds where vid creators and vid watchers alike collaborate and play, working out ideas and arguments about both the source and the art of vidding itself.[52]

What John Hondros calls the LiveJournal vidding community, a group that includes many who came to vidding along the path I've outlined as well as many new vidders from around the world, tends to use YouTube or Vimeo for hosting, but to distribute their vids via embeds on their blog. (That blog was historically LiveJournal, but since the Russian purchase of the site, many fans have moved to Dreamwidth, a fan-run LiveJournal fork site.) Using YouTube only for hosting more or less guarantees that the hosted vids will be invisible on YouTube, but for these vidders, it doesn't matter; the audience for their vids is their friends list. This community keeps itself excited and productive by organizing various vidding conventions, festivals, exchanges, and challenges. These include not only in-person vidding conventions like Vividcon (Chicago, 2002–18) and its European equivalent, VidUKon (Cardiff, 2008–), where one can make and see new work, but also online events like Festivids (2009–), in which vidders make vids in rare and undervidded fandoms as gifts for challenge participants, and Halfamoon (2008–), a festival that solicits fan works about female characters.

Other vidders congregate in fandom-specific social media networks or in ad hoc communities pulled together by subscribing to fandom-relevant tags on sites like Twitter, Tumblr, and the Archive of Our Own. These fan communities make, watch, and share vids alongside other fan artworks like fanfiction, fan art, crafts, and podfic, and will sometimes integrate vids into fandom-specific conventions. This means, for example, that *Supernatural* vids might be found embedded on Tumblr or Twitter and tagged "supernatural" or "spn vids," and those vids would be liked, commented on, or reblogged by *Supernatural* fans looking for *Supernatural*-specific content. Hosting vids on YouTube or Vimeo and embedding them in more fannish context means that the vids will likely be buried by the algorithms on the host site. But again, it doesn't matter. These vidders aren't interested in reaching video watchers; they're interested in reaching the other *Supernatural* fans in their Discord. Moreover, this kind of fannish behavior is no longer limited to old-school genre TV fans. Mainstream network shows like *Scandal*, *Chicago P.D.*, *American Idol*, and *The Big Bang Theory* also have fans who make vids, and if you're a fan of one of those shows, you might watch or scroll past the occasional vid on your Facebook or Twitter or Instagram feed. Even sports fans make hype videos that use many of the techniques of vidding, turning sports into dance and using music to manipulate emotions.

Other fans have developed tactics for surviving, and even flourishing, on YouTube. Some vidders will join a studio, or a small collective of vidders who collaborate and promote each other's solo work. Studios were historically more common in the AMV world, as amateur or preprofessional versions of the professional anime studios of Japan, but the cross-pollination of vidding communities has seen this terminology adopted by some live-action vidders too. Joining a studio usually requires you to apply and show your work, though sometimes an admired vidder is invited to join. Many vidders communicate on Ask.fm or Ask.ru, where they talk vidding tech and aesthetics. Some vidders participate in vidding contests or challenges. Pingvi has run a Test Your Skills challenge for several years; the winners gain visibility and subscribers.[53] Others might join a collab or a MEP (multieditor project); these terms also come from AMV, which historically spoke of editors rather than vidders. A collab is any form of collaborative vid project between vidders (or sometimes between a vidder and a sound editor). A MEP is a more structured collab in which an editor cuts up a song into sections and distributes them among the participants, who each vid their section; the editor then edits all the sections into a coherent whole. There are open MEPs that you can apply to join and closed MEPs produced by a studio or other closed group of vidders. As with any other kind of vidding, there are skills involved that make some MEPs better than others. For instance, a talented MEP organizer will assign more difficult or climactic song sections to vidders with proven skills, which will make it easier for her to create a strong final product.

One of the most admired MEPs in recent history is **BOHEMIAN RHAPSODY** (2016, multifandom) (Video 69 https://doi.org/10.3998/ mpub.10069132.cmp.69), a twenty-five-person collab edited by Grable424 whose participants are basically a who's who of admired YouTube vidders from literally all over the world. Pteyrx, Zurik, Loki (aka SecretlyToDream), voordeel, and many other popular vidders worked on the vid, each discreetly signing their names in the lower right-hand corner of their section. Many of these vidders are Russian or Eastern European nationals (Croatian, Ukranian, Polish); others in the group come from Sweden, Spain, Austria, Italy, Brazil, the Philippines, Australia, the United Kingdom, and of course the United States. If anything proves that vidding is now an international phenomenon, BOHEMIAN RHAPSODY does.

Like the literary vidders of old, these vidders have chosen a song with a strong narrative: Queen's rock opera is related to the heroic ballads and epic folk songs that many vidders of the past chose to use. "Bohemian Rhapsody" is an aria, a musical soliloquy that narrates a situation: "Mama, just killed a man / Put a gun against his head / Pulled my trigger, now he's dead." While in some ways these vidders are worlds away from the literary music videos of Mary Van Deusen, in other ways they're not; we see guns put against heads and triggers pulled, and eyes open on "Open your eyes." However, using a song to tell the story of the text isn't all this vid is doing. Like the Media Cannibals, the vidders of BOHEMIAN RHAPSODY are happily rummaging through fandom's archive of moving pictures, pulling out similar themes and tropes, and making patterns. Where vid like A FANNISH TAXONOMY OF HOTNESS (Video 20 https:// doi.org/10.3998/mpub.10069132.cmp.20) gives us swords, hats, cigars, eyeglasses, straightjackets, and other fetish objects, BOHEMIAN RHAPSODY gives us montages featuring apples, coins, cigarettes, hands, people standing with their faces upturned to the rain—and also swords. (Some things never change.) On a technical level, BOHEMIAN RHAPSODY is a world away from FANNISH TAXONOMY OF HOTNESS; these vidders have high-quality footage and an arsenal of tools that allow for much faster and more precise cutting. In the hands of more skillful vidders, this results in startlingly beautiful musicality. For instance, voordeel's vidding of one of the later guitar solos is masterful, with characters leaping from windows with the perfectly timed synchronicity of dancers in a Busby Berkeley musical.

Because BOHEMIAN RHAPSODY is a MEP, it is, by definition and by design, a hodgepodge; there's an auteurship to FANNISH TAXONOMY OF

HOTNESS that BOHEMIAN RHAPSODY just can't attain, however seamlessly Grable424 stitches together all the individually vidded sections. However, as a collage of smaller vids, BOHEMIAN RHAPSODY reveals much about the sensibilities of the individual vidders. Many of the participants are clearly cinephiles with a more conventional sensibility, as the vid features mainstream hits (*Fight Club, Breaking Bad, Zoolander, The Wolf of Wall Street*) alongside more traditional fannish shows like *Supernatural, Sherlock, Teen Wolf, Doctor Who*, and the MCU. The vid also has a lot of gore and violence, which can partly be explained by the song's murderous theme and the relatively short time that each vidder has (about fifteen seconds) to make an impact. That said, many sections of BOHEMIAN RHAPSODY can be seen to be amplifying the highly choreographed fights scenes and violence of mainstream culture rather than transforming or subverting them, the way vids like A FANNISH TAXONOMY OF HOTNESS or VOGUE (Video 47 https://doi.org/10.3998/mpub.10069132.cmp.47) do.

That said, some sections of BOHEMIAN RHAPSODY are speaking a more traditional, high-context vidding language. The YouTube comments clearly single out Loki/SecretlyToDream for her vidding of the section of the song that includes, "If I'm not back again this time tomorrow / Carry on, carry on / As if nothing really matters." Loki vids the first phrase to two slash pairings, Marvel's Steve Rogers/Bucky Barnes and Sherlock Holmes/John Watson of BBC's *Sherlock*, paralleling the two stories of loss (Bucky's fall from the train in *Captain America: The First Avenger,* Sherlock's fall from the roof in "The Reichenbach Fall"), then cutting to brothers Sam and Dean Winchester at the end of *Supernatural*'s season 5, where Sam falls into hell. Vidding *Supernatural* to the phrase "Carry on, carry on," has particular meaning for fans. "Carry on Wayward Son" is to *Supernatural* what "The Rose" is to *Starsky and Hutch;* it is "the closest thing *Supernatural* has to a theme song. It has been embraced by fandom and is usually sung as the final song at karaoke at *Supernatural* Conventions, and just about any time two of more SPN fans get together!"[54] A fan group called Wayward Daughters was formed to promote "positive female representation in *Supernatural* and other media, and also the idea of fans supporting each other,"[55] and *Supernatural*'s network, CW, later shot a pilot for a proposed *Supernatural* spin-off series called *Wayward Sisters.* (It's also the rejected opening of the 2010 intro vid PREVIOUSLY . . . (Video 52 https://doi.org/10.3998/mpub.10069132.cmp.52), discussed in chapter 4). The fans who watched BOHEMIAN RHAPSODY got this reference and many others. Despite the vid's fast pace, most clips have narrative and emotional significance to fans of the source texts.

Vidders like Loki, Pteryx, voordeel, pingvi, KatrinDepp, and others move between YouTube and other, often older, vidding communities. Their vids circulate to great acclaim on fannish Tumblr and Twitter feeds even as the vidders work to make their work visible on YouTube by conforming to the priorities of the algorithm and working YouTube's "engagement" functionalities—making playlists, liking and commenting, featuring other people's channels on their site, encouraging viewers to subscribe, hosting subscription challenges for others, and, perhaps most important of all, regularly uploading work. They are in contact with multiple vidding ecologies and consequently are conversant in multiple vidding styles. In a 2011 interview at the Supernatural Roundtable, a LiveJournal community, Loki discussed what she took from the various vidding groups she was participating in:

> I can't help but notice that there are two "kinds" of vidders out there. . . . There's the LJ [LiveJournal] vidding community and then there's the YT [YouTube] vidding community and somehow I clearly see the difference in the editing styles vidders try out. For example, YT vidders tend to use more effects, they kind of go crazy about it— not in a bad way :)—and I sometimes catch myself staring at the monitor, watching a video, with my mouth open, like, how did they actually do this? Technically I can imagine how, but the patience!
>
> As for the LJ vidding community—vidders here are a little bit "calmer" if I can say so. The videos are clearer, the editing a little bit simpler but it looks amazing nonetheless. For example, if it's a character study video, vidders tend to dive in into the storyline and the videos, the storyline, the thought behind it—so clear and so straight and amazing, that sometimes the videos are even better than the actual shows/films.

Loki concludes by describing how she has been influenced by both styles:

> At the beginning I kind of wanted to throw into the video whatever effect I could find, like, if it looked cool I'd probably use it, even though if sometimes it wasn't actually that cool. . . . After this phase I kind of went through "calm" phase, when I used a lot of simple editing, my videos were clearer and simpler but I hope not more boring lol I started trying my hands on showing my perception of particular moments in the source I was vidding. And after it I decided to stop somewhere in between I think.[56]

Imagistic Vidding and GIF Sets

While vidders like Loki, Grable424, and KatrinDepp manage to straddle multiple vidding cultures, others are moving toward what could be seen as extremes. For instance, some YouTube vidders have moved increasingly away from fandom's narratives and context and are instead vidding almost pure imagery, almost entirely self-expressively. The result is a kind of audiovisual poetry, a moving musical painting much like experimental art video.

This kind of vidding can be seen as one outgrowth of vidding's emphasis on raccord; for instance, for the second round of pingvi's 2015 Test Your Skills vidding contest, Grable424 submitted a masterfully edited multifandom vid called TESSELLATE (2015). (Video 70 https://doi.org/10.3998/mpub.10069132.cmp.70). The challenge theme was "chemistry," and vidders were asked to "make a video using given elements and create your own video formula." An alphabetized list of thirty elements was distributed to participants, starting with "blood, breaking object, clock, crying, dancing" and ending with "sky, smile, waking up, water, weapon." Grable's submission has the following formula:

(hand) + (falling object) ×2 + (fire) ×4 + (breaking object) + (clock) + (hand) ×2 + (weapon) ×3 + (hitting) ×3 + (breaking object) ×2 + (clock) + (scream) + (crying) ×3 + (breaking object) + (drowning) ×5 + (weapon) + (blood) ×2 + (hitting) + (blood) ×3 + (mirror) ×2 + (fire) + (door) + (eye) + (hand) ×6 + (glass) + (hand) + (musical instrument) ×2 + (hand) + (leg) ×3 + (dancing) ×3 + (kissing) ×3 + (hand) + (crying) + (scream) + (crying) + (clock) + (waking up) + (clock) + (waking up) ×2 + (falling person) + (clock) + (fire) ×4 + (explosion) ×5 + (scream) + (musical instrument) + (dancing) + (musical instrument) + (dancing) ×4 + (glass) ×6 + (eyes) + (flower) ×6 + (scream) ×2 + (crying) + (hand) ×2 + (crying) + (hand) + (glass) ×2 + (eyes) + (hand) + (eyes) + (falling person) + (hand) + (falling person) ×5 + (weapon) ×6 + (shooting) + (blood) + (weapon) ×6 + (laughing) ×4 + (smile) + (hitting) ×3 + (blood) + (sky) + (water) ×5 + (glass) ×4 + (falling person) + (falling object) ×2 + (breaking object) + (falling object) + (breaking object) ×3 + (water)×5 + (weapon) ×12 + (clock) + (running) ×6 + (scream) + (crying) + (kissing) ×2 + (running) ×2 + (sky) + (running) + (door) ×2[57]

Admittedly this formula was produced to meet an editing challenge, and Grable424 used fifty or so sources to make the vid, mostly in recognizable and popular fandoms like *Game of Thrones, Jessica Jones, Harry Potter, Hannibal, Teen Wolf,* and *Star Wars.* However, this is a different way of thinking about vidding—or rather, a way very different from Mary Van Deusen's directive to look at the words of a song and then free-associate about Captain Kirk. The vidders in this challenge are being explicitly challenged to think in shapes and symbols; they are creating a kind of visual poetry by moving from like to like to like. Grable424 is a smart enough vidder that she chose in "Tessellate" a song that explicitly uses geometry and form as a metaphor. Like other experimental video makers—or like painters, for that matter—these vidders can take us on a journey that affects us emotionally. Yet there is a danger that without a strong engagement with the fannish source text or strong point of view from the artist, the poetry of rhyming imagery can devolve into mere doggerel: clock, fire, explosions.

That said, vidding that uses mass media images as both paint and canvas can be as exciting as the very best of experimental cinema, and communities have emerged both on YouTube and on Instagram (where the work is even more imagistic, typically running less than thirty seconds) that explicitly encourage the work of these filmmakers. As I noted in the introduction, many of the younger people who vid in this style have been immersed in the archive of moving pictures since they were children. They were given access to video editing tools right after their first set of crayons, and they have learned to express themselves through manipulating images the way others might write, paint, or draw. As with fanfiction, vidding is a place where creative people can develop as artists. In fandom, you're not considered strange if you want to write or draw or edit video; in fandom, the cry is always "Give us more!" and not "Go away!" While most fans make things simply to satisfy the human hunger to make art, others realize that they're also cultivating skills that have value in the marketplace—or, as with fanfiction, fandom becomes an artistic outlet for women who are already using their skills at work. They vid so that they can make anything they want without commercial restraint. On YouTube, you see commonly see descriptors like "communications designer," "graphic designer," or "video editor" in vidder bios.

On the other side of the spectrum are fandom's GIF set makers, who use some, though not all, of the skills of vidders to many of the same ends. While imagistic vidders are dropping narrative context for the joys of pure form, GIF makers have dropped music and the idea of audiovisual synchronization are instead remaking the stories they love one frame at a time. A GIF is a small moving image of a couple of frames.

It is something more than Laura Mulvey's stilled image; it's enough to capture a movement, a moment. Many vidders—or people who in past eras would have become vidders—are using their discerning fannish eye to make GIFs that isolate, emphasize, and fetishize particular filmic moments, like a significant look or the touch of a hand. See, for example, the *Wonder Woman* GIF, "First Touch, Last Touch" (2017), by Wizhard, which shows, in split screen, the parallel gesture of Diana touching Steve Trevor's face for the first and last time. (See Clip 9. https://doi. org/10.3998/mpub.10069132.cmp.166) This, like vidding, is a way of getting you to see as the fan sees, for she who controls the edit controls the interpretation.

Beyond this, some fans make more elaborate GIFs and combine them into GIF sets, typically of four, six, or eight. Some sets serve the same functionality as old-school slash vidding: they edit together shots to draw a relationship out of the text, emphasizing its importance. In "Just by Your Touch You Make Me Forget the Rest of the World" (2018) (Clip 10 https://doi.org/10.3998/mpub.10069132.cmp.167), lesbiansassemble makes a GIF set that collects significant touches between Steve Rogers and Bucky Barnes of the MCU. One could easily imagine this as the skeleton of a vid. Instead, lesbiansassemble creates what she calls a "lyric poem" by means of her title. Other GIF set makers inscribe text right over the images—usually poetry, either quotes from other fan or professional writers, or written by the fan herself.

Some fans go even further, creating GIFs from frames across television and film and then piecing those GIFs together to form micromovies. By matching color, framing, sight lines, and other formal filmic properties, GIF set makers create entirely new stories, building them up frame by frame. One example is the Wholock (a *Doctor Who* and BBC's *Sherlock* crossover) story by Doomslock wherein *Doctor Who*'s Rose Tyler talks to *Sherlock*'s John Watson (Figure 21 https://doi.org/10.3998/mpub.10069132.cmp.157). Doomslock has cut and lit the GIFs from both shows so as to put the two characters into conversation. Color-coded, subtitled dialogue tells us the new story: one where both Sherlock and the Doctor have been kidnapped.

I've called this six-celled cinema,[58] or film in a petri dish: a new organism that's clearly growing, and growing fast. "When did you last see Sherlock?" is a relatively simple example of the genre, with only a few frames in each GIF and a dark background that isolates the figures, so the vidder can easily make them match. However, GIF sets have gotten increasingly more complicated. Consider the story that PrettiestCaptain

Fig. 21. "When Did You Last See Sherlock?" by Doomslock (c. 2012, Wholock [*Doctor Who* and BBC's *Sherlock* crossover]).

tells in a *Sherlock* and MCU crossover. (See Clip 11. https://doi. org/10.3998/mpub.10069132.cmp.168) In this Avengelock GIF set (c. 2012), each individual GIF is about thirty-seven frames, and most have two or three cuts. The story features Tony Stark coming to the office of DI Lestrade to apologize for the fact that Thor and his lightning have destroyed Big Ben. Tony sits down opposite Lestrade, and they have a conversation invented by PrettiestCaptain, which is plausibly illustrated by the frames she has pieced together: "God, not you again, Stark." "Come on, Lestrade. I already said I'm sorry for that little accident." "Sorry? Little? You and your thunder buddy destroyed Big Ben!" At this point the GIF cuts to Thor, who appears to be calling down lightning to strike Big Ben. "Really very sorry?" Tony hedges. "Out!" Lestrade shouts. "Right," Tony says.

GIF sets have continued to increase in complexity. By 2015, fan mrgaretcarter could make a three-part, twenty-four-panel modern-day Peggy Carter (as in Captain America's girlfriend) alternate universe using footage featuring performances by MCU actors Hayley Atwell, Chris Evans, and others in other, non-MCU roles. (See excerpt, Clip 12. https://doi.org/10.3998/mpub.10069132.cmp.169) Mrgaretcarter uses that footage to piece together a story where Peggy Carter is de-aged and rejoins modern-day S.H.I.E.L.D., and she and Cap resume their relationship. Each GIF in mrgaretcarter's three-part series is crammed with frames, as many as 240. This makes some of the panels run a bit too fast for ideal comprehension, but mrgaretcarter is trying to tell a complex tale that features a network of relationships and friendships, all of which have ups and downs.

In this example, fans strip moving pictures down to their component frames and build them up again into something new, just like Kandy Fong did with her individual *Star Trek* frames more than forty years ago—and some of these mini movies are more radical than anything that Hollywood is dishing out. Consider the phenomenon of so-called chromatic recasting, or (re)casting TV and film with actors of color, which fan GIF storytellers have taken up with enthusiasm. How about a James Bond movie that stars not only Idris Elba as Bond but also Viola Davis as Q? Wouldn't Morgan Freeman make a great Gandalf? What about Cardi B as Harley Quinn? What about a Bollywood Star Wars with Ranbir Kapoor as Luke Skywalker? The real-life casting of Noma Dumezweni as Hermione Granger,[59] of Lashana Lynch as 007, and of Halle Bailey as Ariel in *The Little Mermaid* owes something to the creative imaginations of GIF makers.

Inclusion, Exclusion, and Celebration

But is this vidding? As remix culture expands, as traditions mix, as new tools are released and new forms of creativity are invented and practiced in fan communities, where do we draw the line—or should we even draw lines at all? There are some who feel that the term "vidding" should encompass all forms of fan-made remix video, including not just the particular strand of live-action fan music videos whose history I have been outlining throughout this book, but also AMVs, fan-made trailers, Bollywood epics, Asian vids of Korean-, Chinese-, and Japanese-language sources, video game vids, promos, hype videos and sports highlight reels, political remixes, book trailers, and many other forms. In 2009, vidder bop_radar hosted an energetic and wide-ranging discussion, "On Inclusion and Exclusion in Vidding Fandom," part of which focused on the very definition of "vidding." One commenter to the discussion said, "To me if you manipulate and rearrange video shots (from any source) to create a new work that's vidding." Another fan countered that vidding, as she understood it,

> is predominantly female, and carries with it a particularly female aesthetic. Not that we're a monolith, of course, but there are trends (emphasis on slash, focus on relationships, eroticization of male vulnerability, etc.). It's a particular form that remixes popular culture in a way that appeals to the female id, possibly to the gay id, in a way that mainstream popular culture doesn't.
>
> If you insist that this particular form—genre, if you will—has no boundaries and is just like every other possibility of putting clips to music, then inevitably what happens is that the values and aesthetics of a historically oppressed subculture get erased—again. If you change the meaning of the words we use to define ourselves, you literally make it impossible to talk about ourselves separately.

It was argued that this position was exclusionary: "It's exactly this sort of thing that makes people feel excluded—whether it's because they're a guy and people are going on and on about vidding being a 'female' tradition, or whether it's because they've made a vid that is reverential rather than 'commenting on' the source."[60] But these were the very terms that vidders use to describe and distinguish themselves: a feminine aesthetic, a transformative rather than reverential take on the source. Where does self-definition end and boundary policing begin? This was discussed in another exchange: "Why focus on the differences when we have so much in common?" one fan asked. The reply: "Because we don't have so much in common. And the differences are ones that are valuable to us. Namely, a particular appeal to female interests, and female erotic interests, that have been historically suppressed and denied. And when you insist that we talk about it all as one, you're suggesting that this category doesn't matter."[61]

However, the category clearly matters to many. Much of Katherina Freund's work is about these definitional conversations; see the aptly titled "I Thought I Made a Vid, but Then You Told Me That I Didn't: Aesthetics and Boundary Work in the Fan-Vidding Community." Freund notes that many vidders occupy a position of being "supportive of other new media forms but simultaneously protective of their particular community as a female-dominated and critical response to media texts."[62] That protective element has been there from the start; as I have described throughout this book, live-action fan vidders have taken various steps to preserve their history. From Flamingo's compilation of "*Starsky & Hutch Historical Vids*" to the annual Vividcon history show to bradcpu's Vidder Profiles[63] to the practice of remastering beloved vids with high-quality footage, fans have documented and celebrated their work.

In the wake of the 2007 call to activism, that effort has only increased in ambition and scope. Vids were included as their own category in the 24/7 DIY Video Summit. Vids were showcased alongside mainstream music videos in *Spectacle: The Music Video* (2012–13), a traveling exhibition seen at the Museum of the Moving Image in New York as well as other venues. Vidding took its place alongside collage, remix, and other appropriation arts in the Vancouver Art Gallery's giant multimedia exhibition *Mashup: The Birth of Modern Culture* (2016). Vids now adorn gallery walls, with contextualizing little white cards next to them. (See Image R, https://doi.org/10.3998/mpub.10069132.cmp.189 and Image S, https://doi.org/10.3998/mpub.10069132.cmp.190) This book is just the latest entry in what has become a long and distinguished bibliography.

If vidders have been aggressive about mythologizing their history, it is perhaps because they know what happened to the women of early cinema and television: they were written out of the story once those media grew respectable. In 2000, independent director Allison Anders convened the Women Filmmaker's Summit at the Miramar, a hotel in Santa Barbara, a mere fifteen minutes down the road from the Escapade convention. Anders invited one hundred women to talk about the problems facing women filmmakers and to rehearse the history of "the female pioneers who had shaped the business."[64] That history had been lost to the community. According to Cari Beauchamp, Anders was moved to convene the summit "when she learned that Dorothy Davenport Reid, an acclaimed director in the 1920s, had died in obscurity 50 years later, 'practically in my backyard in Woodland Hills.'"[65] The vidders who organized at Escapade made sure that newer vidders—and the journalists and scholars who interviewed them—knew the names of Kandy Fong, Diana Barbour, Kendra Hunter, Mary Van Deusen, and others.

That's not to say that this history, or any history, is complete or inclusive; it isn't. The history of vidding that has been rehearsed, that this book draws on, is biased toward vidders who have made vids in many fandoms (and thus had the chance to become known outside their individual fannish subcultures[66]) and vidders who have been making work over some number of years. But, partial and incomplete as it is, this history is important. Vidding as a way of seeing mass media differently—subversively, critically, erotically—is a tradition worth preserving.

Ain't I a Woman? Vidding Race

As I argued in chapter 2, the vidding culture that I have been tracing has its roots in the 1970s. Just as fanfiction comes out of the social science fiction (often feminist, often lesbian feminist[67]) of the late 1960s and early 1970s, vidding grew in the same feminist soil that brought us Laura Mulvey and Dara Birnbaum. But the limitations of second-wave feminism have become evident, particularly in terms of race, and a generation of black feminist scholars have subsequently developed a more intersectional feminist analysis. However, the failures of second-wave feminism can still be seen in fan culture,[68] which has developed highly sophisticated genres, tropes, and techniques for thinking through sex and gender in fan works, but has not done comparably sophisticated work rethinking issues of race. While fan works (fanfiction, fan art, vids) fill some representational absences, often radically transforming the gender and sexual politics of mass media, they too often leave the problematic structures of race intact.

That's not to say that vidding has entirely ignored race. Many vids discussed in this book or its online appendix feature characters of color (**SO PURE** [Video 76 https://doi.org/10.3998/mpub.10069132.cmp.76], BRICK HOUSE [Video 48 https://doi.org/10.3998/mpub.10069132. cmp.48]) or make race-based critiques of the source text ("WHITE" AND NERDY [Video 62 https://doi.org/10.3998/mpub.10069132.cmp.62], HOW MUCH IS THAT GEISHA IN THE WINDOW [Video 64 https://doi. org/10.3998/mpub.10069132.cmp.64]), and I do not wish to ignore the many fans of color who make vids and other transformative works.[69] As Benjamin Woo points out, various metrics indicate that between 10 and 33 percent of fans belong to visible-minority groups, though many accounts of fan studies fail to point this out.[70] At the same time, the larger repertoire of vids plainly replicates, rather than alters, the depictions of race in the mass media, which reproduces the racist values of mainstream Western culture.

This blindness in fandom has historically been replicated in studies of fandom. As Abigail De Kosnik notes in her introduction to *Transformative Works and Cultures'* special issue on race, "Fan studies was meant to center people and practices that most Western institutions have long treated as marginal, insignificant, and invisible. But while fan studies has practiced inclusivity in various ways, most notably in its foregrounding of how gender and sexuality operate in fan sites and communities, the perspectives of people of color have not been widely represented or analyzed in fan scholarship to date."[71] Rebecca Wanzo has argued that race disturbs traditional genealogies of fan studies, noting that if the early 1990s gave us *Textual Poachers* (1992), *Enterprising Women* (1991), and *The Adoring Audience* (1992), it also gave us bell hooks's *Black Looks: Race and Representation* (1992), with its chapter[72] on the oppositional gaze of the black female spectator. That essay has not been taken up by fan studies scholars in the same way as those other works, but if we take it as a foundational text, we might conclude that some vidders and vid fans of color (and their allies) take pleasure in reading against the grain and resisting culturally dominant images in ways that overlap with, but are not identical to, the practices of white vidders.

Vidding frequently remakes sexist and homophobic media for the pleasure of the (queer/female) spectator, but vidders rarely think to apply their skills to transforming racist media, or to consider the (queer/female) fan of color who also has her desires marginalized— often doubly or triply marginalized. Vidders tailor-make (and improve) otherwise two-dimensional mass media characters, but leave characters of color on the shelf to everyone's detriment. Worse, some fans will attack or blame those who dare critique or complain about the state of things. But if we take hooks's point as stipulated, then to frame fans or aca-fans who make race-based critiques as (in Wanzo's phrase) "race theorist killjoys, sucking the pleasure out of fan studies by demanding the inclusion of race analysis"[73] is actually to overlook a key axis of fan practice in general and of vidding in particular: that of oppositional reading and media critique. And we have the vids to prove it. (See "Spotlight on: Vidding Characters of Color" in the online appendix.)

Vids about race take pleasure in creating rhythmic, aesthetic critiques both of the mass media and of fan cultures. For example, the bitterly satirical vid ENTER THE WU TANG CLAN: 36 CHAMBERS OF DEATH (2009) by hapex_legomena[74] was made from footage from the Lord of the Rings film franchise but is actually about the ways in which white people in fandom perceive themselves as besieged by swarms of dark, nonhuman creatures. The four-part vid is an elaborate metaphor in which black fans, symbolized as the various faceless armies in Peter Jackson's Lord of the Rings trilogy (who are mostly played by nonwhite actors) attempt to overwhelm white science fiction and fantasy fandom, as symbolized by those whom we might term "the good white peoples of Middle-earth"— that is, the (white) main cast of the film. Although the video source is technically Lord of the Rings, this is not really a Lord of the Rings vid. In fact, in her artist's notes, hapex_legomena warns only for "Spoilers for RaceFAIL '09"—that is, spoilers for a real historical event in which fans of color and their allies engaged in a public debate about racism. Indeed, the vid's central metaphor may have been suggested by some of abusive language used against BIPOC and other race-critical voices during the RaceFail debates because among other insults, fans of color were called "trolls" and "nithings." In her essay, "Thinky Thoughts: A Semi-organized Post Including a Lurker's Belated Thoughts on RaceFail," which accompanied the final "collector's edition" version of the vid, hapex_legomena explains that during discussions like RaceFail, in which "PoC who dare to try to argue their point are labeled irrational, savage, illiterate, elitist, talentless, whiny, drug-addled, backwards, hyper-sexual, emasculated, hyper-masculine, kamikaze jihadists crashing into the ivory tower of clueless people's pure and unsullied beliefs," she is reminded both of Toni Morrison's *Beloved* (the quote she provides includes, "White people believed that whatever the manners, under every dark skin was a jungle") and of the music of the Wu-Tang Clan, "who habitually refer to themselves as the Killa Beez in and out of their lyrics," and who released an album called "The Swarm." The Wu-Tang Clan turns the dehumanized metaphor of "swarming" into a sense of power: We're everywhere, you can't stop us, we're coming for you. Hapex_legomena connects that idea to the epic fantasy world of Lord of the Rings, using hip-hop to transform J. R. R. Tolkien and Jackson's armies of nonwhite creatures into both a revolutionary force and a white person's paranoid fantasy.

Race-Critical Vidding

There are two main race-based critiques of vids and vidding culture, both of which involve failures of what we might otherwise see as vidding's core strengths. First, vidders are experts at creating romances and relationships, but white vidders all too rarely construct or emphasize romances featuring characters of color, black characters in particular. This is not simply because there has historically been a dearth of characters of color in cult science fiction and fantasy media, though there has been. But vidders are geniuses at making something out of nothing; it's what they do. So it has to be significant when vidders, experts at isolating longing looks or the significant brush of a hand, see neither subtext nor text when it comes to characters of color. As Cait Coker and Rukmini Pande have pointed out, white fandom seems to go out of its way to avoid what would otherwise be obvious pairings,[75] be they het, slash, or femslash, when one of the characters is of color. Yes, there are vids shipping Spock and Uhura, or MCU's Steve Rogers and Sam Wilson—but not many, and certainly not as many as there are about white characters, even relatively minor white characters. A rare counterexample is blithesea's TOO GOOD TO BE TRUE (2007, *Stargate: Atlantis*) (Video 71 https://doi.org/10.3998/ mpub.10069132.cmp.71), which painstakingly constructs an on-screen romance between Rodney McKay (a white character) and Ronon Dex (a character of color) by manipulating the footage to create scenes that never happened.

This relates to the second critique: that vidders, who are expert at bringing background characters to the foreground, rarely do this in order to showcase marginalized characters of color. To be fair, this can be difficult; characters of color are rarely well framed or properly lit, and it's only recently that this has even been noticed by white people as an issue.[76] The racism in filmmaking, as in fandom, is pervasive, in content and form alike. But that can't be the end of the argument. If vidders can make fantastic vids about secondary characters like Harry Potter's Neville Longbottom or the women of *Supernatural*, if they can show us a one-night stand between two female characters who aren't even on the same show,[77] then they can make vids about characters of color using the same techniques. But as thingswithwings pointed out in a tweetstorm, this might require a change in aesthetic priorities. After noting that historically it's been "true that to make the slickest, most beautifully framed vid, you have to focus on cis white able-bodied male characters," thingswithwings then adds, "therefore I advise AGAINST prioritizing slickness in vids. The most beautiful shots you have to work with will almost always be white dudes. If you want to make vids about underrepresented minorities, you'll have to massage the footage and accept crappier shots."[78] In response to these tweets, some vidders talked strategy—for example, getting high-definition footage so as to crop the shots to better frame characters of color.

But racism isn't a technical problem, or vidders would have hacked it by now. Vidding culture, like fan culture, feminist culture, queer culture, *culture*, is made of people, so racism is structural and deep rooted. That said, fandom's relative weakness in terms of race is a conversation that fandom has had, and continues to have, with itself. In 2002, Te, an influential fan of color, founded a site called Remember Us devoted to promoting fan works about characters of color. The site's tag line is "Do not adjust your monitors. The color is just fine." A subpage, "Dreaming in Color," features vid recs. In her "Manifesto," Te writes:

> I want people to think about what they're doing when they're canni-balizing media. To consider the reasons—whatever they may be—why they leave the darker characters to rot on the big buffet of fandom as they consume everything White. I want people to feel just as comfort-able objectifying Adebisi [an inmate played by black actor Adewale Akinnuoye-Agbaje on HBO's prison drama *Oz*] as they do Keller [an inmate played by white actor Christopher Meloni]. I want people to acclimatize themselves to the idea of characters of color being valid objects of lust/affection/whatever.[79]

Fans have engaged in this kind of race-based activism over the years, often as a response to a race-based failure either in transformative works fandom (fanfiction, fan art, vidding) or in the broader SFF community. A significant failure resulted in RaceFail '09, alluded to above, which was a more than three-month public argument about race[80] that involved not only a variety of fan communities but also many professional science fiction and fantasy authors. Pande argues that RaceFail was "the first time in online fandom's history when SF/F's racist and imperialist character-izations were debated in a forum where authors and editors of SF/F mag-azines and journals had to engage with those questions,"[81] and also "the first time that alliances between non-white fans were made across forums and platforms."[82] So while some might frame RaceFail '09 as a disrup-tion of community, for fans of color, RaceFail '09 was a transformative event that built a community. N. K. Jemisin, the first African American writer to win the Hugo award for best SF novel, and the first person ever to win it three years in a row, later wrote an essay celebrating the event: "Why I Think RaceFail Was the Bestest Thing Evar for SFF."[83] Elizabeth Ebony Thomas and Amy Stornaiuolo have described how black girls and women organized online afterward, "to connect with other fans, advocate for more and better representation, and even create their own alternatives to popular culture."[84] Fans concerned with social justice have tried to increase the visibility of characters of color through advocacy efforts like Dark Agenda, an attempt to "increase the representation of international, non-English, non-Western fandoms in multi-fandom fic, art and vid exchanges and festivals, as well as promote the responsible writing of characters of colour," and Racebending, a LiveJournal community that developed into "an international grassroots organization of media consumers that advocates for underrepresented groups in entertainment media."[85]

In 2009, Vividcon held an IDIC challenge (IDIC is the Vulcan philosophy of "infinite diversity in infinite combinations") that some hoped would produce vids that showcase diversity. But it didn't; most vidders chose to interpret the theme in other (and in one or two cases highly problematic) ways. In the wake of that failure, there was a public conversation, with Laura Shapiro pointing out the ways in which Vividcon and other fan cons have been "a very safe space for white women in the past, where our gaze is privileged, our opinions are valued, and our sexuality and our bodies are celebrated and safe."[86] But she challenged the con to do better for fans of color. The next year, vidders talitha78 and Deepa D, an Indian fan whose essay, "I Didn't Dream of Dragons," about the dominating whiteness and Eurocentrism of fantasy novels, was an important touchstone in RaceFail '09, curated a vid show called "Race and Representation" and held a panel afterward.

Some socially conscious and/or activist vidders now organize around Wiscon, a long-standing feminist science fiction convention held in Madison, Wisconsin. Since 2010, the Wiscon vid party has become a place to premiere new work, particularly vids that move intersectionally across issues of gender, sexuality, race, disability, and class. The hope was that "having a premieres show associated with Wiscon may, in time, lead to a 'Wiscon vidding aesthetic.'"[87] In fact, some fans have begun to talk about such an aesthetic: vids "created by vidders fluent in the VVC [Vividcon] house style, but they have the DNA of academic research projects in them as well."[88] Vidders interested in the critical aspect of vids have interrogated the line between vids and videographic criticism;[89] for instance, Lori Morimoto made **HANNIBAL: A FANVID** (2016) a "fanvid(eographic essay),"[90] and published it in the online journal *In Transition*. Vidding has been brought into the classroom both as a form of criticism and as a pedagogical approach.[91] There is even talk of a new genre, the database vid, which sifts through large amounts of footage looking for patterns, often beyond what the eye can see or the mind can process.

The term "database vid" was coined by Julie Levin Russo, who vids as Cyborganize, based on Lev Manovich's idea of database cinema. As Russo explains, she adopted "a taxonomic logic that parallels Manovich's description of *Man with a Movie Camera:* 'the process of relating shots to each other, ordering and reordering them in order to discover the hidden order of the world constitutes the film's method. . . . [It] traverses its database in a particular order to construct an argument.'" Russo was also influenced by the remix video genre of the supercut, which simply collects instances of a thing across an archive of cinema, like every use of the word "fuck" in *Scarface* and every lightsaber power-up across the Star Wars saga. As a result, vids like Cyborganize's TRANSMISSION (2018) (Video 73 https://doi.org/10.3998/mpub.10069132.cmp.73), which collects together images of Amazons and their home of Themyscira throughout the Wonder Woman canon and other media, and eruthros's **STRAIGHTENING UP THE HOUSE** (2018),[92] a vid about queer erasure when Marvel comics are translated to Marvel films, are as much digital humanities projects as music videos. Both are accompanied by essays that supplement their intellectual projects. They are also almost casually intersectional. In TRANSMISSION, Themyscira is an explicitly diverse utopia, and Cyborganize concludes with tag lines both from Rita Mae Brown's "Sappho's Reply" ("An army of lovers shall not fail") and Frida Kahlo ("Pies para qué los quiero si tengo alas pa' volar"). STRAIGHTENING UP THE HOUSE is a four-minute rebuttal of *Guardians of the Galaxy* director James Gunn's assertion that "there are probably, you know, gay characters in the Marvel universe, you know, we just don't know who they are yet." But we do know, because gay characters have been a feature of Marvel comics for years, and eruthros proves this by compiling a vast array of queer characters of all races, creeds, and colors. Both TRANSMISSION and STRAIGHTENING UP THE HOUSE, to paraphrase Russo, arise from the database and construct new databases: they create a dense assemblage of images that "assumes access to the most basic interactive video technology: the pause button."[93] Here at the end, we are back to where we started: with the pause button, the single frame, the stilled image as a way of disrupting the propulsive force of narratives and shifting power relations.

Things have improved somewhat when it comes to vidding race, partly because of fan advocacy efforts like the ones I've been discussing, and partly because the larger cultural conversation about race and representation has affected Hollywood a little. Marvel made billions from *Black Panther*, and forthcoming Marvel movies now include a reboot of *Blade* and *Shang-Chi and the Legend of the Ten Rings*, though how the death of Chadwick Boseman and the disruption of shooting schedules due to the Covid-19 pandemic will affect the production of these more diverse blockbusters remains to be seen. But even without these films, there is now enough beautiful footage featuring characters of color in the kind of roles cult media fans love that vidder bironic could make THE GREATEST (Video 74 https://doi.org/10.3998/mpub.10069132.cmp.74), a vid "reveling in the bad-ass wonderfulness of characters of color in SF/F/horror TV and movies of the last 3–5 years." Made at the request of a fan named resolute for the 2017–18 Fandom Trumps Hate charity auction, the vid debuted at the 2018 Wiscon vid party and took first fandom, then the world, by storm; it was a finalist for a 2019 Webby award in the category of remixes and mashups. Crowdsourced by "an army of fan-friends," including many well-known vidders, THE GREATEST includes over a hundred fandoms with central characters of color: from *American Gods*, *Black Panther*, *The Cloverfield Paradox*, and *The Dark Tower* all the way to *A Wrinkle in Time*, *The Walking Dead*, *Z for Zachariah*, and *Z Nation*. Bironic, whose vid STARSHIPS was showcased in the Vancouver Art Gallery's MashUp exhibition, has a particular gift for joyful multi-fandom vids, and it's moving to see a long, fast-cut vid not only made up entirely of characters of color (hundreds of them!) but the kind of wildly heroic genre fiction characters that fandom loves and that exemplify Sia's refrain: "I'm free to be the greatest / I'm alive / I got stamina." It is 4:27 minutes of fabulous power walks, hero shots, bold looks, and big emotions, with characters of color finally getting, en masse, to experience the wonders of saving the world and exploring the universe. There is also love: bironic ends the vid with a montage of hugs and kisses, loving families and sexy relationships, het and slash. Bironic also released the vid with a subtitle track that identifies the characters and shows, so the vid also functions as a recruiter vid for stories featuring diverse characters. Recruiting fans and creating demand can change what gets made.

As fans of all colors vid Idris Elba, Gina Torres, Lucy Liu, Jason Momoa, Anthony Mackie, and other actors of color in their heroic roles, Hollywood seems finally to be realizing that Tessa Thompson, Mahershala Ali, Lupita Nyong'o, John Boyega, Daniel Kaluuya, and Michael B. Jordan are A-list stars. Television is dominated by showrunners like Shonda Rhimes and Donald Glover; as I noted in chapter 4, Rhimes's *Scandal* is an enormous vidding fandom on YouTube. However, fandoms with black protagonists or majority black participants are still segregated in many ways, and differences in genre are not enough to account for it. Kristen Warner has written about the ways in which media fandom and fan studies have ignored or marginalized black women's fan activity, focusing in particular on the creative work black female fans have done in transforming *Scandal*'s protagonist, Olivia Pope, into "a culturally specific black character"[94]—that is, the same sort of creative fixing and remaking in terms of race that white female fans have historically done with gender and sexuality. Writing in 2015, Warner could say, with some fairness, that "few people realize that Black women take part in fandom at all."[95] However, today, Black Twitter, Black Tumblr, Black Geek Girls, Nerds of Color, and other fans of color are being heard, even in mainstream fan spaces like Comic-Con.

Perhaps the biggest factor in the increasing diversification of the media is the rise of streaming television. To convince consumers to spend $10 a month, services like Netflix, Hulu, Amazon Prime, and their competitors are not only opening "television's gates to historically excluded voices" in terms of race, gender, sexuality, and disability (for a season or two, anyway[96]) but are also importing a diverse array of international movies and television shows. These include British country house dramas, Danish spy thrillers, and Spanish comedies, but also works from Korea, China, Taiwan, and Japan. Asian media—including anime and manga, as well as the fan subs, *doujinshi*, fanfiction, and AMVs made by fans—has always been the enormous fandom next door, and today it is bolstered by the surge of C-, K-, and J-drama, much of which is SFF inflected. Although there has always been some crossover between Western and Eastern fandoms, there's now more than ever before. No longer does a fan have to go to extraordinary lengths to get access to these shows (or study Japanese, as many fans once did). Today, viddable shows like South Korea's *Chicago Typewriter* (2017) or like Chinese fantasy dramas *Guardian* (2018) or *The Untamed* (2019) arrive, already subtitled, streaming on Netflix or Viki. There are signs that streaming is in the process of further diversification,[97] commissioning or distributing stories from different cultures, races, and filmmaking traditions.

That said, there is always the danger that this diversification might result only in nichification, stopping new fandoms from having the same impact as the fandoms of old, like the Star Trek franchise or *Starsky and Hutch*. Fandom relies on the creative energies not of the individual but of the group, and the audience is increasingly fragmented in this age of streaming. It's hard for collective energy to form when we're all watching different things at different times. Time-shifting and binge watching have been joined by a sped-up cycle of mass media entertainment. It's no longer this year's big movie or this season's show; it's this weekend's movie and this week's new show—and if you haven't seen it within twenty-four hours of its drop, well, too bad; you've missed it, you'll be spoiled, and everyone will have seen it and moved on. This tends to result in a winner-take-all system (or perhaps it's a Disney-take-all system), where every fandom has to have its own theme park. However, I have great confidence in fans' ability to connect with each other over stories they love, both big and small. Fans have always found like-minded people to make art with, and the recent explosion of fannish energy around Asian dramas can be seen as an optimistic case study for both continuity and change.

The State of the Art

Most of the vidding communities discussed in this chapter are alive and well. Fans who like to watch vids on a big screen can still attend vid shows at fandom-specific conventions, or go to VidUKon or Wiscon (though these were mostly held online in 2020 because of the Covid-19 pandemic). Escapade held a joyful thirtieth anniversary weekend in February 2020, just before lockdowns were announced, though MediaWest's fortieth anniversary convention, scheduled for May 2020, was canceled for lack of attendance even before the pandemic,[98] and the last Vividcon was held in August 2018. However, it's no longer necessary to fly across the country or around the world if you want to gorge yourself on vids, so conventions are having to reimagine themselves. Some of the Vividcon organizers launched a new convention, FanWorks, the integrative purpose of which tells us a lot about the state of things. The FanWorks convention has five tracks—writing, video, audio, art and crafting, and community—and the video track focuses not only on vids but also on AMVs, machinima, fan trailers, reaction videos, fan films, cosplay videos,[99] and supercuts. (GIF sets are part of the art and crafting track.) At the same time, FanWorks will preserve many of Vividcon's most popular features, including a premiere show followed by discussion, and a dance party. The shows will also be broadcast digitally, so fans around the world can stream the vids. VidUKon 2020 was held online using software developed by vidder Lithium Doll, and featured vid shows, panels, and chats. It even offered a new collaborative element enabled by technology: a three-hour group vidding workshop. The Festivids annual vid exchange continues to delight.

YouTube vidders continue to make new work and to fight takedowns, though fighting the machine continues to be grueling and dispiriting. There is a sense among video makers of various kinds that YouTube is—well, no longer for us. Having already prioritized monetizable content over noncommercial video, YouTube is now chasing even bigger money—and alienating small, original content creators in the process. The result is that YouTube looks more and more like television and less and less like the Internet, let alone fandom. Although as of this writing there is not yet a good solution to the problem of vid hosting, I believe that the future of fandom will be federated; that is, that fandom will use its greatest resource—its enormous network of people—to power a decentralized Internet, including distributed video hosting. That technology (Dat, SSB, ActivityPub, PeerTube) is nascent but developing. For the moment, however, we still have millions of vids on YouTube—if you know where to look. Direct links or embeds from your home fannish community will still be your best bet when it comes to finding vids you like.

Today's vidders, like the vidders that came before them, are telling their own stories and developing their own theories and critical apparatus, which they share via vids and video essays, much as film criticism in the age of YouTube has flourished via the visual essay. There is a vast array of vidding meta on YouTube.[100] It includes filmed panels on vidding; Q&As with famous vidders;[101] tips, tutorials, and demonstrations of technique; software evaluations; recommendations of underrated vidders; advice for avoiding takedowns; compilations of best vids of the year; documentaries about vidding;[102] and, of course, vids about vidding. (See "Spotlight: Vids about Vidding" in the online appendix.) Vidding today may be too big to ever support the kind of canon that vidders rehearsed in the predigital age, but individual communities still showcase their best work and their stars. Vidders who started in the early days of YouTube (2007–9) are now grandes dames, though many are still only in their twenties, and they are vidding their own stories through memes like "My vidding journey so far," "What vidding means to me," or "Why I am a vidder." YouTube vidder LullabyProductions made an emotional vid called **WE ARE THE HEART OF THE VIDDING COMMUNITY** (2013) (Video 75 https://doi.org/10.3998/mpub.10069132.cmp.75) to celebrate what vidding means to her, and her description would likely resonate with generations of vidders and fans of vids (Box 5).

In his book *Watching YouTube*, when Michael Strangelove talks about "the Women of the Tube,"[103] he means videos in which women are on camera, presenting themselves; he does not imagine the case of the

---

Box 5. "What Our Vidding Community Is About" by LullabyProductions

CREATIVITY

> We can be creative and free.
> We can make unique art out of a single scene of a movie or a picture.
> We can make people feel and share our feelings and thoughts.

FRIENDSHIP

> We make new friends and forget about the distance.
> We find a way to connect, share our fandoms, watch show together and
> collab together.
> We build up real friendships where we can talk about everything with
> that person.

ACCEPTANCE

> We accept each other.
> We don't care about the religion our friends have, the way they look—
> the way they might struggle with a foreign language just to connect with
> everyone.

HELP

> We help each other out when we have problems.
> Whether it's a technical problem or private.

GUIDANCE

> We guide each other.
> We help each other to find a way to get better when we need to.

WE ARE THE ♥ OF THE VIDDING COMMUNITY.

---

vidder, who, to paraphrase John Berger, acts but does not appear. The woman who acts but does not appear is almost an impossible object in Western culture, a human Escher illusion: Is she really there? The disappearance of the woman artist—the novelist, the painter, the sculptor, the playwright, the film director, the television showrunner—is a recurring story. We lose her because we can't see her; we lose her because we think there's no such thing as a woman who can't be seen. But there is, and I want to end in this place of contradiction: that this is a book meant to bring visibility to this one particular subculture of female filmmaking so that it doesn't get lost, even as it recognizes that the strength of the vidding community may come from its historical refusal to be conventionally visible. Peggy Phelan has written powerfully of the "power of the 'unseen' community," which, she asserts, "lies in its ability to cohere outside the system of observation which seeks to patrol it. So the 'in-jokes,' the 'secret' codes, the iconography of dress, movement, and speech which can be read by those within the community, but escape the interpretative power of those external to it, can create another expressive language which cannot be translated by those who are not familiar with the meanings of this intimate tongue."[104] Vidding has been like that: a place where women, unleashed, reassemble images that, in Berger's words, have become "ephemeral, ubiquitous, insubstantial, available, valueless, free."[105] It is not that there are no female editors in mainstream cinema; the history of film editing is a roster of female talent, including Dorothy Spencer, Anne Coates, Verna Fields, Thelma Schoonmaker, Sally Menke, and Marcia Lucas. But that talent has been put at the service of the male directorial vision.

Vidders edit for themselves, for their own vision, their own eye.

Notes

Introduction

1. Tat-Seng Chua, Juanzi Li, and Marie-Francine Moens, *Mining User Generated Content* (London: Chapman and Hall/CRC Press, 2014), 7.

2. Similarly, the LLC formed to administer the conference is Vivid Constructed Realities, or VCR.

3. Signal/Noise 2k5: Creative Revolution briefing book, table of contents, http://cyber.law.harvard.edu/archived_content/events/SignalNoiseBBFINAL .pdf

4. "The Awakening" can still be seen online: https://www.youtube.com /watch?v=Vpjzg9DUEz0, https://www.youtube.com/watch?v=R60YzcW19pk, https://www.youtube.com/watch?v=T91RudWaYps

5. Jonathan McIntosh, "A History of Subversive Remix Video before YouTube: Thirty Political Video Mashups Made between World War II and 2005," in "Fan/Remix Video," ed. Francesca Coppa and Julie Levin Russo, special issue, *Transformative Works and Cultures*, no. 9 (2012), https://dx.doi.org/10.3983/twc .2012.0371

6. Interview with Jim Kaposztas, AnimeCons TV Extras, Otakon 2011, https://animecons.tv/extra/17/jim-kaposztas-interview

7. Including some men and transmen, nonbinary/enby people, and a range of queer, asexual/ace, poly, and other identities.

8. Thanks to fan Azure Lunatic, who no longer identifies as a woman but who caucuses with women, "especially for the celebration and grief of space travel" (personal correspondence, May 17, 2020).

9. Rachael Sabotini, quoted in "What Is Vidding?," part 1 of Vidding, a six-part series for the New Media Literacies project, https://www.youtube.com/wat ch?v=UbxFt35edWo

10. Luminosity, "Thinking about Vidding, What You Need to Know," LiveJournal, April 6, 2007 (since deleted; page archived by author).

11. Lim, Tumblr, 2014, http://limblogs.tumblr.com/post/84905844671/hi -sorry-if-you-think-im-intruding-but-i-was#84905844671

12. See, e.g., Louisa Ellen Stein, "Vidding: Remix as Affective Media Literacy,"

in *Intermédialités/Intermediality* 23 (2014), https://doi.org/10.7202/1033338ar; Tisha Turk, "Transformation in a New Key: Music in Vids and Vidding," *MSMI* 9, no. 2 (2015): 163–76; Alexis Lothian, "Living in a Den of Thieves: Fan Video and Digital Challenges to Ownership," *Cinema Journal* 48, no. 4 (2009): 130–6; Katherine E. Morrissey, "Vidding and/as Pedagogy," in *The Routledge Companion to Media Fandom*, ed. Susanne Scott and Melissa Click (New York: Routledge, 2017), 55–62; John Hondros, *Ecologies of Internet Video: Beyond YouTube* (New York: Routledge, 2018); Sarah Fiona Winters, "Streaming Scholarship: Using Fan Vids to Teach *Harry Potter*," *Children's Literature in Education* 45, no. 3 (2014): 239–54; Katharina Freund, "'I Thought I Made a Vid, but Then You Told Me That I Didn't: Aesthetics and Boundary Work in the Fan-Vidding Community," in *The Routledge Companion to Remix Studies*, ed. Eduardo Navas, Owen Gallagher, and xtine burrough (New York: Routledge, 2014), 283–94; Sarah Trombley, "Visions and Revisions: Fanvids and Fair Use," *Cardozo Arts and Entertainment Law Journal* 25 (2007): 647–86; Rebecca Tushnet, "I Put You There: User-Generated Content and Anticircumvention," *Vanderbilt Journal of Entertainment and Technology Law* 12 (2010): 889–946.

13. Henry Jenkins, "Layers of Meaning: Fan Music Video and the Poetics of Poaching," *Textual Poachers* (New York: Routledge, 1992); Camille Bacon-Smith, "Visual Meaning," in *Enterprising Women* (Philadelphia: University of Pennsylvania Press, 1992).

14. Note that the guys who made the famously remixed viral trailers like "Shining" were already professionals. Robert Ryang was working at the PS260 editing house; it was also his response to a professional editing contest. See Jonathan Cohn, "All Work and No Play: Trailer Park, the Mash-up, and Industrial Pedagogies," in *Sampling Media*, ed. David Laderman and Laurel Westrup (Oxford: Oxford University Press, 2014), 184–98.

15. Or, in the case of Art Binninger, maker of the claymation *Star Trix* (1974–75), after he approached Paramount looking for permission to show his films on public-access television. Paramount said no; Binninger protested and screened his films anyway.

16. See Jim Windolf, "Raiders of the Lost Backyard," *Vanity Fair*, March 2004, https://archive.vanityfair.com/article/2004/3/raiders-of-the-lost-backyard

17. Browncoats Movie, http://browncoatsmovie.com/?page_id=425 (available through the Wayback Machine).

18. Lucas Hilderbrand, *Inherent Vice: Bootleg Histories of Videotape and Copyright* (Durham, NC: Duke University Press, 2009), xviii.

19. Hilderbrand, *Inherent Vice*, 197.

20. *Sony Corp. of America v. Universal City Studios, Inc.*, 464 US 417 (1984), https://supreme.justia.com/cases/federal/us/464/417/

21. Clinton Heylin, *Bootleg! The Rise and Fall of the Secret Recording Industry* (London: Omnibus, 2004). Heylin is careful to distinguish the bootleg from the pirated; a person who owns a bootleg is likely to have bought everything that was for sale and still wants more.

22. Tashery Shannon, "Move Over MTV: Here Come the Song Vids! Fan Music Videos," *Strange New Worlds* 9 (1993), http://www.strangenewworlds.com/issues/feature-09f.html

23. Shannon, "Move Over MTV."

24. Paul Marino, "Interview with Paul Marino," conducted by Geoffrey Long, *Transformative Works and Cultures*, no. 2 (2009), https://dx.doi.org/10.3983/twc.2009.0111

25. *Campbell v. Acuff-Rose Music, Inc.*, 510 US 569 (1994), https://supreme.justia.com/cases/federal/us/510/569/

26. See Radical Software Group (RSG)'s page at the Electronic Arts Intermix gallery, http://www.eai.org/title.htm?id=10821

27. Counteragent's statement on her Blu-ray vid, RADIOACTIVE, submitted as part of the 1201 EFF OTW Reply Comments Class 7, served May, 2015, A12.

28. Obsession_inc, "Affirmational Fandom vs. Transformational Fandom," Dreamwidth, June 1, 2009.

29. "Curative Fandom," Fanlore (fan wiki), https://fanlore.org/

30. Obsession_inc, "Affirmational Fandom vs. Transformational Fandom."

31. Answer: evidence on the Marvel wiki indicates that Cap can lift 800 pounds over his head but bench press 1,100 pounds.

32. Bob Rehak, "Franz Joseph and Star Trek's Blueprint Culture," Graphic Engine (blog), March 11, 2012, https://graphic-engine.swarthmore.edu/franz-joseph-and-star-treks-blueprint-culture/

33. Matt Hills, "From Dalek Half Balls to Daft Punk Helmets: Mimetic Fandom and the Crafting of Replicas," in "Materiality and Object-Oriented Fandom," ed. Bob Rehak, special issue, *Transformative Works and Cultures*, no. 16 (2014), https://doi.org/10.3983/twc.2014.0531. See also Victoria Godwin, "Mimetic Fandom and One-sixth-scale Action Figures," *Transformative Works and Cultures*, no. 20 (2015), https://dx.doi.org/10.3983/twc.2015.0686

34. Hills provides the example of a fan saying that a particular Dalek on *Doctor Who* "was a bit of a let down to be honest" and building his own on the basis of an earlier "official" design. Hill calls this a "man bites dog" story—fan beats pro—but he also notes that the fan is seeking validation from the show makers: "I'm hoping that the BBC will take notice and maybe use it in the new series." Hills, "From Dalek Half Balls," 2.9.

35. Fans were knitting and selling each other ugly wool hats like those worn by the character Jayne, played by Adam Baldwin, on Joss Whedon's cult show *Firefly* until they were told to stop. See Ellie Hall, "Firefly Hat Triggers Corporate Crackdown," Buzzfeed, April 9, 2013, https://www.buzzfeednews.com/article/ellievhall/firefly-hat-triggers-corporate-crackdown. Still, they persisted. One Etsy shop marketed the hat simply as "Controversial Hat," telling a coded story about the item as a signal to fans. The story begins, "There once was a girl named Jane. . . . She liked simple things, like catching fireflies with her father." The story goes on to talk about the father's "brown coat" (*Firefly* fans are called Browncoats) and how her father was killed by a fox (Fox was the network that canceled *Firefly*). Then the fox tries to take even the grieving girl's hat. The shop owner declares that she doesn't want to live in that kind of a world: "So in Jane's stead, I will handknit similar hats and sell them to you." See Ellie Hall, "Etsy Community Responds to *Firefly* Hat Crackdown," Buzzfeed, April 10, 2013, https://www.buzzfeednews.com/article/ellievhall/etsy-community-responds-to-firefly-hat-crackdown

36. See the IMDb listing of names for *The People vs. George Lucas*, https://www
.imdb.com/title/tt1325014/?ref_=fn_al_tt_1

37. One of the big fanzine archives, created and run by Ming Wathne and now held as a collection at the University of Iowa, was called the Corellian Archives, based on Han Solo's home planet of Corellia. Star Wars zines formed the basis of the collection.

38. Henry Jenkins, *Convergence Culture: Where Old and New Media Collide* (New York: NYU Press, 2006), 153.

39. Kristina Busse, *Framing Fan Fiction* (Iowa City: University of Iowa Press, 2017), 199.

40. Avi Selk, "A Men's Rights Activist Edited *The Last Jedi* to Remove the Women. It's Bad," *Washington Post*, January 7, 2018, https://www.washingtonpost
.com/news/comic-riffs/wp/2018/01/17/a-mens-rights-activist-edited-the-last-je
di-to-remove-the-women-its-bad/

41. Daniel White Hodge and Joseph Boston, "The Racism Awakens," in *The Myth Awakens: Canon, Conservatism, and Fan Reception of Star Wars*, ed. John C. Lyden (Eugene, OR: Wipf and Stock, 2018), 74–91.

42. Kelly Marie Tran, "I Won't Be Marginalized by Online Harassment," *New York Times*, August 21, 2018, https://www.nytimes.com/2018/08/21/movies/ke
lly-marie-tran.html

43. Eve Kosofsky Sedgwick, *Epistemology of the Closet* (Berkeley: University of California Press, 1990), 156.

44. Davis Willis, "False Equivalence," Shortpacked (blog), December 2, 2011, https://www.shortpacked.com/comic/false-equivalence

45. Hazel Southwell, "MCU Retrospective Review: *Captain America: The First Avenger*," April 22, 2015, http://www.needtoconsume.com/film/mcu-retrospect
ive-review-captain-america-first-avenger-2011/

46. Ogi Ogas and Sai Gaddam, *A Billion Wicked Thoughts: What the Internet Tells Us about Sexual Relationships* (New York: Plume, 2012), 72.

47. Andy Medhurst, "Batman, Deviance, and Camp," in *The Many Lives of the Batman*, ed. Roberta Pearson and William Uricchio (New York: Routledge, 1991), 159.

48. Robert Vorlicky, *Acting Men: Challenging Masculinities in American Drama* (Ann Arbor: University of Michigan Press, 1995), 7.

49. THE PRICE can be seen on YouTube at https://www.youtube.com/watch
?v=Ks2si4wE6jA

50. Thingswithwings, "Some Thoughts on Manpain," Dreamwidth, June 16, 2011.

51. Joanna Kucharska, "Also These Voices: Technology and Gender in the Practice of Fanvidding," *Kultura Popularna* 4 (2013): 14–29.

52. No, really. See Angie Pedersen, *The Star Trek Craft Book: Make It So!* (New York: Pocket Books, 2013), for directions on how to make your tricorder purse or a "Spock Monkey."

Chapter 1

1. Michel Chion, *Audio-vision: Sound on Screen* (New York: Columbia University Press, 1994), 69.

2. M.V.D. quoted in Jenkins, *Textual Poachers*, 244.

3. The title comes from the fact that Buffy and her friends call themselves the Scooby Gang, itself a reference to the ghost-hunting teenagers of *Scooby-Doo*.

4. Jason Mittell, "Understanding Vidding," Just TV (blog), November 21, 2007, https://justtv.wordpress.com/2007/11/21/understanding-vidding/

5. See my "One Pringle, One Dorito, One Oreo," in *The Fanfiction Reader: Folk Tales for the Digital Age* (Ann Arbor: University of Michigan Press, 2017), for a more elaborate description of the hunger with which fans consume fan works.

6. Kandy Fong, "Fan Vid History Panel 2008," notes for the "Vidding History: 2000–2004," panel at Vividcon.

7. Jenkins, "Ten Ways to Rewrite a Television Show," *Textual Poachers*, 174.

8. If vidding is a form of participatory culture in which spectators become makers, then Townsend's Lifehouse was also conceived as a stab at passive consumerism. The idea of Lifehouse is that people would stop being passive, programmed consumers through the liberatory, participatory Dionysian experience of "personalized" rock music.

9. M. Blake Wilson, "Behind Zarathustra's Eyes: The Bad, Sad Man Meets Nietzsche's Prophet," in *The Who and Philosophy*, ed. Rocco J. Gennaro and Casey Harison (Lanham, MD: Lexington Books, 2016), 162.

10. Wilson, "Behind Zarathustra's Eyes," 166.

11. "Clam," Fanlore, https://fanlore.org/

12. Turk, "Transformation in a New Key."

13. Flamingo, personal correspondence, October 19, 2017.

14. "Starsky & Hutch," Fanlore, https://fanlore.org/

15. Here's luck & cereta, "The Language of Vidding," handout for Vividcon 2004.

16. Flamingo says that the frame comes from the episode "Class in Crime." Starsky, who has picked up a girl while on the case, is trying to prevent Hutch from coming inside his apartment; the girl is inside, and he is wearing no pants. Flamingo doesn't believe that this farcical moment is what's being evoked by the song (personal correspondence, October 19, 2017).

17. Hutch, for what it's worth, also has blue eyes, and he was once called "Blue Eyes" by Starsky in canon.

18. The slash or virgule conjoining Kirk/Spock is distinguished from the ampersand: Kirk & Spock. The latter indicates friendship or canon-level intimacy, however you define that.

19. Description of WOULDN'T IT BE NICE on YouTube, https://www.youtube.com/watch?v=L7Oe7BzoqHc

20. My discussion of the instrumentation of "Wouldn't It Be Nice" is indebted to the YouTube documentary series Behind the Sounds, June 14, 2008, https://www.youtube.com/watch?v=ofByti7A4uM

21. Chris Higgins, "Beach Boys' 'Wouldn't It Be Nice' Has 2 Accordionists, 2 Drummer, 3 Bassists + 13 More Musicians," Mentalfloss, June 9, 2012, http://

mentalfloss.com/article/30875/beach-boys-wouldnt-it-be-nice-has-2-accordionis
ts-2-drummers-3-bassists-13-more

22. Walter Pater, *The Renaissance: Studies in Art and Poetry* (London: Macmillan, 1910).

23. Pater, *Renaissance*, 130.

24. Yes, I know—it's a misquote. Thompson was actually talking about the television business, but the quote fitted the music business better and stuck.

25. Annabel J. Cohen, "Music as a Source of Emotion in Film," in *Handbook of Music and Emotion: Theory, Research, Applications*, ed. John Sloboda and Patrik N. Juslin (2001; reprint, Oxford: Oxford University Press, 2010), 881.

26. M. M. Marks, *Music and the Silent Film: Contexts and Case Studies, 1895–1924* (Oxford: Oxford University Press, 1997), 9.

27. And of variable quality, as in today's remix culture. Marks cites complaints of the "lamentably deficient" music heard in "nearly every moving picture theatre in New York City" in 1909. Marks, *Music and the Silent Film*, 66.

28. Hugo Munsterberg quoted in Cohen, "Music as a Source of Emotion in Film," 882–83.

29. Ben Model, "Moving Day for Count Orlock," Silent Film Music Blog, October 31, 2017, http://www.silentfilmmusicblog.com/2017/10/moving-day -for-count-orlock.html (via the Wayback Machine).

30. Cohen, "Music as a Source of Emotion in Film," 884.

31. Lawrence Kramer, *Musical Meaning: Toward a Critical History* (Berkeley: University of California Press, 2001), 135.

32. Siegfried Kracauer, *Theory of Film: The Redemption of Physical Reality* (Oxford: Oxford University Press, 1960), 138–39.

33. Karen Pearlman, *Cutting Rhythms: Shaping the Film Edit* (Waltham, MA: Focal Press, 2009), xxvi.

34. Bernard Herrmann, *A Lecture on Film Music* (1973), in *The Hollywood Film Music Reader*, ed. Mervyn Cooke (Oxford: Oxford University Press, 2010), 209, 211.

35. That said, there was respect for a good accompanist in the days of silent film. For example, the pianist at the Bijou on Fourteenth Street was praised for entering "into the spirit of the pictures shown. She absolutely adapts her music to them. Every emotion, every sentiment, every movement, every mood illustrated on the screen, is duplicated by the tones of the piano." Marks, *Music and the Silent Film*, 66.

36. A. M. Baranowski and H. Hecht, "The Auditory Kuleshov Effect: Multisensory Integration in Movie Editing," *Perception* 46, no. 5 (2017): 624–31.

37. Fans are still crying over *Wiseguy*, whose operatic season 1 ending was memorably scored to "Nights in White Satin" by the Moody Blues, which, because of performance rights, was replaced in some later airings and the DVD release.

38. For more on temp scores, see Andrew Liptak's discussion of Tony Zhou, "Every Frame a Painting," Verge, September 12, 2016, https://www.theverge .com/2016/9/12/12893622/hollywood-temp-scores-every-frame-a-painting-film

39. K. Kalinak, *Settling the Score: Music and the Classical Hollywood Film* (Madison: University of Wisconsin Press, 1992).

40. Cohen, "Music as a Source of Emotion in Film," 884.

41. *Lord of the Rings: Return of the King* (2003) and *The Shape of Water* (2017) are the only two SFF films to have won best picture; *Star Wars* (1977) lost to *Annie Hall* (1977), and *Black Panther* lost to *Green Book*. Excellent SFF movies like *2001: A Space Odyssey* (1968), *Blade Runner* (1982), and *Children of Men* (2006) weren't even nominated.

42. Rick Lyman, "Watching Movies With: Michael Bay; A Connoisseur of Illusions," *New York Times*, May 18, 2001, https://www.nytimes.com/2001/05/18/movies/watching-movies-with-michael-bay-a-connoisseur-of-illusions.html

43. Pauline Kael, "Keep Going," *New Yorker*, January 3, 1970, 58.

44. Kael, "Keep Going," 57.

45. D. A. Miller, *Place for Us* (Cambridge, MA: Harvard University Press, 2000), 90.

46. Stacy Wolf, *A Problem Like Maria* (Ann Arbor: University of Michigan Press, 2002), 22.

47. Wolf, *Problem Like Maria*, 214.

48. For more on the comparison between slash fans and gay male subculture, see my "Slash/Drag: Appropriation and Visibility in the Age of *Hamilton*," in *A Companion to Media Fandom and Fan Studies*, ed. Paul Booth (New York: Wiley, 2018), 189–206.

49. Wolf, *Problem Like Maria*, 4.

50. Wolf, *Problem Like Maria*, 40–41.

51. Lim, "Demystifying Vidding," Videlicet, 2017, https://vidders.github.io/articles/vidding/demystifying.html

52. Kramer, *Musical Meaning*, 188.

53. Annette Davison, "Title Sequences for Contemporary Television Serials," in *The Oxford Handbook of New Audiovisual Aesthetics*, ed. John Richardson, Claudia Gorbman, and Carol Vernallis (Oxford: Oxford University Press, 2013), 147.

54. David Johansson, "Homeward Bound: Those *Soprano* Titles Come Heavy," in *Reading The Sopranos: Hit TV from HBO*, ed. David Lavery (London: I.B. Tauris, 2006), 27.

55. Johansson, "Homeward Bound," 35.

56. Johansson, "Homeward Bound," 35.

57. Davison, "Title Sequences," 147.

58. Johansson, "Homeward Bound," 33.

59. Thomas Pettitt, "Before the Gutenberg Parenthesis: Elizabethan–American Compatibilities," Plenary: Folk and Digital Cultures, presented at Media in Transition 5: Creativity, Ownership, and Collaboration in the Digital Age, 2007, http://web.mit.edu/comm-forum/legacy/mit5/papers/pettitt_plenary_gutenberg.pdf

60. Abigail De Kosnik (as Abigail Derecho), *Illegitimate Media: Race, Gender and Censorship in Digital Remix Culture* (PhD diss., Northwestern University, 2008), 2.

61. Mel Stanfill, "The Unbearable Whiteness of Fandom and Fan Studies," in *A Companion to Media Fandom and Fan Studies*, ed. Paul Booth (Oxford: Wiley, 2018), chap. 19.

62. De Kosnik (as Derecho), in *Illegitimate Media*, argues that unlicensed sampling was a wildly influential and economically successful musical practice before

it was smacked down by *Grand Upright vs. Warner Bros. Records* (1991), which "defined sampling as uncategorically, absolutely, unquestionably equivalent to theft," and which changed hip-hop forever. See *Grand Upright Music v. Warner Bros. Records, Inc.*, 780 F. Supp. 182 (S.D.N.Y. 1991), https://law.justia.com/cas es/federal/district-courts/FSupp/780/182/1445286/. By contrast, as I describe in the introduction, white female fandom chose self-censorship and low visibility, and thus remained small and subcultural for another three decades or so.

63. De Kosnik (as Derecho), *Illegitimate Media*, 21.

64. BIN LADEN can be seen at https://www.youtube.com/watch?v=RJ4iZE2 yoLk

65. Kevin Glynn, "Visibility, Media Events and Convergence Culture: Struggles for the Meaning of 9/11," in *Mediated Geographies and Geographies of Media*, ed. Susan P. Mains, Julie Cupples, and Chris Lukinbeal (Amsterdam: Springer, 2015), 307.

66. Glynn, "Visibility," 305–6.

67. HIP HOP SPA can be seen at https://www.youtube.com/watch?v=VsbG4p Xrhr8

68. Catherine Grant and Kate Random Love, eds., *Fandom as Methodology: A Sourcebook for Artists and Writers* (London: Goldsmiths, 2019), 22.

69. THE GRAY VIDEO can be seen at https://www.youtube.com/watch?v=3zJq ihkLcGc

70. Kevin Young, *The Grey Album: On the Blackness of Blackness* (Minneapolis, MN: Graywolf Press, 2012), 395.

71. Consider Henry Jenkins's famous formulation: "Fan fiction is a way of the culture repairing the damage done in a system where contemporary myths are owned by corporations instead of owned by the folk." Quoted in Amy Harmon, "In TV's Dull Summer Days, Plots Take Wing on the Net," *New York Times*, August 18, 1997, https://www.nytimes.com/1997/08/18/business/in-tv-s-dull-summer -days-plots-take-wing-on-the-net.html

72. Young, *Grey Album*, 395.

73. Young, *Grey Album*, 396.

74. Paul J. Booth, "Mashup as Temporal Amalgam: Time, Taste, and Textuality," in "Fan/Remix Video," ed. Francesca Coppa and Julie Levin Russo, special issue, *Transformative Works and Cultures*, no. 9 (2012), https://doi.org/10 .3983/twc.2012.0297

75. Booth, "Mashup as Temporal Amalgam."

76. Bell hooks, "The Oppositional Gaze: Black Female Spectators," in *Black Looks* (Boston: South End Press, 1992), 116.

77. Ara Osterweil, in *Barbara Rubin and the Exploding NY Underground* (dir. Chuck Smith, 2019).

78. Carolee Schneemann, for instance, made *Fuses* (1965) because she was unhappy with the way her lovemaking had been documented by her mentor, Stan Brakhage. Similarly, Rubin and Ono made works that equalized male and female bodies as landscapes for the camera, and Rubin went further and explicitly marked both male and female bodies as sensual and penetrable. See Ara Osterweil, "'Absently Enchanted': The Apocryphal, Ecstatic Cinema of Barbara

Rubin," in *Women's Experimental Cinema: Critical Frameworks*, ed. Robin Blaetz (Durham, NC: Duke University Press, 2007), 127–51.

79. Barbara Rubin, quoted in Osterweil, "Absently Enchanted," 133.

80. Barbara Rubin, "Projection Instructions," quoted in catalog copy for *Christmas on Earth* (1963), Filmmakers' Coop, available at https://film-makersco op.com/catalogue/barbara-rubin-christmas-on-earth

81. Catalog essay by JoAnn Hanley for *The First Generation: Women and Video, 1970–1975* exhibition (New York: Independent Curators Incorporated, 1993), excerpted at https://curatorsintl.org/exhibitions/the-first-generation-women -and-video-1970-75

82. Hanley, catalog essay.

83. Dot Tuer, "Mirrors and Mimesis: An Examination of the Strategies of Image Appropriation and Repetition in the Work of Dara Birnbaum," *n.paradoxa* 3 (1997): 9.

84. Dara Birnbaum, "Talking Back to the Media," *Stichting de Appel 3*, no. 4 (1985): 52.

85. Dara Birnbaum, quoted in *This Is Not a Dream* (dir. Gavin Butt and Ben Walters, 2012); clip available on YouTube at https://www.youtube.com/watch ?v=M6plSiogdDM

86. Birnbaum, quoted in *This Is Not a Dream.*

87. Saul Austerlitz, *Money for Nothing: A History of the Music Video from the Beatles to the White Stripes* (New York: Continuum, 2007), 9.

88. E. Anne Kaplan, *Rocking around the Clock: Music Television, Postmodernism, and Consumer Culture* (New York: Methuen, 1987), 123.

89. Carol Vernallis, *Experiencing Music Video: Aesthetics and Cultural Context* (New York: Columbia University Press, 2004), 45.

90. Steven Shaviro, *Digital Music Videos* (New Brunswick, NJ: Rutgers University Press, 2017), 7.

91. Greg B. Walker and Melinda A. Bender, "Is It More than Rock and Roll? Considering Music Video as Argument," *Argumentation and Advocacy* 31 (1994): 64.

92. TOTAL ECLIPSE OF THE HEART (literal video version) by dascottjr is available at https://www.youtube.com/watch?v=fsgWUq0fdKk

93. Diane Railton and Paul Watson, *Music Video and the Politics of Representation* (Edinburgh: Edinburgh University Press, 2011), 2.

94. Austerlitz, *Money for Nothing,* 6.

95. Will Straw, "Popular Music and Postmodernism in the 1980s," in *Sound and Vision: The Music Video Reader*, ed. Simon Frith, Andrew Goodwin, and Lawrence Grossberg (New York: Routledge, 1993), 5.

96. Andrew Goodwin, *Dancing in the Distraction Factory: Music Television and Popular Culture* (Minneapolis: University of Minnesota Press, 1992), 33.

97. Sérgio Dias Branco, "Music Videos and Reused Footage," in *Cultural Borrowings: Appropriation, Reworking, Transformation*, ed. Iain Robert Smith (Nottingham: Scope e-book, 2009), 113.

98. Or mostly not. Dias Branco, "Music Videos and Reused Footage," gives examples of commercial music videos that use found footage, such as Michael

Jackson's THE MAN IN THE MIRROR (1987) and Public Enemy's FIGHT THE POWER (1990).

99. Kaplan, *Rocking around the Clock*, 62.

100. Brigid Cherry, "From Cult to Subculture: Reimaginings of Cult Films in Alternative Music Video," in *Cultural Borrowings: Appropriation, Reworking, Transformation*, ed. Iain Robert Smith (Nottingham: Scope e-book, 2009), 124–37.

101. Maureen Turim, "Art/Music/Video.com," in *Medium Cool: Music Videos from Soundies to Cellphones*, ed. Roger Beebe and Jason Middleton (Durham, NC: Duke University Press, 2007), 83–110.

102. Cherry, "From Cult to Subculture," 125.

103. Kaplan, *Rocking around the Clock*, 48.

104. Austerlitz, *Money for Nothing*, 4.

105. Austerlitz, *Money for Nothing*, 5.

106. Railton and Watson, *Music Video*, 11–12.

107. Margie, personal communication, October 24, 2006.

Chapter 2

1. Jacqueline Lichtenberg, Sondra Marshak, and Joan Winston, *Star Trek Lives!* (New York: Bantam, 1975), 222.

2. Lichtenberg, Marshak, and Winston, *Star Trek Lives!*, 225.

3. Joan Marie Verba, *Boldly Writing: A Trekker Fan and Zine History, 1967–1987*, 2nd ed. (Minnetonka, MN: FTL Publications, 2003), viii.

4. Laura Mulvey, "Visual Pleasure and Narrative Cinema," in *Feminism and Film Theory*, ed. Constance Penley (New York: Routledge, 1988), 57.

5. Mulvey, "Visual Pleasure," 62.

6. Laura Mulvey, *Death 24× a Second: Stillness and the Moving Image* (London: Reaktion, 2006), 7.

7. Mulvey, *Death 24× a Second*, 161.

8. Mulvey, *Death 24× a Second*, 166.

9. Mulvey, *Death 24× a Second*, 162.

10. Kandy Fong actually made "Amok Time: A Personal Log" in 1974 to entertain the United Federation of Phoenix, a *Star Trek* fan club. When Bjo Trimble, organizer of the Save Star Trek campaign and author of *The Star Trek Concordance*, came to speak at the club, Fong showed her the slideshow, and it was decided that Fong would bring it to the next major *Star Trek* convention, 1975's Equicon (which combined with Filmcon in 1975—hence the phrasing "Equicon/Filmcon"). Fong brought the slideshow to San Diego in 1975 and performed it, over and over, in a basement room, where many fans saw it. This debut is the one that vidding fans use to date the art form.

11. This footage was purchased by Kandy Fong's future husband, John Fong, from Lincoln Enterprises, Gene Roddenberry's *Star Trek* memorabilia company.

12. For more on filk, see Henry Jenkins, "Strangers No More, We Sing: Filk Music, Folk Culture, and the Fan Community," in *Textual Poachers*; and Melissa L. Tatum, "Identity and Authenticity in the Filk Community," *Transformative Works and Cultures*, no. 3 (2009), https://dx.doi.org/10.3983/twc.2009.0139

13. For more about fannish tropes, see Coppa, *Fanfiction Reader*, and Busse, *Framing Fan Fiction*. Busse in particular has written about fanfiction tropes like genderswap, mpreg, conduit fic, noncon, and Alpha/Beta/Omega.

14. Kandy Fong, personal communication, October 14, 2006.

15. Kandy Fong updated the images in her shows as time passed, so the documented versions are not identical to the shows as originally presented. In that way, they are growing, organic things. For instance, the recreated version of IT WAS A VERY GOOD YEAR ends with a lingering shot of Dr. Carol Marcus from *Star Trek II* (1982), a later love interest of Kirk's and the mother of Kirk's son. The show had been updated to take account of new canon.

16. Kandy Fong, interview with Coppa for OTW Vidding History Project, August 18, 2008.

17. Verba's *Boldly Writing* provides a good history of *Star Trek* zine culture.

18. Lichtenberg, Marshak, and Winston, *Star Trek Lives!*, 5.

19. The history of convention skits is being documented on Fanlore; see "Convention Skit," Fanlore, https://fanlore.org/

20. Fong's filmed slideshow vids include BOTH SIDES NOW (c. 1980), MIDNITE BLUE (c. 1983), and THE WAY WE WERE (c. 1983). All were filmed for Gene Roddenberry in 1986.

21. An attempt was made by the OTW (myself included) to document some of these unfilmed slideshows at Vividcon in 2012, though the results are spotty. Many of the slides are reddening and the audiotape is fragile, though Fong did her best to perform from her scripts, which are written in faded ink on yellow pads. Some of the results are hosted online at Critical Commons (https://criticalcommons.org/).

22. For various genealogies of the music video, see Austerlitz, *Money for Nothing*; Beebe and Middleton, *Medium Cool*; Frith, Goodwin, and Grossberg, *Sound and Vision*; Goodwin, *Dancing in the Distraction Factory*; Kaplan, *Rocking around the Clock*; Henry Keazor and Thorsten Wübbena, eds., introduction to *Rewind, Play, Fast Forward: The Past, Present, and Future of the Music Video* (Bielefeld, Germany: transcript, 2010); and Rob Tannenbaum and Craig Marks, *I Want My MTV: The Uncensored Story of the Music Video Revolution* (New York: Plume, 2012).

23. Contenders for the first music video include Tony Bennett's STRANGERS IN PARADISE (1956), in which he was filmed walking moodily down the Serpentine, and Bob Dylan's SUBTERRANEAN HOMESICK BLUES (1967) segment from the film *Don't Look Back* (1967), in which Dylan stands in an alley, peeling off a stack of cue cards featuring significant and sometimes twisted bits of lyrics, seemingly trying to keep up with the pace of the song. Queen's BOHEMIAN RHAPSODY (1975) is also a contender: it uses filmic techniques to visualize music that couldn't be performed (or mimed realistically) as live on such shows as *Top of the Pops*. BOHEMIAN RHAPSODY alternates between avant-garde multiple exposures to convey the song's multiplicity of voice during the choral parts, and more straightforward concert-style footage during the rock sections.

24. Ian MacDonald, *Revolution in the Head*, 3rd ed. (Chicago: Chicago Review Press, 2007), 198.

25. Coppa, "Interview with Kandy Fong" [multimedia], in "Material Fan Culture," ed. Bob Rehak, special issue, *Transformative Works and Cultures*, no. 16 (2014), https://dx.doi.org/10.3983/twc.2014.0535

26. Interview with Jim Kaposztas, AnimeCons TV Extras, Otakon 2011, https://animecons.tv/extra/17/jim-kaposztas-interview

27. Scott Thill, "*The Prisoner*: An All-Star Appreciation," *Wired*, November 13, 2009, https://www.wired.com/2009/11/the-prisoner-an-all-star-appreciation/

28. Richard Lester, "Guardian Interviews at the BFI: Steven Soderbergh Interviews Richard Lester," *Guardian*, November 8, 1999, https://www.theguardian.com/film/1999/nov/08/guardianinterviewsatbfisouthbank3

29. This was a tradition continued by *Monty Python's Flying Circus*, which was regarded as the first television show to satirize the conventions of television itself.

30. Sam Kashner, "Making Beatlemania: *A Hard Day's Night* at 50," *Vanity Fair*, July 2, 2014, https://www.vanityfair.com/hollywood/2014/07/a-hard-days-night-making-of

31. John Lennon has the reputation of being the most avant-garde of the Beatles, but he had a love–hate relationship with the avant-garde, which he often dismissed as bullshit. It was McCartney who, in the mid- to late 1960s, explored the London avant-garde scene.

32. These early films were later stolen from McCartney's London apartment.

33. Barry Miles, *Paul McCartney: Many Years from Now* (New York: Holt, 1997).

34. MacDonald, *Revolution in the Head*, 256.

35. Miles, *Paul McCartney*, 250.

36. Ara Osterweil, "Ang Lee's Lonesome Cowboys," *Film Quarterly* 60, no. 3 (2007): 39.

37. There are exceptions. Lisa Lewis makes a good case that MTV produced some positive models for women in artists such as Cyndi Lauper. Lewis talks about two forms of female address on MTV: access signs (say, women taking over the street, getting access to male spaces) and discovery signs (which celebrate so-called girl culture: talking on the phone, dressing alike, dancing together). Lewis, "Being Discovered: The Emergence of Female Address on MTV," in Frith, Goodwin, and Grossberg, *Sound and Vision*, 129–51.

38. For more, see Coppa, "A Fannish Taxonomy of Hotness," *Cinema Journal* 48, no. 4 (2009): 107–13.

39. Railton and Watson, *Music Video*, 11–12.

40. Meredith Mendelsohn, "Countercultural Icon and 'Father of the Music Video' Bruce Conner Gets His Due in New York," *Artsy*, June 28, 2016, https://www.artsy.net/article/artsy-editorial-how-father-of-the-music-video-bruce-conner-influenced-generations-of-artists

41. Amei Wallach, "The Favorite Word in His Vocabulary Is Undermine," *New York Times*, October 1, 2000, http://www.nytimes.com/2000/10/01/arts/art-architecture-the-favorite-word-in-his-vocabulary-is-undermine.html

42. Wallach, "Favorite Word."

43. Holly Rogers, "Audiovisual Dissonance in Found Footage Film," in *The Music and Sound of Experimental Film*, ed. Holly Rogers and Jeremy Barham (Oxford: Oxford University Press, 2017), 196.

44. Rogers, "Audiovisual Dissonance," 196.

45. There are other isolated examples of cinephiliacs creating vids. For instance, horror fan and director Cortlandt Hull, nephew of *Werewolf of London* Henry Hull, made what is essentially a fan vid out of black-and-white horror

footage to Frank Sinatra's "Strangers in the Night" in the early 1970s. As Harry Knowles describes it in the blurb he wrote for YouTube, Hull's 16mm film "made me want to read *Famous Monsters of Filmland* to learn about all those monsters and the ladies that they loved. It made them tragic romances . . . all of them. Beasts that wanted to love" (https://youtu.be/czwYTzUq95U). Both the emotional tone of Hull's film and its use of image–music conjunctions—these strangers in the night are strange indeed—makes STRANGERS IN THE NIGHT, like Cornell's *Rose Hobart*, fit well into the later vidding tradition. For more, see "Why Harry Knowles Is Harry Knowles . . . *Strangers in the Night* by Cortlandt Hull," March 4, 2011, Ain't It Cool News, http://www.aintitcool.com/node/48755

46. Michael Pigott, *Joseph Cornell versus Cinema* (London: Bloomsbury, 2013), 9.

47. Joe Bob Briggs et al., "Cult Cinema: A Critical Symposium," *Cineaste* 34 (2008): 47.

48. Catherine Corman, "Surrealist Astronomy in the South Pacific: Joseph Cornell and the Collaged Eclipse," *East of Borneo*, November 4, 2010, https://eastofborneo.org/articles/surrealist-astronomy-in-the-south-pacific-joseph-cornell-and-the-collaged-eclipse/

49. Joseph Cornell, "The Enchanted Wanderer: Excerpt from a Journey Album for Hedy Lamarr," *View Magazine* 9, no. 10 (1941), as published in Deborah Solomon, *Utopia Parkway: The Life and Work of Joseph Cornell* (New York: Other Press, 2015), 165.

50. Catherine Corman, "Theatre of the Spirits: Joseph Cornell and Silence," in DJ Spooky That Subliminal Kid, *Sound Unbound: Sampling Digital Music and Culture* (Cambridge, MA: MIT Press, 2008), 369.

51. Quoted in Catherine Corman, "Theatre of the Spirits: Joseph Cornell and Silence," 370.

52. Pigott, *Joseph Cornell versus Cinema*, 70.

53. Pigott, *Joseph Cornell versus Cinema*, 71.

54. Pigott, *Joseph Cornell versus Cinema*, 71.

55. McCartney himself was still being influenced by Cornell as late as 2011, naming his ballet, *Ocean's Kingdom*, after Cornell's assemblage *Hotel Neptune*, which McCartney owns. Paul Du Noyer, *Conversations with Paul McCartney* (London: Hodder & Stoughton, 2012), 155.

56. Neil Aspinall notes that the goal was "to send the album on tour instead of the band"—that is, for the mass media product to replace the live concert experience. Aspinall, interviewed for the documentary *The Beatles Anthology*, episode 6 (1995).

57. Miles, *Paul McCartney*, 300.

58. MacDonald, *Revolution in the Head*, 262.

59. Miles, *Paul McCartney*, 300.

60. Miles, *Paul McCartney*, 301.

61. McCartney continued to have a can-do spirit. In 1996, he made a short film about the Grateful Dead out of his wife's snapshots (much as Kandy Fong made "Amok Time: A Personal Log" out of *Star Trek* slides), although his inspiration was not vidding but Warhol: "If Andy Warhol can film the Empire State Building for three hours, I figure I can do something with four rolls of film."

Quoted in Neil Strauss, "Paul McCartney, Beatle and Deadhead Director," *New York Times*, September 26, 1996, http://www.nytimes.com/1996/09/26/movies/paul-mccartney-beatle-and-deadhead-director.html

62. Du Noyer, *Conversations with Paul McCartney*, 294.

63. *Hearts of Darkness: A Filmmaker's Apocalypse* (dir. Francis Ford Coppola, 1991).

64. Kandy Fong interview by Franzeska Dickson for the Media Fandom Oral History Project, February 2012, "Media Fandom Oral History Project Interview with Kandy Fong and Marnie," Fanlore, https://fanlore.org/

65. Roddenberry claimed to be selling bits of film rescued from the cutting-room floor that would have been trashed otherwise. Fans who purchased this footage were told this and believed it. In fact, it was later claimed that Roddenberry had more or less stolen the film while the show was still actively in production, and that he had sold footage that the show's editors had been planning to use in future episodes. For more, see "Lincoln Enterprises" at the Memory Alpha wiki (http://memory-alpha.wikia.com/); and Herbert Franklin Solow and Robert H. Justman, *Inside "Star Trek": The Real Story* (1991; reprint, New York: Pocket, 1996), 400–401.

66. When I first asked Kandy Fong about BOTH SIDES NOW, she said she thought it was made around 1980; she now thinks that maybe that date is on the late side. In addition, the version filmed for Roddenberry was updated, as were many of Fong's most popular vids, so the 1986 version includes images of Spock from the feature films.

67. Lucinda Franks recalls being a woman journalist in the 1970s, when the ultimate compliment was, "I don't think of you as a woman anymore. You write like a man." Franks, "My Generation Thought Women Were Empowered. Did We Deceive Ourselves?," *New York Times*, December 8, 2017, https://www.nytimes.com/2017/12/08/opinion/sunday/women-empowerment-sexism.html?emc=edit_th_20171210&nl=todaysheadlines&nlid=23624491

68. The unemotional female first officer was present even in Roddenberry's earliest pitch for *Star Trek*, when the captain was neither Kirk nor Pike but rather Robert April. In that 1964 pitch, Roddenberry describes "The Executive Officer," a character who was both sexually and racially othered: "Never referred to as anything but 'Number One,' this officer is female. Almost mysteriously female, in fact—slim and dark in a Nile Valley way, age uncertain, one of those women who will always look the same between years twenty to fifty. An extraordinarily efficient officer, 'Number One' enjoys playing it expressionless, cool—is probably Robert April's superior in detailed knowledge of the multiple equipment systems, departments, and crew members aboard the vessel." Stephen E. Whitfield and Gene Roddenberry, *The Making of Star Trek* (New York: Ballantine, 1968), 29.

69. Melissa Dickinson, "Alexander for the Modern Age: How *Star Trek*'s Female Fans Re-invented Romance and Heroic Myth," in *Boarding the "Enterprise": Transporters, Tribbles, and the Vulcan Death Grip in Gene Roddenberry's "Star Trek,"* ed. David Gerrold and Robert J. Sawyer (Dallas, TX: BenBella, 2006), 170.

70. Kandy Fong interview with Coppa, August 18, 2008, tape C.

71. Others created *Star Trek* slideshows for conventions, mainly random shots of the actors and characters played over a soundtrack. There were no image–

lyric conjunctions, no musical editing or timing, no interpretative framework, no emotional build. Kandy Fong complained about one (male) fan who didn't understand that the images in her shows were synched, that she was actually telling a story, and that "there was a pace for each slide to be shown as far as the words of the song." Kandy Fong interview with Coppa, August 18, 2008, tape C.

72. Lennon in particular does a lot of looking at us as the song's voice and narrator. For example, in a very vid-like moment, Lennon's eye turns to take us in on the lyric "Misunderstanding all you see," positioning him as one who sees even as we watch him.

73. NBC billed itself as the "full color network" (thus the 1956 peacock logo), and *Star Trek* routinely ranked higher among viewers with color TVs. See Solow and Justman, *Inside "Star Trek."*

74. Mervyn Nicholson, "The Star Trek Look," Bright Lights Film Journal, April 30, 2010, https://brightlightsfilm.com/minimalist-magic-the-star-trek-loo k/#.XWPvHpNKj-Y

75. In fact, the two works would have been received nearly simultaneously; STRAWBERRY FIELDS FOREVER was broadcast in the United States on *The Hollywood Palace* (February 25, 1967), a week before the *Star Trek* episode "This Side of Paradise" aired (March 2, 1967).

76. "Where women are investigated, men are tested." Steve Neale, "Masculinity as Spectacle," *Screening the Male: Exploring Masculinities in Hollywood Cinema*, ed. Steven Cohan and Ina Rae Hark (New York: Routledge, 1993), 16.

77. Maurice Berger, *Minimal Politics: Performativity and Minimalism in Recent American Art* (Baltimore, MD: Fine Arts Gallery, University of Maryland, 1997), 8.

78. Marshall McLuhan, *Understanding Media: The Extensions of Man* (New York: McGraw Hill, 1964).

Chapter 3

1. "Between Friends (Starsky and Hutch Zine)," Fanlore, https://fanlore .org/

2. Tisha Turk and Joshua Johnson, "Toward an Ecology of Vidding," in "Fan/Remix Video," ed. Francesca Coppa and Julie Levin Russo, special issue, *Transformative Works and Cultures*, no. 9 (2012), https://doi.org/10.3983/twc.20 12.0326

3. Interview with Kathleen Reynolds by Megan Genovese, 2017.

4. Excerpt from handout, "More than You Wanted to Know about Video Tape and DVD-R," distributed at Escapade 2003; the handout notes that this section, "Part One," "was compiled by Flamingo from The Vidder's List."

5. Excerpt from handout, "More than You Wanted to Know about Video Tape and DVD-R," distributed at Escapade 2003; the handout notes that this section, "Part Two," was written "by Leigh."

6. Interview with Kendra Hunter by Coppa and Morgan Dawn, February 19, 2018.

7. The convention was named for Zebra 3, Starsky and Hutch's radio call sign.

8. Kandy Fong and Sandy Herrold, "Vidding History: 1980–1984," presented at Vividcon, August 15, 2008.

9. Fong and Herrold, "Vidding History."

10. "*Starsky & Hutch* Historical Vids," 2001 booklet and songtape by Flamingo.

11. Flamingo, "*Starsky & Hutch* Historical Vids."

12. Notes to the "Vidding History: 1980–1984" Vividcon vid show, http://Vividcon.info/vidshows/91/

13. Although scholars have examined television's domestication of the viewing experience and the way that VCRs enabled women to time-shift their viewing, insufficient attention has been paid to the filmmaking powers that the VCR bestows. For TV's domestication of the viewing experience, see Lynn Spiegel, *Make Room for TV: Television and the Family Ideal in Postwar America* (Chicago: University of Chicago Press, 1992). For time-shifting, see Anne Gray, "Behind Closed Doors: Video Recorders in the Home," in *Media Studies: A Reader*, ed. Paul Marris and Sue Thornham (New York: NYU Press, 2000), 524–35.

14. "It is possible to love a tape to death," Kandy Fong wryly noted in *Rainbow Noise* #2 (June 1993). "Recently, I borrowed a series from another fan, and I can tell where every one of her favorite scenes is located. Every time she paused the tape—backed it up—paused the tape—replayed it (sometimes in slow motion), the tape stretched a little bit. Now her favorite scenes are bracketed with wavy pictures and rolling images."

15. Coppa, "Fannish Taxonomy."

16. "The Fix," one of the slashiest episodes of *Starsky and Hutch* ever made (which is saying something), still has the power to make fangirls lose their minds. In this episode, Hutch is kidnapped and addicted to heroin by the villain. Starsky finds him a broken man and nurses him back to health. There is a lot of hugging and clutching and being in bed together. Watch the young host of *Fandom on Demand* literally fall to the floor and roll around as she recaps the episode on her YouTube channel in 2013 (https://youtu.be/VI_7VjnbdAc).

17. Flamingo, "*Starsky & Hutch* Historical Vids." See also "The Kiss in the Alley Debate," Fanlore, https://fanlore.org/

18. For more on the history of slash fandom, see Kristina Busse and Alexis Lothian, "A History of Slash Sexualities: Debating Queer Sex, Gay Politics and Media Fan Cultures," in *The Routledge Companion to Media, Sex, and Sexuality*, ed. Clarissa Smith and Feona Attwood, with Brian McNair (New York: Routledge, 2018), 117–29; and Kristina Busse, "Slash," in *The International Encyclopedia of Gender, Media, and Communication*, ed. Karen Ross (New York: Wiley Online Library, 2020), https://doi.org/10.1002/9781119429128.iegmc038

19. The scene in question is the opening of "Targets without a Badge, Part Two" (1979), an episode in which Starsky and Hutch resign after an informant is shot.

20. We cannot hear this dialogue in the vid, of course, but *Starsky and Hutch* fans would likely have known it, particularly because it's a slur against Hutch's masculinity. See "A Starsky and Hutch Canon Compendium," Starsky and Hutch Files, http://starskyhutchfiles.net/compendium/page30/page30.html

21. Though it's hard to imagine what else Terry meant by giving Hutch the bear she used to sleep with. It's even worse when you realize that the bear is

named Ollie; Starsky and Hutch make Laurel and Hardy jokes to each other throughout the series, often calling the other "Ollie."

22. Flamingo, personal communication, October 19, 2017.

23. Flamingo, personal communication, October 19, 2017.

24. "The Rose (Starsky & Hutch Vid)," Fanlore, https://fanlore.org/

25. "ZebraCon/Memories," Fanlore, https://fanlore.org/

26. ZebraCon 2007 program, "Song Vid Show," https://fanlore.org/w/imag es/e/ec/Zebraconlast-7.jpg

27. "Big Emotion," vid show at Vividcon 2011. The playlist is available at https://vividcon.info/vidshows/148/

28. The last ZebraCon was held in 2007.

29. Fong and Herrold, "Vidding History."

30. Flamingo, "*Starsky & Hutch* Historical Vids."

31. "S and H (Starsky and Hutch Letterzine)," Fanlore, https://fanlore.org/

32. The Paul Muni Special is the name of Starsky's favorite meal, which we learn when Hutch cooks it for him in the 1975 episode "Lady Blue." "How'd you know?" Starsky asks. "I called your mother," Hutch replies. "You called my mother," Starsky repeats. "Yeah, she calls it the Paul Muni Special," says Hutch.

33. Mike Loehr reviews the features of editing VCRs versus regular home VCRs. Loehr, "Edit Points: Editing VCRs," *Videomaker Magazine*, December 1, 1995, https://www.videomaker.com/article/c3/1213-edit-points-editing-vcrs

34. Interview with Kendra Hunter by Coppa and Morgan Dawn, February 19, 2018.

35. Fandom metavids include: US, by lim; I LOVE FANDOM, by Barkley; ANYTHING FOR LOVE, by astolat and Speranza; STILL ALIVE, by Counteragent; HARD SUN, by bradcpu and Laura Shapiro; ON THE PROWL, by sisabet and Sweetest Drain; and THE LONG SPEAR by jmtorres, niqaeli, et al.

36. For additional information about PRESSURE, see my "Women, *Star Trek*, and the Early Development of Fannish Vidding," *Transformative Works and Cultures*, no. 1 (2008), https://doi.org/10.3983/twc.2008.0044

37. Lorry remembers: "Regarding PRESSURE, I originally conceived of the idea. I had graduated 2 years earlier from USC. I wrote what shots would be taken, most of the camera work was done by Kathy . . . and lastly my sister physically edited all of it on our machines in our house with shot selection by me and input from Brenda" (personal communication, 2008).

38. Interview with Brenda Wagner by Coppa and Morgan Dawn, May 31, 2018.

39. Interview with Brenda Wagner, May 31, 2018.

40. Lorry, personal communication, 2008.

41. Lorry, personal communication, 2008.

42. See "The Genealogy of Vidding," Fanlore, https://fanlore.org/; and Rachael Sabotini, "VVC Panel: The Genealogy of Vidding," LiveJournal, August 26, 2005, https://wickedwords.livejournal.com/294250.html

43. For more about the split between SFF fandom and media fandom, see my "Brief History of Media Fandom," in *Fan Fiction and Fan Communities in the Age of the Internet: New Essays*, ed. Karen Hellekson and Kristina Busse (Jefferson, NC: McFarland, 2006), 41–59.

44. While SFF fandom is alive and well and still centered around Worldcon and the Hugo awards, the gender-inflected conflicts that resulted in media fans' splitting off into their own spaces are still in evidence. See, for instance, the 2013–17 campaigns of the so-called Sad Puppies and Rabid Puppies promoting old-fashioned (masculinist) SF and decrying the so-called message fiction ostensibly written by women and people of color.

45. Sabotini, "VVC Panel: The Genealogy of Vidding."

46. See Dickinson, "Alexander for the Modern Age." Jacqueline Lichtenberg (*Star Trek Lives!*) was a chemist; Judy Segal (head of the Star Trek Welcommittee) had a master's degree in botany; and Joan Marie Verba (*Boldly Writing*) had a bachelor's degree in physics, went to graduate school for astronomy, and worked as a programmer before becoming an editor and writer.

47. Mary Van Deusen, "My Background in Making Song Videos," 1996, http://www.iment.com/maida/tv/songvids/songbackground.htm

48. Interview with Judith Chien by Franzi Dixon, May 27, 2012, at MediaWest*Con.

49. Interview with Gayle F. and Caren P. by Morgan Dawn, February 10, 2013.

50. Mary Van Deusen, "What Are Literary Music Videos?," http://www.iment.com/maida/tv/songvids/songvids.htm#what

51. Jenkins, *Textual Poachers*, 232.

52. Mary Van Deusen, "Music Video Plans," http://www.iment.com/maida/tv/songvids/plans/index.htm

53. Mary Van Deusen, "What Are Literary Song Videos?," http://www.iment.com/maida/tv/songvids/songvids.htm#what

54. Janice Radway, *Reading the Romance: Women, Patriarchy, and Popular Literature* (Chapel Hill: University of North Carolina Press, 1984), 95.

55. David Halperin, *How to Be Gay* (Cambridge, MA: Belknap, 2012), 99.

56. Sophie Mayer, "Cry Me a River," in *On the Verge of Tears: Why the Movies, Television, Music, Art, Popular Culture, Literature, and the Real World Make Us Cry*, ed. Michele Byers and David Lavery (Newcastle upon Tyne, UK: Cambridge Scholars, 2010), 33. See also Robyn R. Warhol, *Having a Good Cry: Effeminate Feelings and Pop Culture Forms* (Columbus: Ohio State University Press, 2003).

57. Lynn C., quoted in "The Genealogy of Vidding," Fanlore, https://fanlore.org/

58. Personal correspondence with Gayle (June 25, 2018), Tashery Shannon (June 28, 2018), and Jill (June 29, 2018).

59. Jill writes: "I got really into MTV when it launched—I still have collections of favorite bands' videos on VHS that I had to send away for back in the day—so when we started vidding, we were both more influenced by what pros were doing in various media than other fans" (personal correspondence, June 29, 2018). Tashery notes: "We were just coming out of the '80s—the era of MTV and the creative explosion in music videos enabled by an all-music-video cable channel. The editing of many of those music videos was excitingly music-sensitive, especially rhythm-sensitive, and when Jill and I began vidding I'd watched a lot more of these than I'd ever seen of fan vids" (personal correspondence, June 28, 2018).

60. Private correspondence with Tashery Shannon, June 28, 2018.

61. Interview with Gayle F. and Caren P. by Morgan Dawn, February 10, 2013.

62. In the case of *Scandal*, which has a huge vidding fandom, there is also the complicating factor of race. Kristen J. Warner has written about the ways in which both fandom and fan studies have marginalized black women's fan activity, even when it does the same sort of creative fixing in terms of race that white female fans have historically done with gender and sexuality. Warner, "ABC's *Scandal* and Black Women's Fandom," in *Cupcakes, Pinterest, and Ladyporn: Feminized Popular Culture in the Early Twenty-First Century*, ed. Elana Levine (Urbana: University of Illinois Press, 2015), 32–50.

Chapter 4

1. Casey Fiesler, "Tech Ethics Curricula: A Collection of Syllabi," Medium, July 5, 2018, https://medium.com/@cfiesler/tech-ethics-curricula-a-collection -of-syllabi-3eedfb76be18

2. Even today, surprisingly few genre TV shows and movies pass the Bechdel test, the three-part test developed by Alison Bechdel in her comic strip *Dykes to Watch Out For* (1983–2008): whether (1) two (named) female characters (2) talk to each other (3) about something other than a man. *Star Wars*, *Lord of the Rings*, and most of the original Star Trek (TV and movies) fail. Genre TV shows and movies tend either to be buddy-focused (with female characters secondary or absent) or team-focused (where the team is made of a bunch of men and a token woman; hello, Black Widow!).

3. Today slash fans have colonized certain parts of the publishing world, but homoerotic fiction remains a relatively niche interest. Moreover, as fans will be quick to point out, we still haven't had a major superhero, detective, starship captain, or Jedi involved in a same-sex romance, though we now have canonical gay characters on *Star Trek: Discovery* (2017–).

4. See Casey Fiesler, Shannon Morrison, and Amy S. Bruckman, "An Archive of Their Own: A Case Study of Feminist HCI and Values in Design," in *Proceedings of the SIGCHI Conference on Human Factors in Computing Systems (CHI '16)*, 2574– 85, https://doi.org/10.1145/2858036.2858409

5. Maciej Ceglow, "The Fans Are All Right," Pinboard Blog, October 2, 2011, https://blog.pinboard.in/2011/10/the_fans_are_all_right/

6. Rebecca Lucy Busker, "Fandom and Male Privilege: Seven Years Later," in "Appropriating, Interpreting, and Transforming Comic Books," ed. Matthew J. Costello, special issue, *Transformative Works and Cultures*, no. 13 (2013), https:// doi.org/10.3983/twc.2013.0473

7. Relatedly, creators of gen fan works have found it easier to go pro. Wattpad (https://www.wattpad.com/) is premised on this.

8. Constance Penley describes vidding panels at Escapade in *NASA/Trek* (New York: Verso, 1997), 113–15.

9. Beth Greenfield, "Sapphic Princess: Dyke Bar Parties Celebrating Xena's Lesbian Subject Are Flourishing All Over Town. A Report from the Trenches," in *HX for Her: The Totally Biased Politically Incorrect Party Paper for Lesbians*, June 4, 1997, scanned at http://www.ausxip.com/articles/1997/hxforher/index.html

10. Interview by Killa and Jarrow of Sandy, Rache, and Gwyn of the Media Cannibals, plus Mlyn for MIT Vidding Documentary, 2007.

11. Interview by Killa and Jarrow of Sandy, Rache, and Gwyn of the Media Cannibals, plus Mlyn for MIT Vidding Documentary, 2007.

12. Sandy and Rache of the Media Cannibals, interviewed by Coppa, August 2008.

13. Katherine Scarritt, interview at Escapade with Franzeska Dickson for the OTW's Oral History Project, March 7, 2015.

14. Interview by Killa and Jarrow of Sandy, Rache, and Gwyn of the Media Cannibals, plus Mlyn for MIT Vidding Documentary, 2007.

15. Interview by Killa and Jarrow of Sandy, Rache, and Gwyn of the Media Cannibals, plus Mlyn for MIT Vidding Documentary, 2007.

16. Quoted in "Vid Review," Fanlore, https://fanlore.org/

17. Francesca Coppa, "Interview with Sandy and Rache ('The Clucking Belles')," *Transformative Works and Cultures*, no. 6 (2011), ¶ 7.2–7.4, https://doi .org/10.3983/twc.2011.0242

18. These and more were codified by here's luck in her 2004 handout, "The Language of Vidding."

19. "Vid: The FAQ," reposted to VIDDER mailing list, March 17, 1999.

20. Later vidders tried sharing vids using early peer-to-peer networks like Kazaa. In the "About Us" section of Headtilt.com, a now-defunct *Buffy* vidding site, vidder Dr. Dawn teases the other vidders on the site: "You two would be nothing without me. You would still be desperately peddling your videos on Kazaa, and sending scary, stalky emails to anyone that uploaded from you." Headtilt, n.d., http://www.headtilt.com/about_us.htm (via the Wayback Machine).

21. "Digital Vidding on a Budget," http://www.angelfire.com/or/vidding (via the Wayback Machine).

22. Thread, VIDDER post, June 15, 1998.

23. "Internet/Broadband Fact Sheet," Pew Research Center, June 12, 2019, http://www.pewinternet.org/fact-sheet/internet-broadband/

24. Sandy Herrold, quoted in "In the Air Tonight," Fanlore, https://fanlore .org/

25. Katherine Scarritt, interview at Escapade with Franzeska Dickson for the OTW's Oral History Project, March 7, 2015.

26. Gywneth, "No Way Out," Dreamwidth, October 3, 2005, https://gwyn.dr eamwidth.org/293074.html

27. Shoshanna, VIDDER post, February 24, 2002.

28. It also played on *X-Files* creator Chris Carter's logo for Ten Thirteen Productions, in which a child pipes up over the sound of a film reel to declare, "I made this!"

29. Shoshanna, VIDDER post, February 21, 2001.

30. LynnC, VIDDER post, February 21, 2001.

31. Carol S., VIDDER post, February 22, 2001.

32. Lark, VIDDER post, February 22, 2001.

33. Shoshanna, VIDDER post, February 24, 2002.

34. Laura Shapiro, VIDDER post, February 19, 2002.

35. Eliade on her blog, February 18, 2001, quoted in "Escapade/Escapade 2002," Fanlore, https://fanlore.org/

36. Eliade, quoted in "Escapade/Escapade 2002."

37. Astolat/shalott VIDDER post, February 22, 2002.

38. Astolat/shalott VIDDER post, February 25, 2002.

39. Astolat, "About Vividcon," Dreamwidth, June 6, 2017, https://astolat.dre amwidth.org/302253.html

40. My own peripheral recollection is that the word "llama" was evoked by the abbreviation LLC—that is, a limited liability company, because one was needed to administer the convention.

41. Shoshanna, "The Prehistory (and Current Events) of Vividcon," LiveJournal, March 29, 2011, https://the-shoshanna.livejournal.com/335062 .html

42. Jarrow, "New Vid: Paul McCartney," LiveJournal, August 15, 2007, https://jarrow.livejournal.com/957773.html

43. For analyses of I PUT YOU THERE, see Tushnet, "I Put You There"; and Tisha Turk, "Metalepsis in Fan Vids and Fan Fiction," in *Metalepsis in Popular Culture*, ed. Karin Kukkonen and Sonja Klimek (Berlin: De Gruyter, 2011), 213–31.

44. Comment on "YouTube Opinions," Vidding (LiveJournal community), August 2, 2006, https://vidding.livejournal.com/740102.html

45. Comment on "YouTube Opinions."

46. Rosemary Van Deuren, "Top Ten Funny YouTube Links for Insomniacs," IdlerMag, January 12, 2011, https://idlermag.com/2011/01/12/top-ten-funny -youtube-links-for-insomniacs/

47. "I have to push the pram a lot!," MetaFilter thread posted by jonson, July 18, 2006, https://www.metafilter.com/53105/I-have-to-push-the-pram-a-lot.

48. For more on this, see Henry Jenkins's analysis of CLOSER, "How to Watch a Fan-Vid," Confessions of an Aca-Fan (blog), September 17, 2006, http://henry jenkins.org/blog/2006/09/how_to_watch_a_fanvid.html

49. These comments come from the version put up on YouTube by user alex- anderadb on September 8, 2006 (https://youtu.be/3uxTpyCdriY).

50. Julie Levin Russo, "User-Penetrated Content: Fan Video in the Age of Convergence," *Cinema Journal* 48, no. 4 (2009): 125–230.

51. Comments from alexanderab, "Star Trek + Nine Inch Nails = Closer," YouTube, September 8, 2006, https://youtu.be/3uxTpyCdriY

52. Starcrossedgirl, "Stolen Vids on YouTube: FUBAR," Vidding (LiveJournal community), October 21, 2008, https://vidding.livejournal.com/1629542.html

53. Margie, "VVC 2007: Disc Zero—At the Con (1/5)," Dreamwidth, November 16, 2007, https://flummery.dreamwidth.org/2007/11/16/

54. Laura Shapiro, "Vidding Meta: You Can't Stop the Signal," Vidding (LiveJournal community), December 4, 2006, https://vidding.livejournal.com /893694.html

55. Laura Shapiro, "Representing Vidding to the Wider World: Suggestions Needed," Vidding (LiveJournal community), April 8, 2007, https://vidding.livej ournal.com/1035085.html

56. Margie, "VVC 2007."

57. John Hartley, "Bleak House—Beautiful Things," In Media Res, November 17, 2007, http://mediacommons.org/imr/2006/11/17/bleak-house-beautiful -things

58. Jackie K. Jono, comment to Hartley, "Bleak House—Beautiful Things."

59. Joss Whedon, "Me Links to Me," June 30, 2007, Whedonesque, http://wh
edonesque.com/comments/13590

60. Par Avion, "Panel Notes from VVC 2007 Town Hall on Vidding and
Visibility, August 16, 2007," Vividcon (LiveJournal community), https://vividcon
.livejournal.com/119137.html

61. Margie, "VVC 2007."

62. See "Vidding," Organization for Transformative Works, https://www.tran
sformativeworks.org/vidding-index/vidding_en/; and the ProjectNML YouTube
channel Fanvidding, at https://www.youtube.com/watch?v=2xCUw_M_U30

63. See also Henry Jenkins, "Fan Vidding: A Labor of Love (Part One),"
Confessions of an Aca-Fan (blog), December 5, 2008, http://henryjenkins.org
/2008/12/fanvidding.html

64. "The Twenty (Intentionally) Funniest Web Videos of 2007," *New York
Magazine*, November 8, 2007, https://nymag.com/movies/features/videos/406
63/index1.html.

65. Logan Hill, "The Vidder," *New York Magazine*, November 8, 2007, http://
nymag.com/movies/features/videos/40622/

66. Henry Jenkins, "Vidder Luminosity Profiled in *New York Magazine*,"
Confessions of an Aca-Fan (blog), November 20, 2007, http://henryjenkins.org
/2007/11/vidder_luminosity_profiled_in.html

67. Hill, "Vidder."

68. Luminosity's answer: "My favorites were the film noir directors of the for-
ties and fifties—Orson Welles, Jacques Tourneur. On TV, I admire David Nutter,
Kim and Kelly Manners, and Joss Whedon." Hill, "Vidder."

69. Logan Hill, "The Best Fan Vids of 2008," Vulture, November 25, 2008,
https://www.vulture.com/2008/11/best_fan_vids_of_2008_1.html

70. Michael Wesch, "An Anthropological Introduction to YouTube," presented at the Library of Congress, June 23, 2008, https://www.youtube.com/wa
tch?v=TPAO-lZ4_hU

71. Organization for Transformative Works, "Test Suite of Fair Use Vids,"
https://www.transformativeworks.org/legal/vidtestsuite/

72. "Buffy v. Edward: Twilight Remixed," by Jonathan McIntosh, June 20,
2009,   http://popculturedetective.agency/2009/buffy-vs-edward-twilight-rem
ixed

73. Tisha Turk, "DMCA Exemption for Noncommercial Remix Video!,"
LiveJournal, July 26, 2010, https://tishaturk.livejournal.com/7355.html

74. Marybeth Peters, "Recommendation of the Register of Copyrights,"
Copyright.gov, June 11, 2010, 66.

75. Peters, "Recommendation," 66.

76. Peters, "Recommendation," 66–68.

77. Par Avion, "Panel Notes from VVC 2007."

78. Henry Jenkins, "DIY Media 2010: Fan Vids (Part Four)," Confessions of
An Aca-Fan (blog), November 30, 2010, http://henryjenkins.org/blog/2010/12
/diy_media_2010_fan_vids_part_f.html

79. Cathy Cupitt, "Nothing but Net: When Cultures Collide," *Transformative
Works and Cultures*, no. 1 (2008), https://doi.org/10.3983/twc.2008.055

Chapter 5

1. Alexis Lothian, "Living in a Den of Thieves: Fan Video and Digital Challenges to Ownership," *Cinema Journal* 48, no. 4 (2009): 133.

2. The density of vids is such that I must mention that the appearance of Tom Baker, the Fourth Doctor, comes on Spektor's lyric, "We wear our scarves just like a noose / But not 'cause we want eternal sleep." The Fourth Doctor was known for his long multicolored scarf, but in context, the line also suggests that fans aren't looking for trouble. We may be playing dress-up with popular culture, but we're not looking to be hanged for it!

3. Transcript, "City of Death," *Doctor Who* (dir. Michael Hayes, BBC, original airdate September 29, 1979), http://www.chakoteya.net/DoctorWho/17-2.htm

4. Kristina Busse, "'Us'—A Multivid by lim," In Media Res, February 1, 2008, http://mediacommons.org/imr/2008/02/01/us-a-multivid-by-lim

5. The EFF and OTW DCMA filings are archived at Organization for Transformative Works, "Legal Advocacy," http://www.transformativeworks.org/legal/

6. *Mediated*, an exhibit at the California Museum of Photography, January 24, 2009–April 4, 2009, https://ucrarts.ucr.edu/Exhibition/Archive.

7. "Vidders Talk Back to Their Pop-Culture Muses," *All Things Considered*, National Public Radio, February 25, 2009, https://www.npr.org/templates/story/story.php?storyId=101154811; transcript at https://www.npr.org/templates/transcript/transcript.php?storyId=101154811

8. Wesch, "Anthropological Introduction to YouTube."

9. Lawrence Lessig, "Laws that Choke Creativity," TED Talk, 2007, https://www.ted.com/talks/larry_lessig_says_the_law_is_strangling_creativity?language=en#t-1071979

10. Comment on lim, "Us," YouTube, June 2, 2007, https://youtu.be/_yxHKgQyGx0

11. James O'Malley, "Captcha If You Can: How You've Been Training AI for Years without Realising It," Techradar, January 12, 2008, https://www.techradar.com/news/captcha-if-you-can-how-youve-been-training-ai-for-years-without-realising-it

12. Kate O'Neill, "Facebook's '10 Year Challenge' Is Just a Harmless Meme, Right?," *Wired*, January 15, 2019, https://www.wired.com/story/facebook-10-year-meme-challenge/

13. Zeynep Tufeki, *Twitter and Tear Gas: The Power and Fragility of Networked Protest* (New Haven: Yale University Press, 2017), 154.

14. Tufeki, *Twitter and Tear Gas*, 20.

15. Zeynep Tufeki, "We're Building a Dystopia Just to Make People Click on Ads," TED Talk, TEDGlobal>NYC, September 2017, https://www.ted.com/talks/zeynep_tufekci_we_re_building_a_dystopia_just_to_make_people_click_on_ads

16. Zeynep Tufeki, "YouTube, the Great Radicalizer," *New York Times*, March 10, 2018, https://www.nytimes.com/2018/03/10/opinion/sunday/youtube-politics-radical.html

17. Jonah Weiner, "The Great Race to Rule Streaming TV," *New York Times*,

July 10, 2019, https://www.nytimes.com/2019/07/10/magazine/streaming-ra ce-netflix-hbo-hulu-amazon.html

18. Weiner, "Great Race."

19. Weiner, "Great Race."

20. Hondros, *Ecologies of Internet Video*, 97–121.

21. "Simplifying Imeem," Imeem.com, June 25, 2009, http://blog.imeem .com/2009/06/25/simplifying-imeem/ (via the Wayback Machine).

22. Elisa Kreisinger, "Imeem Removes Fan Vids Along with All UGV," Political Remix Video (blog), July 6, 2009, http://www.politicalremixvideo.com/2009 /07/06/imeem-removes-all-fan-vids-along-with-all-other-ugv (via the Wayback Machine).

23. "Copyright and Fair Use," Blip.tv blog, June 22, 2006, http://blog.blip.tv /blog/2006/06/22/copyright-and-fair-use-policy/ (via the Wayback Machine).

24. Luminosity, personal correspondence, November 10, 2014.

25. Katharina M. Freund, "'Veni, Vidi, Vids!' Audiences, Gender and Community in Fan Vidding" (PhD diss., University of Wollongong, 2011), 34, http://ro.uow.edu.au/theses/3447

26. Owen Gallagher, *Reclaiming Critical Remix: The Role of Sampling in Transformative Works* (New York: Routledge, 2017), 24.

27. Patricia G. Lange, *Kids on YouTube: Technical Identities and Digital Literacies* (New York: Routledge, 2016).

28. Matt Gielen, "The Taxonomy of YouTube Videos (And How You Can Develop Original Content that Works)," Tubefilter, February 12, 2019, https:// www.tubefilter.com/2019/02/12/taxonomy-youtube-videos-develop-original-co ntent-that-works/

29. YouTube Advertisers, "Video Identification," YouTube, February 4, 2008, https://youtu.be/xWizsV5Le7s

30. YouTomb, http://youtomb.mit.edu/about (via the Wayback Machine).

31. YouTomb, https://youtomb.mit.edu/about

32. David King, "Content ID Turns Three," YouTube Official Blog, December 2, 2010, https://youtube.googleblog.com/2010/12/content-id-turns-three.html

33. Jonathan McIntosh had vids taken down when he refused to have them monetized; see "Copyright Vampires Attempt to Suck the Lifeblood Out of Fair Use Video," Electronic Frontier Foundation, January 10, 2013, https:// www.eff.org/deeplinks/2013/01/copyright-vampires-attempt-suck-lifeblood- out-fair-use-video

34. Aulia Masna, "YouTube and Its Copyright Trolls," Medium, August 22, 2016, https://medium.com/@aulia/youtube-and-its-copyright-trolls-f6aede65 2340

35. YouTube, "YouTube Copyright School," YouTube, March 23, 2011, https://www.youtube.com/watch?v=InzDjH1-9Ns

36. Corynne McSherry, "YouTube Sends Users to Copyright School: Will Content Owners Have to Go, Too?," Electronic Frontier Foundation, April 15, 2011, https://www.eff.org/deeplinks/2011/04/youtube-sends-users-copyright -school-will-content

37. Jodie Griffin, "My First Day at YouTube Copyright School," Public Knowledge, April 15, 2011, https://www.publicknowledge.org/news-blog/blogs /my-first-day-youtube-copyright-school

38. Electronic Frontier Foundation, "Guide to YouTube Removals," https://www.eff.org/issues/intellectual-property/guide-to-youtube-removals

39. Interview with Zeynep Tufeki, "The Facebook Dilemma: Zeynep Tufeki," *Frontline*, May 22, 2018, https://www.pbs.org/wgbh/frontline/interview/zeynep-tufekci/

40. Hondros, *Ecologies of Internet Video*, 117–19.

41. Hondros, *Ecologies of Internet Video*, 119.

42. Lim, "This Is Not Legal Advice: YouTube, Endemol, and the BBC vs. . . . Me," Videlicet, 2017, https://vidders.github.io/articles/vidding/legal.html

43. Moin Nadeem, "How YouTube Recommends Videos," Medium, July 7, 2018, https://towardsdatascience.com/how-youtube-recommends-videos-b6e00 3a5ab2f

44. Joan E. Solsman, "YouTube's AI Is the Puppet Master over Most of What You Watch," CNET, January 10, 2018, https://www.cnet.com/news/youtube-ces-2018-neal-mohan/

45. Matt Gielen and Jeremy Rosen, "Reverse Engineering the YouTube Algorithm: Part 1," Tubefilter, June 23, 2016, https://www.tubefilter.com/2016/06/23/reverse-engineering-youtube-algorithm/

46. "The YouTube Algorithm Hacks Every Creator Needs to Know," Promolta, n.d., https://blog.promolta.com/the-youtube-algorithm-hacks-every-creator-ne eds-to-know/

47. Sophie Bishop, "Anxiety, Panic and Self-Optimization: Inequalities and the YouTube Algorithm," *Convergence* 24, no. 1 (2018): 69–84.

48. Kevin B. Lee, in a 2018 video presentation, describes similar fears about the video essay, which he argues has gotten standardized and made "effective" rather than "illuminating" by the pressures of YouTube and commercialization. Lee, "The Video Essay: Lost Potentials and Cinematic Futures," Vimeo, November 8, 2018, https://vimeo.com/298734232

49. Tony Zhou, "Postmortem: Every Frame a Painting," Medium, December 3, 2017, https://medium.com/@tonyszhou/postmortem-1b338537fabc

50. Ken Ashcorp is kind of a modern-day filker, a singer-songwriter who creates songs about modern Internet life and memes. The "20 Percent Cooler" meme is based on a quote from *My Little Pony*, in which Rainbow Dash tells someone that her outfit needs to be "about 20 percent cooler."

51. For more on GLITTER AND GOLD, see Speranza, "Glitter and Gold: Sound and Story," Videlicet, 2017, https://vidders.github.io/articles/vids/glitter.html

52. Turk and Johnson, "Toward an Ecology of Vidding," 1.4.

53. For example, Pingvi's "Test Your Skills" (TYS) challenge (https://youtu.be/qeryO8jt2q4) or the "Elements of Vidding (EOV) challenge" (https://you tu.be/3UKyZIwVCmo). See Simone Tosoni and Mariana Ciancia, "Vidding and Its Media Territories: A Practice-Centred Approach to User-Generated Content Production," in *Present Scenarios of Media Production and Engagement*, ed. Simone Tosoni et al. (Bremen: edition lumière, 2017), 48.

54. "Carry On Wayward Son," Supernatural Wiki, http://www.supernaturalw iki.com/

55. "Wayward Daughters," Supernatural Wiki, http://www.supernaturalwiki.com/

56. "Ask the Vidder: Loki (SecretlyToDream)," Spnroundtable (LiveJournal community), October 24, 2011.

57. Grable424, "Multifandom: Tesselate (TYS: Round 2)," YouTube, December 14, 2015, https://www.youtube.com/watch?v=Wcr9xCnstHo

58. Francesca Coppa, "Six Celled Cinema: Remix and Fan Video," for "Cinematic Bricoleurs: Remixing, Restyling, and Repurposing in Contemporary Filmmaking Practice," TRI-PACT event, King's College London, January 8, 2016.

59. The idea of Hermione Granger as Black also has roots in a 2015 Buzzfeed article by biracial fan Alanna Bennett, who thought that Granger's being called a "mudblood" within Harry Potter was akin to a person of color being harassed with the n-word.

60. Freund, "I Thought I Made a Vid," 285.

61. All are comments to bop_radar's post, "On Inclusion and Exclusion in Vidding Fandom: Personal Reflections," LiveJournal, August 20, 2009.

62. Freund, "I Thought I Made a Vid," 293.

63. The Vidder Profiles are a series of video essays made by bradcpu in which vidders discuss their work. Profiled vidders include: kiki_miserychic, dragonchic, charmax, Dualbunny, AbsoluteDestiny, Obsessive24, mranderson71, and Luminosity. Some of these videos are now hosted by the Vidderprofile channel on YouTube (https://www.youtube.com/user/vidderprofile). For more about the series, see bradcpu, "Documenting the Vidders: A Conversation with Bradcpu," interview conducted by Counteragent, in "Fan/Remix Video," ed. Francesca Coppa and Julie Levin Russo, special issue, *Transformative Works and Cultures*, no. 9 (2012), https://doi.org/10.3983/twc.2012.0423

64. Cari Beauchamp, "100 Women, One Hotel, and the Weekend Retreat that Presaged Time's Up by 18 Years," *Vanity Fair*, January 30, 2018, https://www.vanityfair.com/hollywood/2018/01/women-directors-miramar-women

65. Beauchamp, "100 Women, One Hotel."

66. Much less is known about the *Xena: Warrior Princess* vidders of the late 1990s, who met at *Xena*-specific fan gatherings and rarely digitized or shared their work.

67. See, for instance, a linchpin figure like Joanna Russ, who wrote science fiction, fanfiction, and an essay about Kirk/Spock slash fiction that is one of the first critical essays in fan studies. Russ, "Pornography by Women, for Women, with Love" (1985), reprinted in *The Fan Fiction Studies Reader*, ed. Karen Hellekson and Kristina Busse (Iowa City: University of Iowa, 2015).

68. See § 5, "Whose Feminism Is This Anyway? Intersectional Feminism(s), Whiteness, and Fan Studies," of Briony Hannell's "Fan Studies and/as Feminist Methodology," in "Fan Studies Methodologies," ed. Julia E. Largent, Milena Popova, and Elise Vist, special issue, *Transformative Works and Cultures*, no. 33 (2020), https://doi.org/10.3983/twc.2020.1689

69. Warner, in "ABC's *Scandal*," has called out the invisibility of black female fans and their fan works both within mainstream culture and within fandom.

70. Benjamin Woo, "The Invisible Bag of Holding: Whiteness and Media Fandom," in Scott and Click, *Routledge Companion to Media Fandom*, 247.

71. Abigail De Kosnik and andré carrington, "Fans of Color, Fandoms of Color," editorial to their special issue of *Transformative Works and Cultures*, no. 29 (2019), 1.1, https://doi.org/10.3983/twc.2019.1783

72. bell hooks, "The Oppositional Gaze: Black Female Spectators," in *Black Looks* (Boston: South End Press, 1992).

73. Rebecca Wanzo, "African American Acafandom and Other Strangers: New Genealogies of Fan Studies," *Transformative Works and Cultures*, no. 20 (2015), https://doi.org/10.3983/twc.2015.0699

74. Hapex_legomena, "Enter the Wu Tang Clan: 36 Chambers of Death," Archive of Our Own, April 26, 2009, https://archiveofourown.org/works/1098 6699

75. Cait Coker and Rukmini Pande, "Not So Star-Spangled: Examining Race, Privilege and Problems in MCU's *Captain America* Fandom," in *The Darker Side of Slash Fan Fiction: Essays on Power, Consent and the Body*, ed. Ashton Spacey (Jefferson, NC: McFarland, 2018), 97–114.

76. Nadia Latif, "It's Lit! How Film Finally Learned to Light Black Skin," *Guardian*, September 21, 2017, https://www.theguardian.com/film/2017/sep /21/its-lit-how-film-finally-learned-how-to-light-black-skin

77. See THE ADVENTURE (2012), a vid about Neville Longbottom by Greensilver, at https://youtu.be/Rc7Wz03VKfA; WOMEN'S WORK (2007) by Luminosity and sisabet, and STILL ALIVE (2008) by Counteragent, about the women of *Supernatural*; and the crossover vid HURRICANE (2010) by Laura Shapiro.

78. Thingswithwings, tweetstorm on Twitter, at @twwings May 1, 2016.

79. Te, "Remember Us Manifesto, v. 1.0," Remember Us, http://www.dream ing-in-color.net/manifesto.html

80. For more on RaceFail '09, see Siobhan Carroll, "The Fan as Public Intellectual in 'RaceFail '09,'" in *The Year's Work in Nerds, Wonks, and Neocons*, ed. Jonathan P. Eburne and Benjamin Schreier (Bloomington: University of Indiana Press, 2017), 301–25; Helen Young, *Race and Popular Fantasy Literature: Habits of Whiteness* (New York: Routledge, 2016), 171–85; Nathan Rambukkana, "From #RaceFail to #Ferguson: The Digital Intimacies of Race-Activist Hashtag Publics," *Fibreculture Journal*, no. 26 (2015), https://doi.org/10.15307/fcj.26.194.2015; Stanfill, "Unbearable Whiteness"; and Rukmini Pande, *Squee from the Margins: Fandom and Race* (Iowa City: University of Iowa Press, 2018).

81. Pande, *Squee from the Margins*, 33.

82. Pande, *Squee from the Margins*, 33.

83. N. K. Jemisin, "Why I Think RaceFail Was the Bestest Thing Evar for SFF," N. K. Jemisin (blog), January 18, 2010, http://nkjemisin.com/2010/01/why-i-th ink-racefail-was-the-bestest-thing-evar-for-sff/

84. Ebony Elizabeth Thomas and Amy Stornaiuolo, "Race, Storying, and Restorying: What Can We Learn from Black Fans?," in "Fans of Color, Fandoms of Color," ed. Abigail De Kosnik and andré carrington, special issue, *Transformative Works and Cultures*, no. 29 (2019), https://dx.doi.org/10.3983/twc.2019.1562

85. The Racebending LiveJournal community evolved into Racebending. com: Media Consumers for Entertainment Equality, and connects on Twitter at @racebending.

86. Laura Shapiro, "Vividcon 2009: Some Observations about Race, Gender, and Accessibility," Dreamwidth, August 19, 2009, https://laurashapiro.dreamwi dth.org/280845.html

87. "Wiscon Vid Party Info Post," Wiscon-vidparty (Dreamwidth community), August 11, 2010.

88. Seekingferret, untitled post, Dreamwidth, April 17, 2019, https://seekin gferret.dreamwidth.org/298378.html

89. See "Roundtable: Remix and Videographic Criticism," *Cinema Journal* 56, no. 4 (2017): 159–84; Melanie E. S. Kohnen, "Videographic Criticism 101," Antenna, July 9, 2015, http://blog.commarts.wisc.edu/2015/07/09/videograp hic-criticism-101/; Christian Keathley, Jason Mittell, and Catherine Grant, eds., *The Videographic Essay: Practice and Pedagogy*, 2019, http://videographicessay.org

90. Lori Morimoto, "Hannibal: A Fanvid," *In Transition*, October 6, 2016, http://mediacommons.org/intransition/2016/10/06/hannibal-fanvid

91. See Morrissey, "Vidding and/as Pedagogy"; Winters, "Streaming Scholarship"; and Jessica K. Parker's *Teaching Tech-Savvy Kids: Bringing Digital Media into the Classroom, Grades 5–12* (Thousand Oaks, CA: Corwin, 2010).

92. Eruthros's STRAIGHTENING UP THE HOUSE can be found at the Archive of Our Own at https://archiveofourown.org/works/14793695

93. Cyborganize's TRANSMISSION can be found at the Archive of Our Own at https://archiveofourown.org/works/17648882

94. Warner, "ABC's *Scandal*," 35.

95. Warner, "ABC's *Scandal*," 33.

96. Gavia Baker-Whitelaw, "Your Favorite Netflix Show Will Soon Be Canceled," Daily Dot, August 9, 2019, https://www.dailydot.com/parsec/diver se-netflix-shows-canceled/ (So much for diverse voices.)

97. Cedric Thornton, "John Boyega Signs with Netflix to Develop African Films," Black Enterprise, March 17, 2020, https://www.blackenterprise.com/john-boyega-signs-with-netflix-to-develop-african-films/. Streaming service KweliTV offers programming from the worldwide Black diaspora at https://www.kweli.tv/

98. Lori and Gordon, "End of an Era," MediaWest*Con, February 4, 2020, https://mediawestcon.wordpress.com/2020/02/04/end-of-an-era/

99. For more on cosplay video, see Louisa Ellen Stein, "Embodying *Yuri on Ice*: Cosplay Video as Youth Media Authorship," In Media Res, November 21, 2017, http://mediacommons.org/imr/2017/11/21/embodying-yuri-ice-cospl ay-video-youth-media-authorship

100. See, e.g., lim's "Talking about Vidding" playlist on YouTube, at https://www.youtube.com/playlist?list=PLliE8mqiSLjwoQ7sXRXkd-JEmFhtIfaur

101. These are sometimes called tags, in that vidders tag each other to answer questions.

102. See, e.g., Abigail Christensen's 2011 "Vidding: A Documentary about Fanvideos/Vidders," in which she interviews a number of vidders from her community, at https://www.youtube.com/watch?v=3Id-DNHRQXs

103. Michael Strangelove, *Watching YouTube: Extraordinary Videos by Ordinary People* (Toronto: University of Toronto Press, 2010), 84–102.

104. Peggy Phelan, *Unmarked: The Politics of Performance* (New York: Routledge, 2003), 93.

105. John Berger, *Ways of Seeing* (London: BBC and Penguin Books, 1972), 32.

Index